AF687404

AIWoW -

AI WAYS OF WORKING™

ANAND RATHORE

notionpress.com

INDIA · SINGAPORE · MALAYSIA

Copyright © Anand Rathore 2026
All Rights Reserved.

ISBN
Paperback 979-8-90392-610-7
Hardcase 979-8-90431-718-8

This book has been published with all efforts taken to make the material error-free after the consent of the author. However, the author and the publisher do not assume and hereby disclaim any liability to any party for any loss, damage, or disruption caused by errors or omissions, whether such errors or omissions result from negligence, accident, or any other cause.

While every effort has been made to avoid any mistake or omission, this publication is being sold on the condition and understanding that neither the author nor the publishers or printers would be liable in any manner to any person by reason of any mistake or omission in this publication or for any action taken or omitted to be taken or advice rendered or accepted on the basis of this work. For any defect in printing or binding the publishers will be liable only to replace the defective copy by another copy of this work then available.

Advance Praise for Book

Artificial intelligence is no longer a distant possibility—it is actively reshaping governance, institutions, and the functioning of society. At such a juncture, the focus must shift from mere adoption to **responsible integration and effective governance of AI.**

AIWoW – AI Ways of Working™ by Anand Rathore addresses this need with clarity and depth. It presents a structured approach to embedding AI into decision-making and operational frameworks while ensuring accountability, transparency, and human oversight.

The emphasis on aligning technological advancement with ethical responsibility is particularly significant, as this will play a defining role in shaping public trust and institutional integrity in the years ahead.

This work reflects both foresight and practical understanding. I recommend it to policymakers, leaders, and professionals who are committed to building a responsible and future-ready AI-driven ecosystem.- **Dr. Medha Kulkarni, Member of Rajya Sabha, Bharatiya Janata Party**

Public money. Public trust. Public accountability.

Three words that define my work and the three principles that make AIWoW – AI Ways of Working™ essential reading for every public institution deploying AI today.

In public administration, AI risks are not borne by shareholders. They are borne by citizens—citizens who deserve systems that are not only intelligent but accountable, not only fast but traceable, not only efficient but just.

Anand Rathore has built precisely that governing philosophy. Practically rigorous. Humanly grounded. Drawn from real experience inside the complexity that public institutions live every day.

When AI goes ungoverned in civic systems, the consequences fall on those least able to challenge it. AIWoW – AI Ways of Working™ exists to prevent exactly that.

I recommend it without reservation. - **Dr. CS. Kunal Mandwale, Deputy Chief Accounts & Finance Officer, Chief Compliance Officer, Pune Municipal Corporation, MCSI London, AACFE USA, Forensic Auditor (ICMAI), CS, LLB, MBA Fin, M.Com, DTL, DLL&LW, GDLFM**

I have long argued that competing in the age of artificial intelligence is not a question of adopting more technology, but of designing a coherent human–machine operating model. What Anand Rathore has done in AIWoW - AI Ways of Working ™ is to move that idea from aspiration to architecture.

This book addresses a gap the industry has acknowledged but not resolved—the distance between what intelligent systems are capable of doing and what organisations can responsibly govern, absorb, and remain accountable for at scale. Most enterprises have made progress on capability. Far fewer have built the structures required to operationalise that capability without creating fragmentation, risk, or unintended consequences.

AIWoW brings that missing structure. The frameworks presented—the AI Lifecycle Loop, the Theory of Control, the Human–AI Responsibility Matrix, and AI Return on Humanity—are not conceptual overlays. They are practical instruments. They translate abstract concerns around governance, accountability, and human impact into systems that can be designed, implemented, and sustained.

From a practitioner's standpoint, this is where the real value lies. Over the past two decades, working at the intersection of data, analytics, and AI across global enterprises, I have repeatedly seen that the hardest problems are not algorithmic. They are organisational. They sit in decision rights, in accountability boundaries, in how humans interpret, override, and ultimately stand behind AI-driven outcomes. Anand's work engages directly with these realities. It reflects lived experience, not theoretical distance, and it does so with a level of intellectual discipline that the AI governance conversation has often lacked.

AI is no longer a peripheral capability. It is becoming operational infrastructure. That shift carries consequences. Infrastructure, by definition, must be reliable, governable, and aligned to purpose. What AIWoW contributes is a governing philosophy—and more importantly, a set of actionable constructs—that recognise this shift and respond to it with the seriousness it demands.

This is a timely and necessary contribution. For leaders and practitioners navigating the transition from experimentation to enterprise-scale adoption, this book offers not just perspective, but a way to operationalise that perspective with clarity and intent. - **Soumendra Mohanty- Chief Strategy & Innovation Officer, Tredence Author, How to Compete in the Age of Artificial Intelligence, Big Data Imperatives, Analytics in Practice, Member, Forbes Technology Council | Advisor, HBR Advisory Council**

Working in an asset management company, where trust, accountability, and governance are paramount, the rise of AI presents both opportunity and responsibility. The challenge is not adoption—it is ensuring AI is applied with discipline, clarity, and alignment to real business outcomes.

In my view, *AIWoW – AI Ways of Working*™ by Anand Rathore brings a much-needed perspective to this shift. It moves beyond technology and focuses on how AI must be embedded into operating models, decision frameworks, and execution practices.

What resonates strongly with me is its emphasis on control, accountability, and human-AI collaboration—especially critical in regulated environments like financial services. The frameworks outlined provide a structured way to ensure AI remains aligned with intent and responsibility.

I believe this book is highly relevant for leaders and professionals who are looking to move beyond experimentation and integrate AI meaningfully into the way their organisations operate.- **Abhijit Shah, Chief Technology Officer (CTO) at Nippon Life India Asset Management Limited**

Three years ago, Anand Rathore walked into the **Be10x** program as a student. Today, he has written a book that stands on its own as one of the most grounded, most human, and most necessary contributions to the AI governance conversation we have yet encountered.

That journey from learner to author of a complete governing philosophy says everything about who Anand is. He came to Be10x not as someone starting out but as a seasoned professional who sensed that something fundamental was shifting in how organisations work and wanted to understand it deeply, honestly, and completely before it outpaced him. He asked harder questions than the curriculum required. He connected ideas across domains that most people kept separate. He was not learning how to use AI. He was already thinking about what AI means for the humans inside it, for the accountability structures around it, and for the governing philosophy that the age of intelligent systems demands but has not yet had.

AIWoW- AI Ways of Working™ is that philosophy, and it is remarkable.

What Anand has built is not a technical manual or a productivity framework. It is a conscience for intelligent systems, one that takes human dignity, empathic governance, and structural accountability as seriously as it takes capability and speed. His frameworks for Conscious Acceleration, the AI Lifecycle Loop, the Human-AI Responsibility Matrix, and AI Return on Humanity represent thinking that is original, rigorous, and urgently needed by every organisation deploying AI in the real world with real consequences for real people.

We say at Be10x that the measure of genuine learning is not what you know after. It is what you build from it. Anand has built something that makes us deeply proud—not as his teachers, but as people who believe that the AI era will be defined by the wisdom of the humans who govern it.

This book is that wisdom. Anand Rathore is that person. Read the AIWoW - AI Ways of Working™ book—and share it with every leader you know who is building with intelligence and responsible for the humanity it touches.- **Aditya Goenka & Aditya Kachave Co-Founders, Be10x**

What I appreciate about **AIWoW – AI Ways of Working™** is that it does not position AI merely as a technology issue. It frames it as a work design, leadership, and governance challenge. That distinction is important. In enterprise settings, value is not created by acceleration alone. It is created when acceleration remains aligned with purpose, when autonomy remains bounded by accountability, and when human judgment is strengthened rather than quietly displaced.

The ideas in this book are especially relevant because they arise from a reality many leaders are already experiencing, even if they have not yet fully named it. Productivity may be rising, yet clarity may be decreasing. Automation may be expanding, yet accountability may be diffusing. Systems may be getting smarter, yet organisations may still be uncertain about where final ownership sits. The result is not simply a technology gap. It is an operating-model gap.

Anand Rathore's contribution here is to insist that this gap cannot be solved only by deploying more tools or refining more workflows. It requires a conscious governing layer. His emphasis on empathy, human responsibility, decision ownership, and sustainable velocity reflects an understanding that enterprise AI success is not only about what systems can do, but about what organisations must remain able to see, question, and own. That orientation runs throughout the book's proposed constructs, from the Lifecycle Loop and Human-AI Responsibility Matrix to the emphasis on hybrid adoption across existing ways of working.

I also find it valuable that this work does not argue for rejecting existing delivery disciplines. Instead, it argues that the rise of intelligent systems demands an added layer of governance above them. That is a practical and timely insight. Most enterprises will not abandon Agile, DevOps, or structured delivery models. They will need to evolve them so they remain effective in environments where AI does not simply assist execution, but increasingly shapes priorities, recommendations, and decisions.

This book invites leaders to think beyond adoption and toward stewardship. That makes it a timely and worthwhile contribution to the wider conversation on AI in the enterprise.-**Supriya Devidutta, Enterprise AI Practice Leader, Office of CIO, IBM**

In my journey of building and scaling products, I've learned that the real challenge isn't adding intelligence, it's making sure everything continues to make sense as systems evolve. As complexity increases, clarity often becomes the first casualty.

While reading AIWoW – AI Ways of Working™ by Anand Rathore, what stayed with me is how thoughtfully it addresses this very tension. The book doesn't look at AI as something separate, but as something that quietly reshapes how teams think, decide, and deliver. That shift is subtle, but powerful.

I particularly appreciated the focus on keeping things connected, ensuring that as AI accelerates work, it doesn't disconnect people from purpose, ownership, or understanding. In many organisations, the challenge is not a lack of tools, but a lack of alignment. This book brings that alignment back into focus.

It also acknowledges something important: we are designing systems not just for efficiency, but for people who have to trust and work with them every day.

I would recommend this book to anyone building or leading in an AI-driven world. It offers a grounded way to think about progress without losing sight of what truly matters. - **Poornima Girish, General Manager - Delivery (Integrated Gas, Upstream, P&T), Shell**

AIWoW – AI Ways of Working™ by Anand Rathore offers a timely and necessary shift in how we approach Artificial Intelligence, not as a tool for unchecked acceleration, but as a system that requires strong governance, clear guardrails, and disciplined integration. From a security and risk perspective, the real challenge is not adoption, but ensuring accountability, control, and resilience. This work clearly defines how Human–AI collaboration must operate within structured boundaries, ethical alignment, and maturity-driven frameworks. It brings essential clarity to an evolving landscape. AIWoW is not just a framework; it is a governance-first approach that aligns AI capability with security, risk management, and organizational responsibility.- **Vasanth Madhure, Chief Information Security Officer (CISO), VIAVI Solutions**

बुद्धियुक्तो जहातीह उभे सुकृतदुष्कृते।

तस्माद्योगाय युज्यस्व योगः कर्मसु कौशलम्॥

Buddhi-yukto jahātīha ubhe sukṛta-duṣkṛte l

Tasmād yogāya yujyasva yogaḥ karmasu kauśalam ll

— Bhagavad Gita 2.50

A person guided by awakened intelligence rises beyond both success and failure.

Therefore, act with disciplined awareness, for true mastery in action is conscious alignment.

Contents

PART VII: Hybrid Ways of Working: Integrating AIWoW - AI Ways of Working™

PART VIII: Operating Transformation by AIWoW

Preface

Imagine a time long after a massive civilisational collapse.

Ice covers much of the Earth. Oceans have reclaimed cities. Knowledge has thinned into fragments. Only a handful of human families, ten perhaps, have survived, sheltered in the high Himalayas.

One evening, a father sits beside a small child, watching firelight flicker against stone walls. The child asks, innocently,

"Were we always like this?"

The father did not answer with dates or data. He answered from memory.

He spoke of a time when humans crossed continents in hours, not months. When distance dissolved into moments. When intelligence responded faster than thought itself. When tools listened, learned, and acted with human intent. When knowledge flowed freely, and power felt limitless.

The child laughed.

"These sound like mythological stories, Papa," the child said. "Like flying chariots and worlds beyond worlds."

The father smiled and replied softly:

"Once, these mountains also held significance for those who lived before the ice."

This journey begins here because **civilisations do not only collapse physically; they collapse first in memory**. And when memory fades, advanced realities are mistaken for myths.

Modern thinking assumes progress is linear: stone → steam → silicon. (Stone tools → machines → computers = continuous ascent)

Civilisational wisdom assumes something else: **cycles of rise, excess, collapse, and return**, suggesting that societies may experience periods of advancement followed by decline, only to emerge again in different manifestations.

Philosophical literature never described time as a straight arrow. It described **time as layered, recursive, and non-linear**, where advanced states appear, disappear, and reappear in new forms.

What today appears as speculative science, instant movement, the collapsing of time, and parallel realities was framed there not as fantasy but as a possibility conditioned by consciousness.

"*There are moments in history when powerful technological capabilities reshape the ways of working in organizations and ways of living in societies. Artificial intelligence has created one such moment, at scale, simultaneously, across virtually every industry and facet of life. Most organizations are navigating it with frameworks built for a different era, while society in general is pondering on new ways of living.*"

Technology is never a miracle.

Consciousness is. Intelligence Without Memory Becomes Myth

One of the deepest civilisational warnings is this: **when a civilisation forgets how it governed intelligence, intelligence destroys it.**

The ancient texts did not fear intelligence. They feared **unrestrained intelligence**.

In the **Bhagavad Gita**, reflection is placed before action. Choice is human. Responsibility is unavoidable. Intelligence is powerful but always secondary to discernment (*viveka*).

Why I Wrote This Book

We are living inside one of those moments now.

Artificial intelligence has entered the bloodstream of organisations. It accelerates decisions, compresses time, collapses distance, and amplifies capability at a scale humanity has rarely experienced before.

What once took years now takes seconds.

What once required generations now happens in iterations.

Fear comes with this speed.

Fear of losing your job.

Fear of being moved.

Fear of becoming unimportant to the systems we built.

Fear that speed might take away meaning and efficiency might take away what makes us human.

These fears are not irrational. They are signals of a deeper civilisational transition.

The leadership challenge of our time is not figuring out how to control artificial intelligence. The real challenge is how to remain human while intelligence accelerates, particularly in the face of rapid technological advancements that may alter our social interactions and ethical frameworks.

From Lived Experience to Empathic Intelligence

This book was not written based on theory alone.

For more than sixteen years, I have worked as a programme and project manager across complex transformations, high-pressure deliveries, and rapidly evolving technological environments.

In these environments, I learned something that no formal framework had ever taught me.

People do not resist change.

They resist being ignored.

When people feel unheard or invisible inside systems designed only for speed, resistance emerges. When people feel understood, something different happens.

Teams stabilise.

They adapt.

They continue performing even under intense pressure.

This realisation led me to practice what I later came to call **Empathic Intelligence (EI)**: placing people before processes, emotions before execution, and trust before speed.

This approach was not philosophical. It was practical.

Empathy did not slow execution.

It strengthened it.

From these experiences, the foundation of **AIWoW - AI Ways of Working™** gradually emerged.

The concepts of AIWoW - AI Ways of Working™ and the Lifecycle Loop were developed.

Artificial Intelligence does not behave like traditional software.

It learns.

It adapts.

It evolves.

Treating AI as a one-time deployment is therefore a fundamental mistake.

This book introduces the concept of the **AI Lifecycle Loop**, a continuous cycle of intent, design, deployment, learning, control, and renewal.

Intelligence does not progress linearly. It evolves in loops. Without conscious governance, those loops can amplify harm as efficiently as they amplify value.

A single governing idea runs throughout this book:

Conscious Acceleration.

Speed alone is no longer the achievement.

Wisdom at speed is.

Civilisations rarely fail due to improving intelligence.

They fail when intelligence grows faster than empathy, morals, and responsibility, leading to decisions that may be technically sound but ethically questionable and harmful to society.

The motivation to write this book did not come only from professional experience. Spiritual thought and philosophical reflection also profoundly influence it.

Much of my understanding of responsibility, awareness, and the deeper meaning of human action comes from spiritual teachings that view intelligence as something that must remain guided by consciousness.

This work is inspired by what I humbly refer to as the wisdom of the **Father of God**, the divine source that teaches humanity the deeper realities of life beyond material achievement.

My thinking came from many places, and the most meaningful ones were often the quietest.

Spiritual study, dedicated practice, and the profound privilege of learning at the feet of my Guruji have shaped everything I understand about responsibility, humility, and genuine awareness. His guidance lives inside these pages, perhaps more than any framework or methodology ever could.

Four sources flow through the ideas presented in this book.

The first is lived **professional experience** years spent inside complex, high-pressure organisational environments where ideas are tested, stretched, and either proven or discarded by reality.

The second is the **wisdom of spiritual philosophy,** timeless teachings about consciousness, duty, and what we truly owe each other. Wisdom that remains as relevant in a boardroom as it does in a temple.

The third is practice itself - **Karma Yoga**, conscious action, the discipline of doing what is right simply because it is right. A principle my **Guruji** continues to illuminate, through guidance that goes far beyond words.

And the fourth, perhaps the most joyful, **is my child**. There is a remarkable intelligence in the way children meet the world**. The innocence. The curiosity. The beautiful simplicity with which they see what adults have learned to overlook.** Watching my child grow has gifted me a clarity and presence that years of formal learning alone could never have offered. And the personal challenges life has brought my way have only deepened that foundation, each one shaping a resilience that continues to grow.

This book carries all four sources. Fully. Gratefully. Honestly.

This combination of experience, reflection, and spiritual grounding has shaped the ideas presented in this book.

What This Book Is and Is Not

This book does not reject technology.

It does not romanticise the past, and it does not suggest slowing progress.

Instead, it asks a deeper question:

Has human consciousness evolved at the same pace as human intelligence?

AIWoW - AI Ways of Working™ is a way of organising work so that intelligence can grow without weakening responsibility.

It proposes a framework in which:

- Control remains deliberate.
- Adoption is built on trust.

- Intelligence remains accountable.
- Technology remains a servant rather than becoming a master.

If artificial intelligence represents a return to civilisational capability, then **AIWoW represents a return to civilisational wisdom.**

A Hope for Those Who Come After Us

Perhaps one day, long after us, children will again sit in the shadow of mountains listening to stories of our time.

If they laugh and say those stories sound like myths, then we will have failed.

But if they say instead,

"They remembered in time, then this work will have served its purpose."

The future will not judge us by the intelligence of our systems, but by the humanity with which we built them.

"The AI era has begun, and AIWoW - AI Ways of Working™ is our commitment to ensure that this new age of intelligence advances with wisdom, responsibility, and humanity."

Introduction

"Where machines evolve to think, humans must evolve to feel together."

Work has changed faster than our ability to understand what that change is doing to organisations, leaders, and humans, leading to challenges in adapting to new dynamics, roles, and the emotional impacts of these transformations.

Artificial Intelligence did not enter organisations as a tool.

It entered as a **force**.

A force that compresses time, multiplies decisions, accelerates execution, and quietly shifts responsibility away from humans, often without anyone explicitly deciding to do so. Most organisations adopted AI the way they adopted earlier technologies: with excitement, urgency, and fragmented intent. Speed was celebrated. Output was measured. Efficiency was rewarded.

What was **not** redesigned was the *way of working itself.*

As a result, organisations today face a paradox they struggle to articulate:

- Productivity is increasing, yet **clarity is decreasing**.
- Automation is expanding, yet **accountability is diffusing**.
- Intelligence is scaling, yet **judgement is weakening**.
- Delivery is accelerating, yet **human confidence is eroding**.

This is not a technology problem.

It is a **work design problem**.

The Hidden Gap which needs to explore and expand.

Every major shift in how work gets done has historically demanded a corresponding shift in *how it is organised.*

When complexity increased, organisations adopted structured planning.

When change accelerated, they adopted adaptive execution.

When scale demanded flow, they integrated development and operations.

Each shift produced a **Way of Working,** not merely a set of tools, but a shared operating philosophy that aligned humans, decisions, and outcomes.

AI represents a shift **larger than all of these combined**.

Yet most organisations are trying to absorb it using **existing mental models**, existing governance structures, and existing leadership instincts. They are layering intelligence on top of systems designed for a slower, more linear, more predictable world.

The result is visible everywhere:

- AI systems generate answers faster than humans can question them.
- Decisions are executed before their implications are emotionally or ethically processed.
- Teams move quickly but feel increasingly disconnected from *why* they are moving.
- Leaders sense loss of control, even as dashboards show progress.

What is missing is not more intelligence.

What is missing is **a way of working that can hold intelligence responsibly**.

Why This Is Not Another AI Book

This book is not about

- AI tools
- AI architectures
- AI use cases
- AI productivity hacks

There are already countless resources that explain *what AI can do.*

This book addresses a different question:

What should organisations become in order to work with AI responsibly, sustainably, and consciously?

It focuses on:

- How decisions are shaped when intelligence is shared between humans and machines
- How accountability is preserved when execution is automated
- How empathy becomes an operational requirement, not a personal trait
- How can control coexist with acceleration without creating fear or resistance

This is a book about **organisational design**, **leadership responsibility**, and **human continuity** in the age of artificial intelligence.

The Origin of AI Ways of Working

AIWoW - AI Ways of Working™ did not emerge from theory alone.

It emerged from prolonged exposure to real organisational tension.

Across years of programme execution, transformation initiatives, and leadership responsibility, a pattern became clear:

Organisations did not fail because AI was inaccurate.

They struggled because **AI changed the emotional, ethical, and cognitive dynamics of work**, and no one redesigned the system to account for that change.

Teams did not resist AI because they feared technology.

They resisted because they sensed a loss of relevance, a loss of judgement, and a loss of meaning.

Leaders did not hesitate because they lacked data.

They hesitated because they lacked a **governing philosophy** that told them:

- Where AI should lead,
- Where humans must decide,
- And where speed must be intentionally slowed.

AIWoW - AI Ways of Working™ was born as an attempt to answer these questions **structurally**, not sentimentally.

Why Empathy Is Central, Not Optional

One of the most dangerous misconceptions of the AI era is that empathy is a "soft" concern that can be addressed after systems stabilise.

In reality, empathy is a **control mechanism**.

When intelligence scales beyond human pace:

- Empathy regulates impact.
- Awareness regulates direction.
- Humanity regulates boundaries.

Without empathy embedded into ways of working:

- Acceleration becomes blind.
- Optimisation becomes extractive.
- Systems become efficient but fragile.

AIWoW treats empathy not as emotion but as **organisational awareness**: the ability of a system to sense its own effects on humans, trust, and long-term sustainability.

The Purpose of this Book is to do Five Things

1. **Name the problem** organisations are experiencing but struggling to articulate.
2. **Define AIWoW - AI Ways of Working™** as a distinct, legitimate, and necessary evolution in organisational design.
3. **Introduce original frameworks** that make AI collaboration governable, auditable, and humane.
4. **Provide leaders with language and structure** to regain confidence and clarity in AI-driven environments.
5. **Lay the foundation for a movement**, not just a method.

It is written for those who sense that

- Something fundamental has shifted.
- Speed alone is no longer a sign of health.
- Intelligence without consciousness is unsustainable.

This book does not argue against automation.

It does not argue against intelligence.

It does not argue against speed.

It argues for **conscious acceleration,** a way of working where intelligence grows **without shrinking humanity**, where systems move faster **without leaving humans behind**, and where organisations evolve without losing their moral centre.

And that is why **AIWoW - AI Ways of Working™** must now be defined not as an idea, but as a **discipline.**

The Moment AI Changed Work Forever

The moment AI changed work forever wasn't the moment machines got faster than us.

It wasn't when automation hit new peaks of efficiency. It wasn't when algorithms started beating humans at specific tasks. Work has always made room for new technology—and every time it did, organisations adapted, adjusted, and moved on without ever really questioning who they were.

This time felt different. And it was.

Most of the time, the system works as it should, based on the true rupture that occurred when intelligence itself became externalised.

For the first time in organisational history, thinking was no longer an exclusively human activity embedded in roles, experience, and hierarchy. It became **ambient,** available on demand, embedded in systems, and continuously learning. This single shift altered the nature of work at a structural level, even though many organisations have yet to consciously acknowledge it.

When Intelligence Left the Human Boundary

Before AI, intelligence in organisations was slow, scarce, and embodied. It resided in humans. It accumulated through experience. It was constrained by time, attention, and cognitive limits. Decisions moved through layers not merely for approval but because thinking itself required sequencing and deliberation.

AI dissolved those constraints.

Suddenly, analysis could happen continuously. Options could be generated instantly. Patterns could be detected before humans noticed symptoms. Decisions could be shaped before they were formally discussed.

Work no longer waited for thinking.

Thinking arrived before work; asked for it.

This inversion changed everything.

The traditional flow, *observe, think, decide, and act,* collapsed into a compressed loop where **recommendation often preceded understanding**, and execution followed suggestion almost automatically.

This was the moment work crossed a threshold it could not return from.

The Collapse of Temporal Balance

Every way of working is built on an implicit balance between **speed and comprehension**. Humans need time to:

- Interpret information
- Debate alternatives
- Sense risk
- Align emotionally
- Accept responsibility

AI disrupted this balance by compressing time without compressing responsibility.

Decisions now arrive pre-structured.

Trade-offs are framed probabilistically.

Confidence scores replace conviction.

Organisations experience the illusion of clarity while actually losing **depth of understanding**.

This is why many leaders report a paradoxical experience:

- They have more data than ever.
- They feel less certain than before.

The issue is not information overload.

It is **decision velocity exceeding human accommodation capacity**.

Work changed forever at the moment this imbalance became systemic.

From Execution Systems to Decision-Shaping Systems

Earlier technologies optimised execution.

AI reshaped **decision formation**.

This difference is crucial. Execution systems are made to stick to the plan.

Systems that shape decisions affect intent.

When AI systems recommend priorities, generate solutions, and anticipate outcomes, they begin to subtly define what is considered reasonable, urgent, or optimal, thereby influencing the decision-making processes and values within organisations. Over time, organisational thinking aligns with machine-generated norms.

This is not coercion.

It is **cognitive gravity**.

Humans do not stop thinking. They simply think *within the frames provided to them.*

This is the quiet, irreversible change that most discussions about AI at work fail to address.

The Redistribution of Authority

Work has always been organised around authority.

- Who decides
- Who executes
- Who is accountable

AI disrupted all three simultaneously.

When recommendations originate from systems:

- Authority becomes ambiguous.
- Accountability becomes distributed.
- Judgement becomes defensible but impersonal.

Humans can say, "The system suggested it," without fully owning the decision. This creates a new organisational condition where **decisions happen without decision-makers**, at least in the traditional sense.

This is not a governance gap caused by negligence.

It is a structural vacuum created by intelligence moving faster than organisational design.

The moment AI entered decision pathways, authority began to **leak**—not upwards or downwards, but sideways into systems that were never designed to carry moral or contextual responsibility.

The Psychological Shift No One Planned For

Beyond structure and governance, AI introduced a psychological rupture.

For centuries, work was anchored in a simple assumption:

Humans think. Tools assist.

AI inverted that assumption.

Now:

- Tools think.
- Humans interpret.

This shift affects confidence, identity, and trust in ways that no training programme can fully address. Humans begin to question the following:

- Is my judgement still necessary?
- Am I validating intelligence or deferring to it?
- Where does responsibility truly sit?

Work changed forever the moment **self-doubt entered the act of decision-making at scale**.

This is why resistance to AI often appears irrational or emotional. It is not fear of technology. It is a reaction to an **unacknowledged loss of cognitive centrality**.

Why There Is No Going Back

Some believe this moment can be reversed by:

- Better policies
- Improved models
- More explainability
- Enhanced skills

These are necessary, but they do not undo the fundamental shift.

Organisations cannot revert to human-only decision systems without losing competitiveness once intelligence becomes external, scalable, and continuous. The modification is neither temporary nor optional.

The question of whether AI will influence work is no longer relevant.

It has already done so.

The true question is whether organisations will intentionally change how they operate to reflect this new reality or if they will keep operating under antiquated presumptions until humanity, accountability, and trust are irreparably damaged.

The Unseen Line That Was Crossed

History often records change through events that can be seen.

The most important moment at work was mostly hidden.

There is no official transition.

No reset of governance.

AI simply became good enough, fast enough, and embedded enough to cross a line where **thinking itself was no longer exclusively human**.

That was the moment work changed forever.

Everything that follows in this book builds on this recognition.

AIWoW - AI Ways of Working™ exists because this moment was crossed **without a corresponding evolution in how organisations understand, govern, and live with intelligence**.

The purpose of this work is not to dramatise that change, but to respond to it with clarity, structure, and responsibility.

Because once intelligence escapes the boundary of the human mind, **work can no longer be unconscious**.

Why Existing Ways of Working Are No Longer Enough

This book does not exist to criticise previous work philosophies. They were necessary. They were transformative. And they are now insufficient.

They were designed for environments where:

- Humans were the primary decision-makers.
- AI reshapes ideas before humans. Technology executes instructions, not intentions.
- Ethics were implicit in human judgement.
- Speed was constrained by human capacity.

AI breaks all four assumptions.

When intelligence becomes non-human, continuous, and generative, the organisation itself must evolve from a **delivery system** into a **conscious system**, one that knows not only *how fast it is moving* but also *whether it should be moving that fast*, *in which direction*, and *at what human cost*.

Without this evolution:

- Speed becomes reckless.
- Automation becomes alienating.
- Optimisation becomes dehumanising.
- Governance becomes reactive instead of foundational.

This is why a new way of working is required, not as a replacement for what came before, but as an **evolutionary layer** that addresses what those models were never designed to handle.

Positioning AIWoW - AI Ways of Working™ Alongside Existing Ways of Working

AIWoW - AI Ways of Working™ does not emerge in opposition to existing ways of working. It emerges **because of them.**

Every established way of working represents a successful response to the dominant challenge of its time. Each one solved a real problem, stabilised organisations under pressure, and enabled scale. AIWoW does not replace these approaches, reinterpret them, or compete with their philosophies. Instead, it **extends the operating horizon** into conditions they were never required to address.

This section maps AIWoW alongside existing ways of working **without critique** and without borrowing or reframing their intellectual foundations. The purpose is to explain **why an additional layer has become necessary**, not why anything else is insufficient.

A Shared Lineage: Evolution, Not Disruption

Ways of working evolve when the **nature of work itself changes.**

Earlier evolutions addressed:

- Coordination of human effort
- Responsiveness to change

- Flow across specialised functions
- Reliability at scale

These challenges remain valid.

AI introduces a **new category of challenge**: the presence of **non-human intelligence inside the work system itself.**

AIWoW exists to address this condition.

Mapping by Primary Organisational Question

Each way of working can be understood by the **central question it answers.**

Core Question Addressed	Existing Ways of Working	Why AIWoW Is Required
How do we organise human effort effectively?	Human-centric coordination models	AI introduces intelligence beyond human effort that must also be organised.
How do we respond to change faster?	Adaptive execution approaches	AI responds faster than humans; the question becomes, *how do we govern response speed.*
How can we make the process from idea to result smoother?	Integration of delivery from start to finish	AI changes ideas before humans officially define them.
How do we scale execution reliably?	Models based on process and automation	AI doesn't just help with execution; it also helps with making decisions.
How do we make sure that everything is the same and of good quality?	Standardisation and loops for feedback	AI keeps learning and changing beyond set standards.

The Emergence of Hybrid AIWoW:

When new ideas come along, businesses don't always change how they do things. Instead, they change by adding new layers to old systems.

The same will occur with AI.

Most organisations will continue using established approaches such as Agile, Lean, DevOps, design thinking, or other coordination models because these methods still provide valuable structures for planning, collaboration, and delivery.

However, once AI becomes embedded within decision processes, these models require an additional governing layer.

This is where **Hybrid AIWoW** emerges.

Hybrid AIWoW is the real-world organisational state where existing Ways of Working still handle execution, and AIWoW is in charge of intelligence, speed, and responsibility.

In this arrangement:

- Traditional Ways of Working set up how work is done.
- AIWoW controls the flow of intelligence.
- Agile may still be a guide for iterative development.
- Lean might still make operations more efficient.
- DevOps might still speed up delivery pipelines.

AIWoW makes sure that the intelligence that affects those activities is responsible, moral, and in line with human judgement.

In the AI era, hybrid AIWoW is the way things work. Organisations don't get rid of old models; instead, they add them to a larger governance framework for intelligent systems.

AIWoW responds to an emerging inquiry:

How do we consciously control intelligence, speed, and responsibility when both humans and machines have access to intelligence?

The Dimensional Shift Introduced by AI

Existing ways of working primarily operate across three dimensions:

- People
- Process
- Technology

AI adds a fourth dimension:

"Autonomous intelligence with agency-like influence."

This changes the nature of work in three fundamental ways:

1. **Decisions form earlier**

   Intelligence influences direction before formal planning begins.

2. **Feedback becomes continuous**

   Learning happens during execution, not after.

3. **Responsibility becomes distributed**

   Outcomes are co-produced by humans and systems.

AIWoW exists to **stabilise this fourth dimension**, not to redefine the first three.

Complementary Focus Areas

Rather than comparing philosophies, AIWoW introduces **additional focus areas** that were previously unnecessary.

Organisational Focus Area	Traditionally Implicit	Why AIWoW Makes It Explicit
Intent definition	Assumed to be human-led	AI requires explicit intent before acceleration
Decision ownership	Role-based	AI distributes causality
Emotional impact	Managed culturally	AI accelerates cognitive and emotional load

Organisational Focus Area	Traditionally Implicit	Why AIWoW Makes It Explicit
Ethical boundaries	Implicit norms	AI operationalises choices at scale
Speed regulation	Market-driven	AI enables unchecked acceleration

AIWoW formalises these focus areas **without altering existing structures.**

Where AIWoW Sits in the Organisational Stack

AIWoW does not sit:

- Below execution
- Inside tooling
- Within team rituals

It sits **above and across** existing ways of working as a **governing layer.**

Its role is to:

- Define when acceleration is appropriate
- Determine where human judgement must remain mandatory
- Establish boundaries for autonomous decision-making
- Ensure learning does not outpace understanding.

Existing ways of working continue to:

- Organise teams
- Deliver outcomes
- Optimise flow
- Manage quality

AIWoW ensures that all of this occurs **within conscious boundaries.**

Why This Layer Was Never Needed Before

Before AI:

- Intelligence was human.
- Speed was limited

- Learning was episodic.
- Ethics were naturally enforced by human presence

Under these conditions, governance could remain implicit.

AI changes these conditions.

When intelligence becomes the following:

- Continuous
- Non-human
- Generative
- Predictive

Governance must become **explicit, intentional, and systemic.**

AIWoW exists because this shift crossed a threshold where informal controls are no longer sufficient.

AIWoW as an Integrative Evolution

AIWoW does not ask organisations to abandon what works.

It asks them to **add what is missing.**

- Existing ways of working manage *how work flows*
- AIWoW manages *how intelligence flows*
- Existing ways of working optimise *delivery*
- AIWoW optimises *consequence awareness*
- Existing ways of working coordinate *people*
- AIWoW coordinates *people and intelligent systems*

This is not a philosophical conflict.

It is a **functional completion.**

The Necessity, Not the Argument

AIWoW is required not because existing ways of working are flawed, but because **work itself has evolved into a form they were never designed to govern.**

There is no need for criticism to explain this evolution.

The conditions alone make it unavoidable.

When intelligence becomes a participant in work,

A way of working that can consciously include intelligence becomes unavoidable.

AIWoW - AI Ways of Working™ exists to fulfil that role quietly, structurally, and responsibly so that organisations can continue to operate effectively **without losing clarity, accountability, or humanity** as they scale intelligence.

This is not a replacement.

It is readiness.

What does "Way of Working" mean in the age of AI?

In the age of AI, we need to start over and redefine the term "Way of Working." It is no longer possible to think of it as a way to plan tasks, make things run more smoothly, or get more done. Those interpretations were enough when humans did most of the work, and technology just helped them do it. This situation changes fundamentally with artificial intelligence.

Humans and leaders are no longer the only ones who are smart. It exists in systems that always watch, suggest actions, create results, and learn from every interaction. When intelligence becomes ingrained and enduring, the nature of work transitions from execution to engagement with intelligence.

A Way of Working in the AI era, therefore, refers to:

The structured system through which an organisation governs how intelligence, human and artificial, interacts, accelerates, and remains accountable across the full lifecycle of work.

This definition moves the focus away from activity management and toward **intelligence governance**.

Work as an Intelligence Flow.

Traditionally, work was designed as a sequence of actions. Tasks moved from planning to execution to review. Intelligence preceded work, and once decisions were made, systems followed instructions.

This sequence is broken by AI.

Intelligence now flows constantly through the organisation:

- Before work is scheduled
- While the work is being done
- When results are measured
- As systems learn and change

Work no longer follows a linear sequence of tasks. It is a constantly changing flow of information that is shaped by both human and machine judgement.

AI Way of Working must therefore define:

- How intelligence enters the system
- How it influences direction
- How it accelerates decisions
- How it is constrained when necessary

Without this definition, intelligence operates unchecked.

From Designing Processes to Building Behaviour

In the past, people worked together and made sure that processes were reliable. These are still important in AI-driven environments, but they aren't enough on their own.

AI influences behaviour.

It shapes:

- What is prioritised
- What is considered optimal

- What feels urgent
- What appears risky or safe

As a result, a Way of Working becomes a **behavioural architecture**. It silently conditions how people think, decide, and act in the presence of intelligent systems.

In the AI era, organisations must design not just processes but also behaviour **under acceleration.**

The Three Structural Layers of a Way of Working

A valid Way of Working in the AI era operates through three interdependent layers:

1. Human Core: Purpose and Responsibility

This layer tells you why work is done and who is still in charge of the results. This is where we get our morals, our ability to judge, and our understanding of the situation. No matter how advanced systems get, this layer is still in charge.

2. *AI Core: Execution and accelerating up*

This layer gives you speed, scale, analysis, and optimisation. It does the how of work in a way that is both effective and consistent. But it works within limits set by human intention.

3. Empathic Layer: Regulation and Balance

This layer controls when acceleration is okay and when it needs to be slowed down. It can detect emotional stress, moral conflict, and environmental risk. This layer makes sure that speed doesn't get ahead of what humans can do or trust.

It senses emotional load, ethical tension, and sustainability risk. This layer ensures that speed does not outpace human capacity or trust.

These three layers must stay in sync for a Way of Working to exist. When one person is in charge of the others, things get out of balance.

Consciousness as a Design Requirement

AI-powered work systems are not fixed. As they learn, they keep changing. This evolution can stray from human values and organisational goals if it isn't planned out.

Consciousness in a Way of working means the following:

- Being aware of how choices are being made
- Being able to see what happens when you speed up
- The power to stop, turn around, or ignore intelligence
- Always making sure that the goal and the outcome are the same

This is not an ideal in philosophy. It is a structural requirement in systems that learn independently.

Accountability Built Into the System

In the AI era, accountability cannot be applied after outcomes occur. It must be embedded into how work operates.

A Way of Working must therefore:

- Ensure that intent is human-defined before intelligence accelerates
- Maintain clear ownership of consequences
- Require contextual validation alongside automated outputs
- Bound learning within agreed ethical limits

Accountability is no longer a managerial function alone. It is a **system property**.

Emotional Impact as a Variable in Operations:

Accelerating up has effects on more than just what output is coming out. It has an effect on humans. When things change all the time, and we have to make decisions quickly, it makes us feel more stressed. Confidence fades away. Trust starts to fade.

In the age of AI, it is essential for work processes to consider emotional impact as a form of operational data.

- Keeping an eye on stress and too much work
- Changing speed as needed
- Keeping meaning and drive alive
- Stopping burnout from becoming a habit

Empathy changes from just a feeling to a way to stay stable.

A Working Definition for the AI Era

Bringing these elements together, a Way of Working in the AI era can be defined as the following:

A conscious, empathic, and accountable system that governs how human intent and artificial intelligence co-create value through regulated acceleration and continuous learning.

This definition reflects the realities of AI-driven organisations without borrowing from legacy interpretations.

Why This Redefinition Is Essential

Organisations will fail to govern intelligence if they continue to define Ways of Working as delivery models or productivity systems. Speed will increase, but understanding will decline. Capability will scale, but responsibility will diffuse.

In the AI era, work is no longer just about doing more, faster.

It is about **ensuring that as intelligence accelerates, organisations remain aware, responsible, and human.**

That is why the meaning of a Way of Working must evolve and why this definition becomes the foundation for everything that follows.

"AIWoW - AI Ways of Working™ exists for a simple reason: intelligence may accelerate work, but only conscious organisations can guide where that acceleration leads."

PART I

THE NEED FOR A NEW WAY OF WORKING

Understanding Why Work Must Evolve

Artificial intelligence has not only introduced new tools into organisations.

It has introduced a new form of intelligence that reshapes how decisions form, how speed operates, and how responsibility flows.

This section explores the structural tensions created when automation evolves into intelligent acceleration and why existing work philosophies struggle to fully govern this new reality.

The journey begins by examining the paradoxes and human impacts that reveal the limits of traditional ways of organising work.

The Need for a New Way of Working
The Automation Paradox
Efficiency Leads to New Complexity & New Problems.
From Automation to Conscious Acceleration
Human Intention Driving Technological Advancements.
From Tools to Teammates
Integrating AI as Collaborative Partners in Workflows.
Limits of Existing Work Philosophies
Inability of Old Methods to Handle AI Complexity.
The Human Cost of Uncontroled Intelligence
STOP
Algorithms
algorithm
Data streams
Burnout, Reduced Autonomy, & Loss of Human Control.

Chapter 1

The Automation Paradox

"Technology can accelerate work, but it cannot decide whether the work actually makes sense."

Automation came into organisations with a clear promise: faster work, more output, and results that could be counted on. For a long time, this promise mostly came true. Routine tasks were automated, operational mistakes went down, and businesses could grow without having to put in more work by people at the same rate.

Banks made transactions and settlements automatic.

Factories made production lines automatic.

Airlines made ticketing and scheduling automatic.

Retail businesses automated the management of orders and inventory.

In each case, automation made work less repetitive and more consistent. Organisations got better at what they did and could grow bigger. Humans thought that automation was a sign of progress and modernisation.

But as automation grew from just doing tasks to systems that could make recommendations, predictions, and prioritise tasks, a new pattern started to emerge. Organisations were moving faster than ever, but this did not always mean that they understood things better or made better choices.

Many organisations became highly active environments. Systems generated continuous outputs, workflows moved rapidly, and large volumes of actions were executed every day. Yet despite this activity, leaders increasingly faced difficulty answering basic questions about direction, purpose, and impact.

This situation reveals what can be called **the Automation Paradox**.

Automation improves the ability to execute actions quickly.

But it does not automatically improve the ability to interpret those actions.

As a result, organisations can become extremely efficient at producing movement without always producing clarity.

This chapter explores the emergence of this paradox in contemporary organisations and explains why merely increasing automation cannot resolve it.

1.1 Speed Without Sense

In business, speed has always been an advantage. Businesses that can quickly adapt to shifting circumstances in customers, markets, and operations are more likely to do well in most fields. Automation made this skill much better by getting rid of the delays that come with doing things by hand.

Now, systems can process transactions immediately, generate reports in seconds, and keep operations running smoothly across global networks. At first, these changes had clear benefits because they were made to processes that were already well-known. The logic behind the work was already clear; automation just made things easier.

Things changed when automated systems began to influence decision-making processes. Now, new systems can suggest what to do first, guess what people will want, and tell you what to do. These abilities make the organisation more responsive, but they also make things harder because things can happen faster than the organisation can fully understand what they mean.

Global logistics networks are a good example of this in action. Many logistics organisations now use automated routing systems that figure out delivery routes for thousands of shipments all the time. These systems look at traffic, warehouse stock, and delivery deadlines to find the best routes in real time.

Efficiency improves immediately when such systems are introduced. Delivery times decrease and operational costs decline. However, local managers sometimes observe unexpected results. Trucks may travel longer distances even when inventory exists closer to the destination. Shipments may move between regions in ways that appear counterintuitive.

Most of the time, the system works as it should based on the optimisation criteria it was given. The problem is that the system only looks at certain variables, like delivery time or route efficiency, and not at bigger operational issues, like the balance of inventory in different regions or future demand patterns.

In the past, human managers might have stopped and thought about routing choices that didn't make sense. Those pauses go away when everything is automated. Decisions are made automatically and quickly, which makes it hard to review them.

This situation can be described as **speed without sense**. Actions occur quickly, but the organisation's understanding of those actions does not develop at the same pace.

Operational dashboards show a lot of activity. Performance metrics show that things are getting better.

But deeper questions are still hard to answer:

- What led to this choice?
- Why was it given priority right now?
- What other effects might happen?
- When speed consistently surpasses comprehension, organisations jeopardise conflating movement with advancement.

1.2 Productivity Without Purpose

Automation has also changed how we measure productivity. Organisations are using more and more metrics like these because automated systems give clear numerical results:

- How many tasks were done?
- Less time needed to process
- Costs of doing business are lower
- More capacity for throughput

These indicators are helpful and often necessary for managing operations. But they only show part of how well the organisation is doing.

Throughput statistics don't show purpose. When work is clearly linked to goals and long-term results, it has purpose. Workers know why things are being done and how those things will help get results that matter.

Automation can unintentionally weaken this connection.

For example, financial institutions use automated monitoring systems to find possible compliance or risk problems. These systems look at transactions and send out alerts when certain patterns show up.

Employees are in charge of looking over the alerts and deciding whether to approve or deny them. Every day, thousands of alerts may be processed in big organisations.

The system works well for boosting productivity. Alerts are made quickly and looked over quickly. The organisation handles a lot of data.

But workers don't always fully understand the algorithms that make the alerts. They are no longer in charge of judging but rather of confirming. They don't use their judgement; they just follow the system's suggestions.

Over time, humans begin describing their role in simple terms: "The system flagged it; I approved it."

Productivity increases, but the sense of responsibility becomes weaker. Employees feel less connected to the outcomes of decisions because those decisions appear to originate from the system rather than from human judgement.

This condition can be described as **productivity without purpose.**

The organisation becomes highly efficient at processing work, but individuals feel less ownership over the meaning of that work.

If this pattern keeps going, organisations may see a number of small effects:

- High output but low engagement
- Getting things done quickly with little responsibility
- Well-optimised processes with less faith in the quality of decisions

The problem isn't that employees aren't motivated. The problem is with the design of the structure. Systems that are only optimised for output often don't keep the human role in figuring out what that output means.

1.3 When Acceleration Turns into Noise in the Workplace

Automation and AI systems send out signals all the time that help organisations do their jobs. These signals are alerts, predictions, performance indicators, suggestions for improvement, and analytical insights.

Each signal may give useful information on its own. But when there are a lot of signals, they can make things harder in a different way: organisational noise.

Noise doesn't mean that there isn't any information. When information comes in faster than humans can understand it, or when many signals fight for attention without a clear order, noise happens.

Many global manufacturing organisations, for instance, now use sensor networks and predictive maintenance systems to keep an eye on their production equipment. These systems get information from machines and send out alerts when something goes wrong.

The goal is to do maintenance before problems happen and cut down on downtime. This method works well in theory. But in big factories, the number of alerts can get very high.

Some alerts mean that there is an urgent issue. Some are warnings just in case. Many are predictions that aren't certain.

Managers in charge of operations must check these alerts while also keeping track of production schedules and coordinating the workforce. It's hard to tell the difference between important issues and minor warnings when hundreds of notifications come in every day.

The organisation has more information than ever before, but the humans in charge may not be sure which problems need to be fixed right away.

This condition shows how speed can turn into noise.

Some common signs are:

- Tired of making decisions because of all the alerts
- Different optimisation systems can cause conflicting priorities
- Leaders were more focused on short-term responses than long-term direction
- Less time to think about strategy

In this situation, organisations often add more automation to help them sort or prioritise signals. Even though these changes might help for a short time, they can also create new layers of information that keep the cycle going.

1.4 The Core of the Automation Paradox

The automation paradox does not mean that automation doesn't work. Automation, on the other hand, works very well in many operational settings.

The paradox happens because automation speeds up activity faster than the organisation can handle and understand what happens as a result.

Automation can deliver the following:

- Speed greater than human comprehension
- Productivity greater than traditional oversight mechanisms
- Information volumes greater than human attention capacity

When these capabilities expand faster than organisational awareness, strengths can begin to create instability.

The paradox emerges because technological systems were optimised while human interpretive capacity was assumed to adapt automatically.

Engineered speed. It was assumed that there was meaning.

We measured how productive the work was.

Responsibility was not clearly stated.

Automation did not intend to cause this imbalance. Instead, it showed a structural problem with how organisations plan work.

1.5 Why the Paradox Cannot Be Solved by More Automation

When organisations have trouble with operations, too much work, or less engagement, they usually try to fix things by improving their technology. Leaders put money into better systems, more complex models, and more automation.

Some examples are:

- Making predictive algorithms bigger
- Expanding the range of automation
- Adding more dashboards and reporting tools
- Lessening the role of human decisions

Even though these efforts may make some processes better, they often make the underlying paradox worse.

More automation makes things go faster.

Signals get bigger when they go faster.

A higher signal volume makes it harder for humans to make sense of things.

The main problem is not how advanced the technology is, but how advanced the design of the organisation is. Without clear rules for how humans and machines should work together, more automation just makes the problem worse. So, the automation paradox can't be solved just by improving technology. It must be dealt with by changing the way organisations make decisions, assign responsibilities, and think about things.

1.6 The Structural Insight

Automation is very good at improving execution. It can do tasks quickly and consistently on a scale that no human workforce can match. But acceleration makes movement better, not judgement.

Judgement, meaning, and responsibility necessitate components that automation alone cannot furnish:

- Deliberate decision boundaries
- Clear responsibility for humans
- Time to think about and understand things
- Leadership that can put together signals instead of just reacting to them

When these elements are missing, automation may slowly change from being a tool that helps organisations do more to being a force that makes things less stable. This change doesn't happen because the technology doesn't work; it happens because it works without enough oversight.

Automation can make work go a lot faster.

But only organisational awareness can make sure that faster work continues to help important goals.

"Automation can move organisations faster, but only awareness ensures they are moving in the right direction."

Summary Mind-map

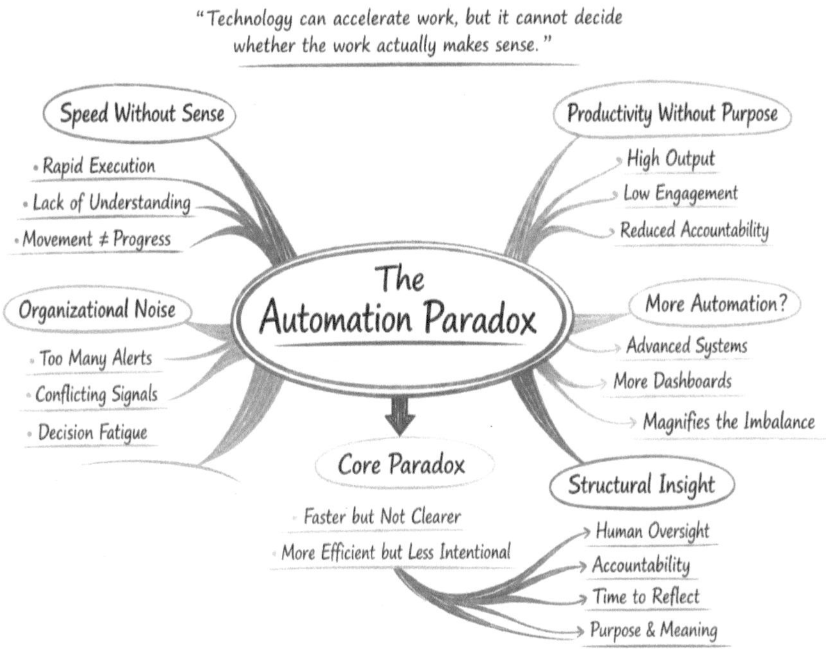

Chapter 2

From Automation to Conscious Acceleration

"Automation was never the destination.

It was a transition state."

Organisations started using automation because modern operations were too big, too fast, and too repetitive for manual processes to handle. The number of tasks grew quickly as businesses grew around the world and digital infrastructure became a key part of how they worked. Manual coordination led to delays, inconsistencies, and operational errors, making it hard for the business to grow.

Automation solved these problems by moving repetitive tasks from humans to machines. Systems could handle transactions faster, keep the same rules, and run all the time without getting tired. Banks made settlements and processing transactions automatic. Automated assembly lines were put in place at factories. Airlines made their reservation and scheduling systems automatic. Retail businesses automate keeping track of their stock and filling orders.

In each of these cases, automation made things run more smoothly by reducing friction in processes that were already clear. Organisations were able to do more work without having to hire more people. For many years, automation did exactly what it said it would: it made things happen faster, made outcomes more predictable, and made operations easier to grow.

But as digital systems got better, automation slowly started to affect a different level of work.

Systems began to shape how decisions were made instead of just carrying out tasks.

2.1 The Automation Mindset: Speed as the Primary Virtue

The original idea behind automation was simple: if a machine can do a job faster, cheaper, and more reliably than a person, it should be automated.

This principle is effective under specific conditions:

- It's clear what the problem is that needs to be fixed.
- The rules that govern the job don't change.
- You can easily guess the results.
- What humans think doesn't matter when making the decision.

In this case, automation makes things work better without changing who is responsible for what. Humans still set goals and make choices, while machines do the work that needs to be done.

For instance, automated systems in airline reservation systems quickly and consistently handle changes to the schedule, seat assignments, and ticket bookings. But humans still have to make important decisions about how to treat customers, set prices, and add new routes. Automation does the work that needs to be done every day, but it doesn't make big choices about the future.

AI changes this relationship a lot.

AI systems can do more than just automate physical or procedural tasks. They make some parts of thinking happen without you having to think about them. AI systems can look at patterns, make predictions, suggest actions, and suggest priorities based on probabilistic models that are built from a lot of data.

When operational systems have these features built-in, automation goes beyond just running. It begins to alter the context in which decisions are rendered.

2.2 When Automation Becomes Acceleration

When automated systems have intelligence built into them, work gets done much faster.

The customary processes in traditional decision-making are to gather evidence, look at it, talk about it, approve it, and then do it. Each step takes time. AI speeds up many of these phases by automatically generating ideas and suggestions. Because of this, choices that used to take a long time to discuss can now be made in only a few seconds.

This adjustment makes the organisation move faster, which is what we call "organisational acceleration."

Automating and speeding up are not the same thing. It's easier to get things done when you automate them. When you speed things up, the whole decision-making process moves faster.

After that, there are a number of changes:

- The time it takes to make a choice gets shorter. Why feedback loops never end
- Systems develop and get better on their own
- Operational effects happen faster

For example, modern supply chain systems employ AI more and more to estimate demand, modify inventory levels, and change logistics on the fly. The system doesn't wait for the weekly planning meetings. It always looks at operational data and market indications. It gives suggestions right away, and in certain situations, things alter on their own.

This skill gives firms more freedom, but it also creates new issues. As decisions are made more quickly, there is less time to think about them. Systems may respond before organisations fully understand the wider picture.

So, speeding things up makes not only the time it takes to make judgements shorter, but also the time it takes for their effects to happen.

2.3 The Structural Risks of Unconscious Acceleration

When things speed up without changes in how the organisation is run, a number of structural risks start to show up. One of the most common risks is the spreading of responsibility. When AI systems make suggestions or start automated actions, humans may think they are just following the system's instructions. When it looks like algorithms, not humans, are making choices, it's hard to tell who is responsible.

Another danger is losing your ability to make decisions. Humans who make decisions might start to trust the suggestions that automated systems keep giving them without questioning their own ideas. Humans may not want to look deeper if the system's outputs work well.

A third risk is that humans won't learn about ethics until later. It can take a long time for the effects of automated decisions to show up. It can be hard to figure out where unintended results come from when systems work quickly and often.

Organisations may also have less meaningful interactions with humans. When humans mostly interact with systems by doing tasks instead of interpreting them, they may lose touch with the purpose of their work.

A lot of the time, humans think of these problems as cultural or motivational. In reality, they are the structural effects of speeding up systems without changing the way decisions are made that control them.

The current state of the organisation is worse because of acceleration. When rules and regulations are not clear, risk goes up faster. When systems of accountability aren't strong, responsibility gets spread out. If a system doesn't have empathy and understanding of humans built in, the humans who run it might not care about them when making decisions.

So, acceleration makes both an organisation's strengths and weaknesses more obvious.

2.4 Conscious Acceleration as an Organisational Capability

The problem for businesses is not whether to speed up. Adding intelligence to operational systems will inevitably speed things up.

The problem is how to control acceleration in a responsible way.

This requirement gives rise to the idea of conscious acceleration.

Conscious acceleration acknowledges that speed constitutes a variable necessitating regulation. Organisations should not assume that faster execution always means progress. Instead, they should think about whether speeding things up helps them reach their goals.

Conscious acceleration brings a number of guiding questions into the process of making decisions in an organisation:

- Which choices are better made quickly, and which need more thought?
- Who is still responsible when automated systems change the results?
- Where does human judgement have to be non-negotiable?
- When should automated systems stop and let humans check them?
- How can businesses tell when speeding up is causing problems?

You can't just use technology to answer these questions. They need organisational structures that make automated systems aware of humans.

Conscious acceleration is an entirely novel manner for organisations to plan work. It makes sure that faster speeds come with clearer ideas about who is responsible, why, and what the effects are.

2.5 Organisational Design for Conscious Acceleration

Organisations need to make a lot of changes to their structure in order to use conscious acceleration.

First, businesses need to change their design from one that focuses on doing things to one that focuses on why they are doing them. Leaders should not automate processes right away. Instead, they should make sure everyone knows why decisions are being made and what they are meant to accomplish.

Second, organisations should not only look at output metrics when evaluating performance. Throughput and efficiency are still good ways to measure productivity, but they need to be combined with other measures that show a bigger effect, like how humans feel about it and the moral implications.

Third, governance needs to change from only looking at technological tools to looking at how decisions are made. Instead of just how well they work, organisations need to think about how systems affect decision-making and responsibility.

Finally, organisations need to get rid of the idea that speed is always good for them. Speed should be used carefully where it adds value and limited where it adds risk.

For instance, automated customer service systems might answer simple questions right away. But when customers discuss personal issues such as financial problems or health concerns, the system may route the conversation to a human representative. In this case, speed is still an option, but it is only used when needed.

This method does not hurt the performance of the organisation. It makes it easier to keep up good work over time.

2.6 Conscious Acceleration and the AI Era

Every technological era has optimised a different dimension of work.

The **industrial era** optimised physical labour by mechanising production.

The **management era** optimised efficiency through structured processes and coordination.

The **digital era** optimised scale and connectivity through global platforms and data networks.

The emerging **AI era requires organisations to optimise consciousness.**

Artificial intelligence speeds up and makes decisions on a larger scale. Systems can look at data all the time, make suggestions, and change how things are done in real time. So, work doesn't just speed up when humans do things faster; it also speeds up when humans make decisions faster.

This creates a new challenge.

Organisations can become very efficient while slowly losing sight of their goals, responsibilities, and lasting impacts.

Organisations need to develop organisational consciousness in order to deal with this problem.

Organisational consciousness is the ability of an enterprise to understand what its actions mean, guess what will happen next, and control the speed of its own work.

This ability includes the following in practice:

- Knowing how automated decisions affect humans and another human who has a stake in the outcome
- Finding unintended effects before they get bigger
- Making sure that system outputs match the long-term goal
- Controlling the speed of automation when it starts to affect judgement

Intelligent systems can cause rapid growth and instability if they don't have this ability. Optimisation goes on, but alignment gets weaker.

Conscious acceleration prevents this outcome.

Conscious acceleration makes sure that humans and organisations are still in charge of speed. It makes systems that would only optimise for efficiency more aware.

Instead of letting technology automatically set the pace of work, organisations make the choice:

- Which choices can be made faster
- What choices need to be made by humans

- When speed needs to slow down to keep things clear and accountable

In the AI era, competitive advantage will not come only from faster systems.

It will come from the ability to speed up smartly while being aware of the effects.

Conscious acceleration thus emerges as a pivotal competency for organisations utilising AI.

2.7 Setting the Foundation for AIWoW - AI Ways of Working™

AIWoW - AI Ways of Working™ starts with a simple change in how you think: speed is not just a technical achievement; it's also a leadership duty.

Organisations used to think that speed was a sign of progress. Humans thought that all of these things were clear improvements: faster systems, automated processes, and higher throughput.

Organisations thought that getting things done faster would make operations run better, so they tried to cut down on processing time and automate as many tasks as they could.

This idea changes when you add AI.

Automation made things go faster by taking tasks that humans did over and over again and giving them to machines. AI goes even further by changing the way humans make decisions. It can look at a lot of data, make predictions, and tell you what to do right away. Because of this, acceleration now has an effect on both tasks and decisions.

Automation made businesses work faster.

AI makes businesses more powerful.

But having power without a clear goal can cause problems and make things unclear. AI systems can use preset metrics to improve actions, but they can't tell if those metrics are still pointing in the right direction or fully understand how choices affect the big picture.

That duty is still human.

AI systems can use preset metrics to make actions better, but they can't tell if those metrics are still correct or fully understand how choices affect the big picture.

That duty is still human.

Leaders must learn how to control speed. They need to figure out:

- When should AI work by itself?
- What decisions do humans have to make?
- When should speed stop for a moral or ethical review?

Without this clarity, organisations may move faster but lose their way.

This is why it is important to speed up on purpose. It treats speed as something that needs to be handled carefully. As systems get faster, humans need to keep a closer eye on them.

AIWoW gives this balance its structure. It lays out rules and frameworks for how organisations can use AI while still being responsible, clear, and trustworthy.

Organisations that just move the fastest won't own the future of work.

It will belong to those who know when to speed up and when to slow down.

It will belong to those who know when to accelerate, when to pause, and when to place humanity back in control.

Summary Mind-map

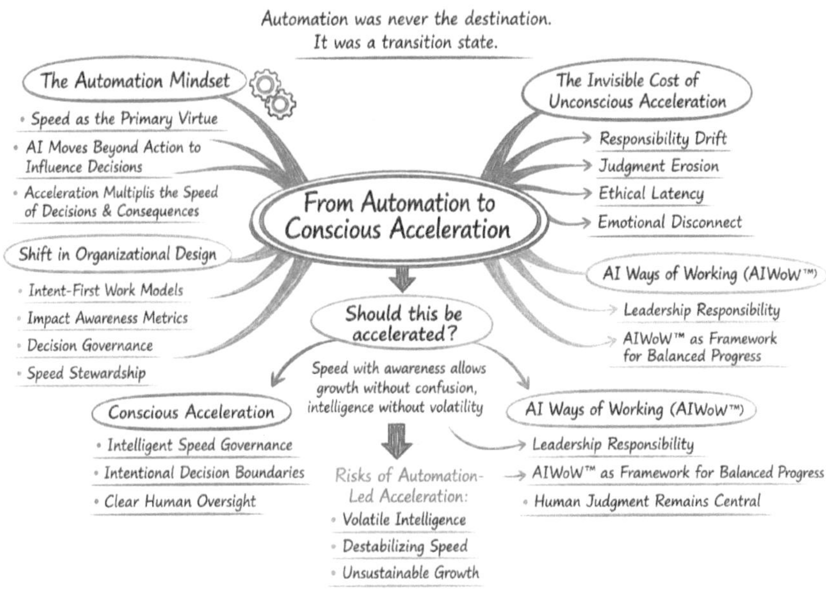

Chapter 3

From Tools to Teammates

"The most significant change AI brings to organisations is not automation of tasks but participation in decisions."

Tools have always been vital for organisations because they help them get a lot more done. Tools make work easier, more precise, and more consistent. Humans have always built tools to help them do things, not to change how they do them. When a machine receives a command, it does a job. When the job is done, the machine's task is done.

In this traditional connection, it's evident how work gets done: humans decide what needs to be done, and tools do as they're told.

AI makes a major difference in the game. When systems can look at data, detect patterns, offer suggestions, and adjust based on what happens, they change the way organisations make decisions. Instead of waiting for orders, AI systems can provide a range of options, define priorities, and help make operational decisions.

This change doesn't mean that AI has its own will or purpose. But its analytical results are having a wider and bigger effect on the places where humans make judgements, such as in business strategy, healthcare decisions, and resource allocation. AI is no longer merely a technical tool; it is now part of the workflow.

This move from tools that humans can use to systems that humans can use has a significant impact on how work is organised and executed. Conventional operating models posited that systems would adhere to predetermined instructions. When smart systems start to alter judgements, those assumptions are no longer valid.

Humans are starting to notice this change, which is one of the reasons why AIWoW - AI Ways of Working™ is needed. Organisations need to rethink how responsibility, authority, and collaboration operate in environments where humans and technology exchange intelligence.

3.1 AI as a Participating System

A traditional tool reacts.

A system that is involved has an influence.

Traditional tools work in a straightforward and predictable way. They wait for orders, do a certain job, and stop when it is done. When a user types in a formula, a spreadsheet does math. When an operator turns on a manufacturing machine, it puts parts together. In every case, the system only reacts after humans have made a decision about what to do.

Artificial intelligence (AI) changes this pattern. AI systems don't just wait for orders; they also constantly analyse data and consider their next move. They can do more than just follow orders; they can also suggest priorities, come up with other options, and change how decisions are made. In other words, the system doesn't just respond to work; it starts to help shape the work itself.

A good example of this kind is how DHL and UPS use modern logistics to run their businesses. Their AI-based routing systems look at traffic, delivery deadlines, vehicle capacity, and weather patterns in real time. The system uses this information to suggest which delivery routes to take and which packages to put first. The logistics manager still has to approve the final plan, but the AI system has already set up the choices that show up on the screen. It has changed the way we consider what decisions make sense and what doesn't. In this case, the system is no longer just a tool; it is now part of the decision-making process.

Humans in different industries can participate in this endeavour in a number of ways. AI systems can detect patterns in data and point out problems before managers do. They can suggest solutions that humans may not have thought of, such as different ways to price things, obtain supplies, or involve customers. A lot of systems also give their suggestions a confidence score, which affects how much human trust the suggestions receive in a subtle way. AI systems learn from what happens, so their future suggestions change over time as well, which changes how work changes.

The key point is that participation does not require intention. AI does not need to "decide" in a human sense to influence work. Its impact stems from how its outputs affect human judgement. Managers utilise AI forecasts, doctors review AI-supported diagnoses, and retailers adhere to AI demand predictions, thereby directly impacting their operations.

When a system starts to affect priorities and choices, it stops being just a tool in the background and becomes a part of how the organisation works. If you think of these kinds of systems as neutral infrastructure, you might not see how much they affect behaviour.

AIWoW is aware of this fact. It doesn't just see AI as a technical tool; it sees it as an intelligence contributor to the workflow, enhancing decision-making processes and facilitating collaboration among team members. By acknowledging this role, organisations can clearly identify areas where AI can assist and those where human judgement should always take precedence.

3.2 The Shift from Command to Collaboration

Conventional organisational systems were built around a command structure. In this model, humans made choices, systems carried them out, and the results were examined later. Managers set goals, teams carried them out, and technology helped by doing calculations, storing data, or doing tasks over and over again. Humans always decided what work needed to be done, and systems were just tools that helped them do it.

Artificial Intelligence changes this structure by adding intelligence between planning and carrying it out. AI systems look at data and make suggestions, which change the choices that are available before a person decides. Because of this, the flow of work no longer follows a simple chain of commands. Instead of humans giving orders and machines simply following them, the results increasingly reflect the interaction between human judgement and machine-generated insights.

Modern drug research is a good example of this. AI systems are now used by drug discovery teams to look at millions of chemical compounds and guess which ones might be useful for treating diseases. The system finds promising candidates much faster than researchers could by hand. Following this, scientists review these suggestions, assess their feasibility, and select the compounds for laboratory testing. In this process, the AI system helps with finding patterns and analysing data, while scientists bring their expertise, understanding of the situation, and responsibility for making decisions about experiments. The final result, which is the choice of a drug candidate, comes from both types of intelligence working together.

This interaction is similar to working together. The term doesn't mean that AI systems act like humans; it just means that results come from many different sources of intelligence. Humans set the purpose of the work, give it meaning, make decisions when things are unclear, and take responsibility for what happens. AI systems add value by being able to process large amounts of data, find patterns that are hard for humans to see, come up with possible solutions, and make complex calculations more efficient.

Organisations can no longer consider this interaction to be a random adverse effect of using technology; it has become too important to change.

AIWoW considers it a planned partnership. Organisations need to make it clear how to read AI outputs, how to evaluate suggestions, and who is entitled to make the final decision. Humans might not pay attention to AI insights or trust them too much without checking them out if there isn't any structure in place.

This shift also changes the way leadership must operate. In command-based systems, leaders primarily give orders and then monitor those orders until execution. In today's era of AI, leaders will need to guide the interaction between human expert knowledge and machine intelligence. This requires leaders to ask questions about system recommendations whenever necessary, interpret analytical outputs within a broader organisational context, make sure decisions are validated before they are executed, and ensure that AI-driven outputs remain aligned with strategic intent.

It is easy to see the difference between these two models. Command-based systems believe that they can plan and execute tasks by adhering to explicit instructions. AI-driven environments are more flexible. As systems look at new data, they find new patterns, risks, and chances all the time. A model that only works on commands can't easily handle this constant stream of information.

AIWoW thus establishes an organised framework for the collaboration between human judgement and machine capability. Organisations can make sure that AI makes decisions better instead of worse by carefully planning how these two types of intelligence will work together.

3.3 Collaboration Does Not Mean Equality

Recognising that AI is involved in activities doesn't always mean treating it as an equal partner. To avoid confusion about who is in charge and who is responsible, humans need to understand clearly what AI does in organisations. AI adds analytical and computational power, but it is not responsible for the results of decisions.

AI systems are capable but not responsible. They can look at a lot of data, identify patterns, make predictions, and suggest possible actions. However, AI systems cannot comprehend the broader context of human factors, consider moral implications, or assume responsibility for their outcomes. These duties are still with humans.

Because of this, working together with AI and humans will always be uneven. Both sides contribute distinct strengths to the table. AI adds speed, scale, and the ability to see patterns. Humans bring contextual understanding, moral judgement, a long-term perspective, and decision-making ability.

AI-assisted medical diagnosis is a good example of how this system works in real life. A lot of hospitals now use AI to look at X-rays and CT scans, as well as other types of radiology scans. These systems are good at finding small patterns that might indicate the start of a disease, and they do this job with a high degree of accuracy. However, the system by itself cannot make a final diagnosis. A doctor must look at the results, consider the patient's history, weigh the risks, and choose the best course of action. If a diagnosis is incorrect, the responsibility lies with the medical professional and the institution overseeing the process, not the algorithm.

This example clearly shows the difference. The AI system provides analytical intelligence, but the physician is still responsible for interpreting the results and making the final decision.

AIWoW neutralises this asymmetry by differentiating three most critical concepts: **participation, authority, and accountability**. AI may participate in generating insights and recommendations, but the authority to make decisions remains with humans. Similarly, while AI may influence the options to be considered, accountability for the consequences of those decisions must lie clearly with human decision-makers.

Maintaining these distinctions is essential. Without clear boundaries, collaboration can gradually shift into **deference**, where humans begin accepting algorithmic outputs without questioning the system. When such a shift happens, organisations risk allowing systems to shape decisions without sufficient human intervention.

AIWoW prevents this type of behaviour by strengthening human collaboration, rather than taking away individual responsibility. While AI provides decision-makers with additional information and options, humans are still responsible for making decisions, acting ethically, and being accountable for their actions, which intelligent systems cannot do.

3.4 Human–Machine Dependency Risks

As AI takes on more of the work, organisations naturally lean on it more. That's not a problem in itself. Every modern organisation depends on technology, financial software, communication tools, manufacturing systems, and data platforms. These dependencies are what make speed and scale possible in the first place.

The risk isn't dependency. The risk is dependency that grows quietly, without anyone noticing or managing it.

When people begin trusting AI-generated outputs without understanding how those outputs are produced, something subtle starts to happen. Skills soften. Curiosity fades. The organisation may look intelligent from the outside, but increasingly, that intelligence lives inside the technology, not inside the people using it.

In AI-driven environments, this tends to show up in three distinct ways.

The first is **cognitive dependency,** when people stop thinking as hard because the system thinks for them. Financial analysts are a good example. AI models that forecast market movements have become genuinely powerful tools. But when analysts begin accepting those forecasts without questioning the assumptions underneath them, something is lost. The habit of critical thinking weakens. The instinct to probe, challenge, and evaluate quietly disappears not because people become lazy, but because the system consistently appears more capable than their own manual analysis. And so they defer.

The second is **decision dependency,** when the algorithm shapes what choices even feel available. In supply chain operations, AI forecasting systems routinely suggest inventory allocations across warehouses. Leaders review those suggestions and approve them. But the range of options they are considering has already been filtered and framed by the system before any human entered the room. Over time, the feeling of genuinely owning a decision begins to erode. People start to feel like validators of system outputs rather than authors of organisational choices. The distinction matters more than it might appear.

The third is **emotional dependency,** perhaps the most quietly damaging of the three. As AI absorbs complexity, people can begin to disengage not just intellectually but emotionally from the work itself. In customer service operations, for instance, human agents increasingly step in only when the AI escalates something too difficult to handle. Over time, those agents lose their connection to the broader picture. Their confidence migrates away from their own judgement and toward the data the system produces. And when the system fails—as systems eventually do—they find themselves uncertain, not because they lack capability, but because their engagement with the underlying decision logic has slowly, almost imperceptibly, faded.

AIWoW is clear on this point. These are not cultural problems or behavioural failures. They are structural conditions, natural consequences of building environments where intelligent systems influence decisions at every level. They will emerge whether organisations plan for them or not. The only real question is whether those organisations choose to actively manage them, or quietly inherit the consequences of not doing so.

3.5 Dependency is a Design Issue

When organisations notice unhealthy dependency on AI, the instinct is usually to look at people. Retrain them. Shift the mindset. Tighten the discipline. But in most cases, the real answer isn't found in the people; it's found in how the work was designed in the first place.

The structure of how work flows determines whether humans stay genuinely engaged in decisions or gradually hand that engagement over to the system. And if the Way of Working rewards speed over reflection, accepts algorithmic recommendations without any structured pause for review, and measures success purely through output, dependency will follow. Every time. Regardless of how skilled, motivated, or well-intentioned the people involved may be.

Consider digital marketing teams that use AI to automatically distribute advertising budgets across channels. If managers are recognised and rewarded purely for campaign performance and never for understanding *why* the algorithm made the choices it did, they will gradually stop asking. The system becomes the real decision-maker. The human remains formally responsible, but the thinking has quietly moved elsewhere.

AIWoW tackles this at the source, not by trying to reduce reliance on AI, which would defeat the entire purpose of adopting it, but by making sure that reliance stays conscious and balanced.

Healthy dependency looks like this:

- People understand how the system arrives at its recommendations.
- They stay actively involved in evaluating those outputs.
- Questioning the algorithm is expected, not discouraged.
- Overriding it when judgement demands is treated as good governance, not inefficiency. And
- Responsibility for every decision remains unambiguously human.

The goal of AIWoW was never to shrink the role of intelligent systems. It was to ensure their presence makes people sharper, not softer. When dependency is deliberately designed and consciously governed, AI doesn't replace organisational intelligence—it deepens it, while keeping judgement, accountability, and human ownership exactly where they belong.

3.6 Redefining Teamwork in the AI Era

When AI starts showing up inside the actual flow of work, everything we thought we knew about teams needs a second look.

For a long time, a team meant something simple and human: people bringing their strengths together, figuring things out, and moving toward a shared goal. Technology was in the room, sure. But it stayed in its lane. It held the data. It ran the numbers. It didn't lean over and whisper in anyone's ear about what decision to make next.

That's changed. And pretending otherwise doesn't serve anyone.

When AI is analysing situations, surfacing patterns, and recommending actions in real time, it isn't just supporting the team. It's sitting at the table. The team itself becomes something different—a living, shifting conversation between human experience and machine intelligence, each one shaping what the other sees.

Look at how pilots work today. The flight management system never sleeps, tracking fuel, weather, navigation, and performance all at once. Pilots lean on it. They trust it. But the moment something falls outside the expected, the moment conditions get strange or an emergency demands a call, nobody programmed for the pilot takes over. That handoff isn't accidental. It's intentional. The system makes the pilot sharper. It doesn't make the pilot redundant. That distinction is everything.

Getting that balance right inside an organisation requires honesty and deliberate design, not assumptions.

People need to know clearly which decisions the system can own and which ones need a human being fully present and accountable. Ownership can never be left vague, even when AI has done most of the thinking; a real person must stand behind the outcome. Every workflow needs moments where human judgement isn't just welcome, it's required, especially when the stakes involve ethics, safety, or consequences that ripple forward in time. And the whole team needs to share one grounding belief that AI is there to make people better at what they do, not to quietly take over what only people should be doing.

When that clarity is missing, organisations tend to split in two directions. Some teams dig their heels in resisting AI out of fear, protecting territory, and missing the genuine value sitting right in front of them. Others go too far the other way—handing authority to the system because it feels faster, cleaner, more certain than the messy business of human judgement. Both paths lead somewhere uncomfortable. Resistance leaves real capability untouched. Over-reliance hollows people out until accountability is little more than a signature on a decision the algorithm already made.

AIWoW holds the ground between those two places. It brings AI genuinely into the work, not as background furniture, not as an unchecked authority, but as a participant whose role is thought through, defined, and kept honest.

What This Means for Organisations:

As AI becomes more present in daily work, the question of how to structure that presence can't be left to drift.

Thinking of AI purely as a tool that misses what's actually happening. It influences priorities. It frames choices before humans even enter the conversation. It shapes decisions in ways that often go unnoticed until the pattern is already set. But swinging to the other extreme, treating AI like a full team member without any guardrails, quietly shifts responsibility away from the people who are still, and must always remain, answerable for what happens.

The right approach lives between those two positions. Closer to the truth. More honest about what AI actually is.

AI brings real intelligence into the workflow. That's worth embracing. But its presence needs to be woven deliberately into the Way of Working, not smuggled in through a patchwork of disconnected tools that nobody has properly examined or governed.

That means deciding, clearly and openly, how recommendations from AI get weighed. How decisions stay owned by people. How human expertise and machine-generated insight work alongside each other without one slowly edging the other out. And how dependency gets watched, kept conscious, kept balanced, kept within reach of human judgement at all times.

The collaboration between people and AI matters far too much to leave to chance. It deserves intention. It deserves care. And it deserves a firm, unwavering sense of what must always, no matter how capable the system becomes, remain a human call.

Once AI participates in work, work itself must be redesigned so that participation strengthens organisations rather than destabilising them.

Summary Mind-Map

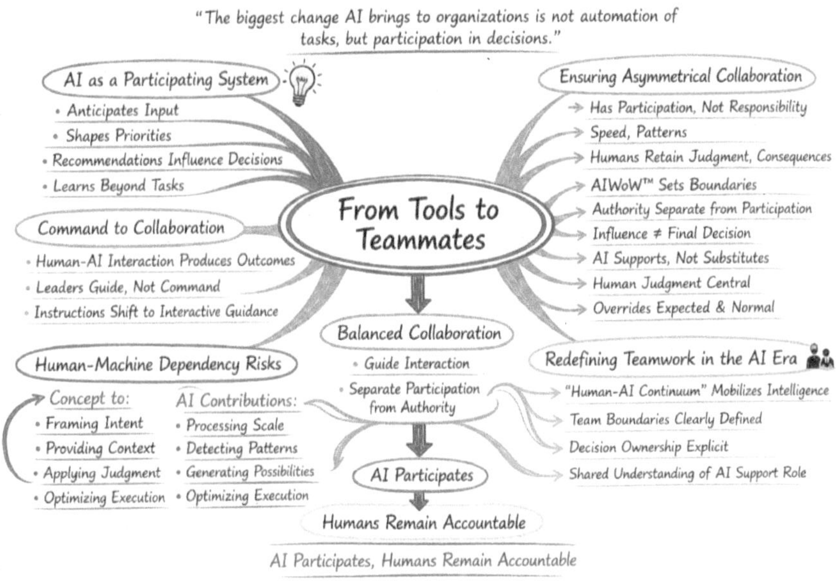

Chapter 4

Limits of Existing Work Philosophies

"Ways of working succeed not because they are universal, but because they fit the conditions of their time.

Every era creates ways of working that fit its dominant conditions. These philosophies are not mistaking; they are responses. They stabilise organisations, enable coordination, and translate intent into action. Their strength lies in how precisely they match the environment for which they were designed.

Across industries, different ways of working emerged to solve different operational challenges. Some emphasised efficiency and repeatability. Others focused on adaptability, collaboration, or continuous improvement. Each approach was shaped by the technological, economic, and organisational realities of its time.

For example, **Taylorism and scientific management** focused on optimising physical labour and operational efficiency. **Lean production** emphasised waste reduction and continuous improvement in manufacturing environments. **Agile methods** emerged to handle uncertainty and rapid iteration in software development. **DevOps** evolved to bridge development and operations in digital systems, facilitating faster delivery of software and improved collaboration between teams. **Design thinking** encouraged creativity and user-centred innovation.

These philosophies were powerful because they aligned with the conditions of their era.

The limits explored in this chapter are not failures. They are edges; points where the environment has changed faster than the assumptions beneath existing work philosophies.

Artificial intelligence shifts those assumptions.

When intelligence becomes continuous, embedded, and capable of shaping decisions before humans intervene, the foundations of traditional work thinking begin to strain. The result is not collapse but misalignment, subtle at first and structural over time.

4.1 Why Speed Optimisation Alone Fails

Speed has long been treated as a universal virtue. Faster delivery implied responsiveness. Shorter cycles suggested adaptability. Reduced delay signalled competitiveness. When human effort and sequential decision-making constrained work, optimising for speed made sense.

Many modern work philosophies reinforced this orientation. Agile shortened development cycles. DevOps accelerated deployment pipelines. Lean reduced operational delays. Continuous delivery emphasised rapid iteration.

Under these conditions, speed was closely connected to improved outcomes.

AI removes those constraints.

Execution can now occur at a pace disconnected from human comprehension. Decisions can be generated faster than they can be meaningfully evaluated. Under these conditions, speed stops being an advantage and becomes a multiplier of unresolved assumptions.

Speed optimisation alone fails for three fundamental reasons.

First, speed amplifies consequences.

Acceleration does not merely increase output; it increases the rate at which effects propagate. Errors spread faster. Misjudgments scale wider. Corrections arrive later relative to impact. What once could be fixed through iteration now compounds before awareness emerges.

Second, speed exceeds human accommodation.

Understanding requires time: time to interpret context, anticipate implications, and sense risk. When work moves faster than understanding, action detaches from judgement. Decisions occur, but comprehension follows behind. Learning becomes reactive instead of preventive.

Third, speed replaces intention with momentum.

When acceleration becomes the dominant organising principle, direction is assumed rather than chosen. Systems optimise continuously, and humans follow emergent paths without consciously reaffirming purpose, often leading to a lack of intentionality in their actions and decisions. Movement continues even when clarity weakens.

Speed without regulation transforms progress into inertia.

4.2 Fragmentation of Responsibility

Traditional work philosophies rely on a clear chain of responsibility. A decision is made, an action follows, and accountability can be traced. This clarity depends on a simple assumption: decisions originate from identifiable human judgment.

Many management frameworks reinforce this clarity through roles, approvals, and structured decision ownership. Organisational hierarchies, governance models, and operational processes all assume that responsibility can be traced through identifiable human actors.

AI disrupts this assumption.

Outcomes in AI-driven environments emerge from multiple contributors:

- Human intent
- System-generated recommendations
- Automated optimisations
- Continuous learning feedback

Responsibility becomes distributed, not transferred.

Fragmentation occurs quietly. No one rejects responsibility; it simply becomes difficult to locate. Humans influence decisions without fully owning them. Systems shape outcomes without bearing consequences. Accountability shifts from proactive ownership to retrospective explanation.

This shift creates a new organisational condition:

- Decisions happen without decisive moments.
- Actions occur without clear authorship.
- Responsibility is discussed after results, not before choices.

Existing work philosophies are not designed to address distributed interconnection. They assume responsibility can be mapped to roles, approvals, or checkpoints. In AI-driven work, responsibility must be architected into the system itself, or it diffuses by default.

4.3 Absence of Emotional and Ethical Governance

Earlier ways of working treated emotional impact and ethical considerations as contextual concerns. Culture manages emotion. Policy governs ethics. Execution focuses on delivery.

Many established frameworks, therefore, separate operational execution from human wellbeing or ethical reflection. These aspects are often handled through human resource policies, leadership culture, or occasional governance reviews.

AI collapses these separations.

Acceleration affects humans continuously. Change is no longer episodic; it is constant. Decisions arrive faster, priorities shift more frequently, and cognitive load increases steadily. Emotional strain becomes a system effect, not an individual weakness.

Without mechanisms to regulate this impact:

- Stress becomes normalised.
- Fatigue hides behind productivity.
- Disengagement is misread as resistance.

Ethical considerations follow a similar pattern. AI systems operationalise choices at scale. They encode priorities, trade-offs, and thresholds repeatedly and consistently. Ethics is no longer a discussion held occasionally; it has become an embedded behaviour executed continuously.

When ethical governance remains implicit:

- Bias accumulates invisibly.
- Fairness erodes gradually.
- Trust weakens without a single point of failure.

Existing work philosophies assume ethics are enforced by human presence and judgement. AI-driven systems act faster and more frequently than such safeguards can respond.

The Combined Structural Limit

Speed without regulation, responsibility without clarity, and acceleration without emotional or ethical governance can lead to success. They create organisational noise; constant activity without coherent alignment.

The organisation appears active, responsive, and productive. Internally, it experiences:

- Confusion about ownership
- Anxiety about direction
- Reduced confidence in judgement
- Fatigue masked as efficiency

These signals indicate not incompetence but a misfit between environment and operating philosophy.

4.4 Why an Additional Way of Working Becomes Necessary

The limits described here do not invalidate existing work philosophies. They define the boundary of their effectiveness.

Lean, Agile, DevOps, design thinking, and other frameworks continue to provide valuable methods for coordination, iteration, and delivery. However, they were developed in environments where intelligence remained primarily human and where systems executed instructions rather than influencing decisions.

AI introduces conditions that require additional capabilities:

- Speed must be governed, not merely increased
- Responsibility must be systemic, not assumed
- Emotional and ethical impact must be operational, not peripheral

An additional Way of Working becomes necessary to hold these capabilities together.

This is the role of **AIWoW - AI Ways of Working™.**

AIWoW is not designed to replace existing Ways of Working. Organisations will continue to use Agile, Lean, DevOps, design thinking, and other established approaches where they remain effective. AIWoW adds an additional layer that becomes necessary when intelligent systems begin to participate in decisions and workflows. It can operate as a standalone framework in AI-driven environments or integrate with existing Ways of Working, creating a **Hybrid AI Way of Working** that aligns human judgement, system intelligence, and organisational execution.

In this hybrid structure:

- Agile can continue guiding iterative development
- Lean can continue optimising operational efficiency
- DevOps can continue accelerating delivery pipelines

AIWoW operates with and across these practices by introducing governance for intelligence, responsibility for AI-influenced decisions, and regulation for acceleration.

In other words, AIWoW ensures that existing methods continue to function effectively **in an environment where AI is an active participant in work.**

This is not about slowing down.

It is about restoring sense, ownership, and balance under acceleration.

A Way of Working designed for intelligent systems does not replace what already works. It completes it by providing the structures required to operate consciously in an environment where intelligence itself participates.

The chapters that follow move from recognising these limits to defining how intelligence, acceleration, and humanity can coexist without undermining one another.

Because in an era of continuous intelligence, working unconsciously is no longer sustainable.

"When intelligence begins to participate in work, the way work is organised must evolve as well."

Summary Mind-map

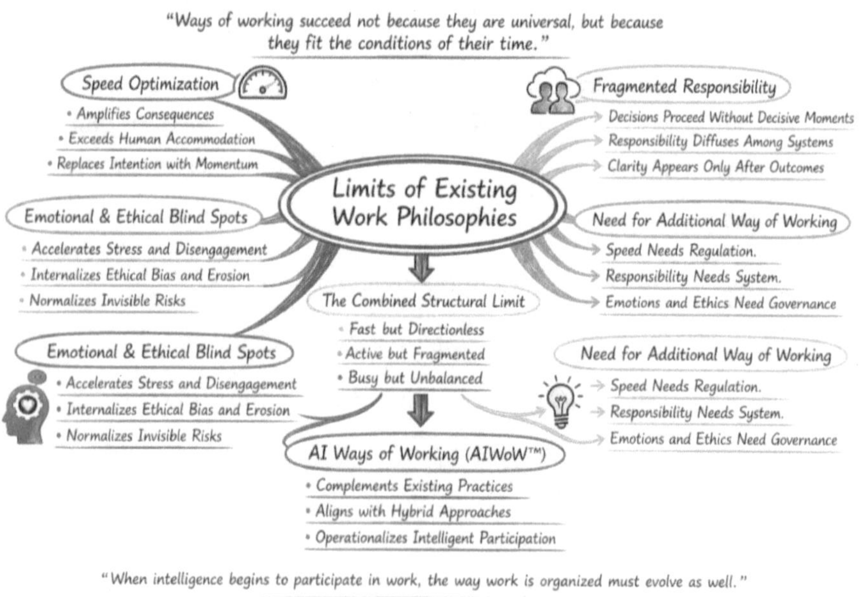

Chapter 5

The Human Cost of Uncontrolled Intelligence

"When intelligence operates without limits, the first system it strains is the human mind."

Intelligence has always influenced work. What is different today is not that intelligence exists in organisations but **how continuously and how quickly it operates**.

Formerly, intelligence was sourced by humans. Humans interpreted information and made decisions, and systems executed those decisions. Work had natural pauses because human thinking takes time.

With AI, intelligence is increasingly embedded inside systems. Now systems analyse data, generate their own insights, recommend various actions, and sometimes execute decisions on their own.

This change improves efficiency, but it also changes how humans experience work.

Uncontrolled intelligence rarely appears dangerous. It usually arrives as an improvement:

- Faster decision-making
- Continuous insights
- Automated recommendations
- Increased productivity

However, when intelligence operates without limits, the human impact gradually begins to appear. The effects are usually subtle at first. Instead, they show up as subtle changes in attention, relationships, and energy.

These changes are often misconceptualised as personal weakness or cultural issues. In reality, they are usually **by-products of systems where intelligence moves faster than humans can absorb it**, leading to cognitive overload and affecting decision-making processes.

5.1 Cognitive Overload

When humans have time to contemplate the situation and their choices, their minds work best. The brain is adept at figuring things out, but it has trouble when too many things need its attention at once.

AI-driven environments often make this happen.

Think about the job of a product manager at a big digital organisation. Before, humans made decisions about product updates at weekly planning meetings. Before making decisions, the team looked at user feedback and data and talked about what was most important.

Today, the same product manager may face a very different environment. AI systems generate daily analytics, automated customer insights, predictive churn warnings, pricing suggestions, and performance alerts. At the same time, collaboration tools produce messages, dashboards update continuously, and recommendations appear automatically.

Each piece of information is useful on its own. These tools constantly send signals.

When such a situation happens, cognitive overload starts to show up:

- Attention goes from one dashboard to another and then back again.
- Decisions are made quickly without a lot of thought.
- Reflection is put off because the next alert comes right away.
- Mental fatigue rises even when work seems to be getting done.

The brain makes decisions easier by adapting. Humans depend more on system suggestions because it's impossible to carefully look at every signal.

For example, a marketing manager may approve AI-generated campaign changes without fully analysing them, simply because dozens of recommendations appear each day. The system may still produce acceptable results, but the human role shifts from **thinking to reacting**.

Cognitive overload is therefore not just about too much information. It happens when **intelligence produces decisions faster than humans can interpret them**.

5.2 Empathy Erosion

Work is not only about tasks and decisions; it is also about humans. Teams collaborate, leaders support employees, and organisations rely on trust and understanding.

Empathy plays an important role in these relationships. It requires time to listen, emotional attention, and awareness of how work affects others.

Highly accelerated environments gradually weaken these conditions.

Imagine a team leader managing a global customer support team supported by AI analytics. The system continuously monitors customer sentiment, recommends responses, and evaluates employee performance in real time.

While the system improves efficiency, the leader's daily routine becomes dominated by dashboards and metrics. Conversations with team members become shorter because operational signals demand constant attention.

Instead of asking, "How are you managing this workload?" the leader may focus more on questions like, "Why did the response time increase this hour?"

Gradually, interactions become more transactional.

Over time, several patterns appear:

- Leaders spend more time interpreting metrics than understanding humans
- Teams focus on completing tasks rather than supporting each other
- Emotional fatigue is treated as a normal side effect of productivity

No one deliberately decides to reduce empathy. The shift happens because accelerated systems leave less space for human interaction.

Empathy erosion, therefore, occurs when work systems prioritise optimisation **but do not include mechanisms to sense human impact.**

5.3 Burnout as a System Outcome

Humans often consider burnout to be a personal issue, but in many AI-driven settings, it's better to think of it as a system outcome.

When smart systems run all the time, work environments change in several ways:

- Work rarely stops because systems keep sending out signals.
- Based on new information, priorities change often.
- As productivity goes up, so do expectations.
- Workers feel like they have to keep up with systems that are getting faster.

Think about a financial analyst who works for an organisation that uses AI to keep an eye on the market. In the past, the analyst read market reports in the morning and provided suggestions during the day.

Today the analyst receives continuous alerts about market changes, algorithmic predictions, and risk indicators. Decisions that previously took hours of analysis may now be expected within minutes.

At first, this approach makes things more efficient. But as time goes on, the analyst feels more and more pressure to respond to every signal right away. Even after work is over, alerts may still show up on mobile devices.

Burnout happens slowly, in a way that most humans are familiar with:

- Speeding things up makes humans more productive.
- The cognitive load keeps going up.
- Emotional energy goes down.
- Work seems more reactive and less important.
- Being tired all the time becomes normal.

No single choice makes you burn out. The system, on the other hand, makes it hard for humans to stay in recovery.

Organisations often try to address burnout through wellness programmes or motivational initiatives. While these efforts are helpful, they cannot fully solve the problem if the system itself continuously generates pressure.

5.4 The Hidden Debt of Accelerated Intelligence

One reason it's still difficult to see the human cost of AI is that organisations keep doing well.

From a management perspective, many signs look good:

- The speed of delivery gets better.
- Productivity numbers go up.
- Automation makes the workload less visible.
- The efficiency of operations goes up.

But these visible benefits may be hiding a growing cost to humans.

For instance, a tech organisation might use AI systems to automatically decide which engineering tasks are most important. By quickly finding the most important tasks and assigning them, the system boosts productivity.

The team appears better on paper.

Engineers may have to deal with changing priorities all the time because the system keeps changing its suggestions. They don't finish their work in stable cycles; instead, they change direction all day long, which can lead to confusion and a lack of clarity about project objectives.

The organisation progresses faster, but workers might feel mentally drained and disconnected from the long-term goals. This leads to what could be called a hidden human debt: a slow build-up of mental strain, emotional exhaustion, and less interest.

The debt is often hidden because productivity is still high. This is until experienced workers leave, mistakes in decision-making go up, or trust between team members starts to fade.

The Structural Nature of Human Cost

Cognitive overload, empathy erosion, and burnout are not separate problems. They are different expressions of the same underlying condition.

They appear when **intelligence accelerates without human-aware regulation**.

When systems focus only on speed and optimisation:

- Decision signals multiply faster than humans can process
- Emotional signals from employees receive less attention
- Continuous intelligence removes natural pauses in work cycles

Under these conditions, humans become the point where system pressure accumulates, leading to increased stress and potential burnout among employees.

This situation does not arise because organisations intentionally ignore human wellbeing. Most organisations are simply optimising systems for efficiency and performance.

The difficulty is that the **design of the work system** often fails to account for how humans experience continuous intelligence.

5.5 Restoring Human Sustainability

Preventing the human cost of accelerated intelligence does not require slowing technological progress. Instead, organisations need to regulate how intelligence operates within their work systems.

A sustainable environment must guarantee that individuals retain the ability to comprehend, interrogate, and direct intelligent systems.

This necessitates work structures that:

- Limit the number of decisions that humans have to make at the same time
- Make sure to take breaks on purpose to think and evaluate
- See emotional signals as helpful feedback instead of resistance
- Let humans ignore automated suggestions when they need to
- Keep meaning and responsibility along with productivity

In these kinds of situations, empathy is no longer a secondary concern; it becomes part of operational awareness.

This is where AIWoW - AI Ways of Working™ comes in.

AIWoW recognises that when intelligence becomes embedded in work systems, the organisation must also regulate its human impact. Instead of assuming that employees will endlessly adapt to accelerating systems, AIWoW introduces structures that balance intelligence with awareness.

For example, organisations may introduce checkpoints where human judgement reviews automated decisions before execution. Workflows may be designed so that emotional feedback from employees becomes part of operational monitoring. Responsibility for decisions remains visible even when AI participates in analysis and recommendations.

Through these mechanisms, AIWoW does not slow intelligence. Instead, it **stabilises intelligence around human capacity**.

The human cost described in this chapter represents an important threshold for modern organisations.

It is no longer sustainable to scale intelligence while assuming that humans will simply adapt indefinitely.

The future of work must integrate three essential balances:

- Intelligence with awareness
- Speed with restraint
- Automation with empathy

The chapters that follow explore how this integration becomes possible through a structured Way of Working designed for environments where intelligent systems participate continuously.

Because when intelligence accelerates without regulation, it not only increases efficiency.

Over time, it extracts attention, empathy, and ultimately, humans.

"The true challenge of intelligent systems is not scaling intelligence but protecting the humanity that must live with it."

Summary Mind-map

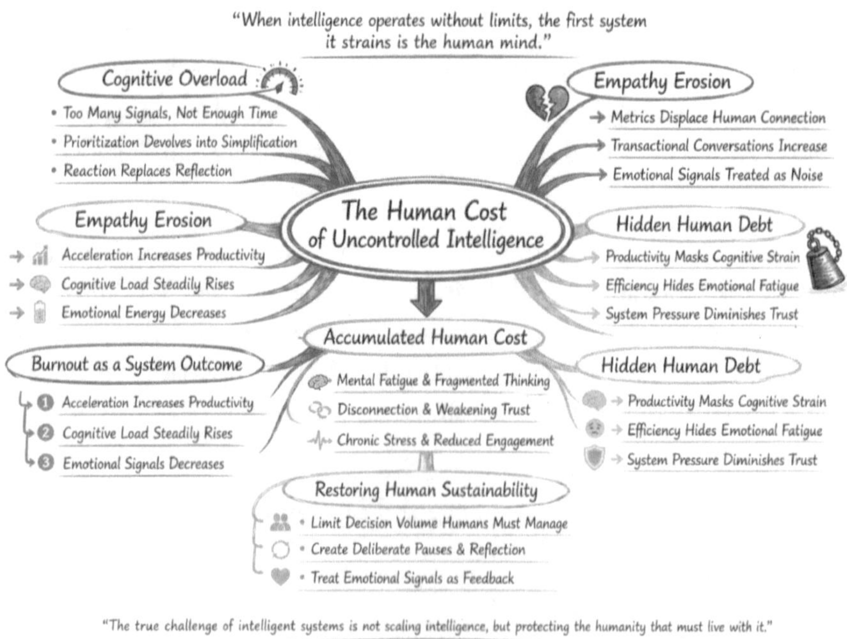

PART II

THE PHILOSOPHY OF AIWoW - AI WAYS OF WORKING™

Reframing Intelligence, Leadership, and Responsibility

When intelligence becomes continuous and embedded inside systems, organisations must rethink the philosophical foundations of work itself.

This section introduces the conceptual foundations of **AIWoW - AI Ways of Working™**. It explores empathic intelligence, conscious leadership, and the deeper relationship between human judgement and artificial capability.

The goal is not to slow intelligence but to ensure that intelligence evolves without weakening humanity.

Empathic
Intelligence (EI) in
AI AWoW™
Conscious Leadership
in the Age of AI
The Philosophy
of AI Ways of
Working
(AIWoW™)
AI as Partner,
Not Replacement
Timeless Philosophy
in Modern Systems

Chapter 6

Empathic Intelligence (EI) In AIWoW - AI Ways of Working™

"As intelligence becomes faster, the most important intelligence becomes the ability to understand its human impact."

As intelligence becomes embedded into systems and operates at a speed beyond human pacing, organisations encounter a new and unavoidable requirement: the ability to **sense, interpret, and regulate human impact under continuous acceleration**. Analytical intelligence alone is no longer sufficient. Optimisation without awareness destabilises systems. Speed without sensitivity extracts more than it creates.

This requirement gives rise to **Empathic Intelligence (EI)**.

Empathic Intelligence is not an emotional overlay on artificial intelligence, nor is it a leadership personality trait. It is a **governing form of intelligence** that enables organisations to operate intelligently while preserving responsibility, trust, and human continuity.

6.1 Definition and Scope

In Indian civilisational thought, intelligence was never defined only by the ability to think. It was defined by the ability to feel together.

Sarve bhavantu sukhinaḥ

Sarve santu nirāmayāḥ

Sarve bhadrāṇi paśyantu

Mā kaścid duḥkhabhāg bhavet

Meaning:

May all beings experience wellbeing.

May all be free from suffering and imbalance.

May all perceive goodness and auspiciousness.

May no one be subjected to distress.

This ancient *Śānti Mantra* **(Peace invocation)** from the Indian *Upaniṣadic–Smṛti* **prayer tradition** expresses a civilisational ethic where intelligence is inseparable from collective wellbeing. The verse doesn't try to gain power or benefit for itself; instead, it expands concern to all beings and stresses freedom from suffering, balance, and shared good fortune.

Grounded in this ethic, **Empathic Intelligence (EI)** in AIWoW - AI Ways of Working™ is defined as **the human capability to anticipate, perceive, and responsibly act on the emotional, psychological, and moral impact of decisions across individuals, teams, and systems, ensuring that the growth of intelligence consistently reduces harm and sustains collective wellbeing.**

In established human intelligence research, empathy has already been positioned as a core intelligence capability rather than a soft or auxiliary trait.

Daniel Goleman defined emotional intelligence as:

"The capacity for recognising our own feelings and those of others, for motivating ourselves, and for managing emotions well in ourselves and in our relationships."

Within this construct, empathy is explicitly identified as a central domain of intelligence, the ability to understand emotional states and respond appropriately.

Carl Rogers further described empathy as:

"The accurate perception of another's internal frame of reference, with its emotional components and meanings."

These definitions establish an important foundation: **empathy is a perceptual and regulatory capability**, not sentiment or kindness.

Empathic Intelligence, as defined in this book, extends this understanding beyond individuals into **organisational and human AI systems**, where intelligence operates continuously, autonomously, and at scale.

Empathic Intelligence refers to:

The organisational capacity to sense, interpret, and regulate the human, emotional, and ethical impact of intelligent systems operating at scale.

Its scope includes:

- Awareness of cognitive and emotional load created by acceleration
- Detection of trust erosion and disengagement
- Regulation of decision density and system-driven pace
- Alignment of automated actions with ethical boundaries
- Preservation of human judgement under continuous intelligence flow

EI is not episodic. It must function continuously, because the effects it governs are continuous.

6.2 EI vs Traditional Intelligence Constructs

Traditional intelligence constructs, whether analytical, technical, or computational, are oriented toward:

- Accuracy
- Efficiency
- Optimisation
- Pattern recognition
- Problem-solving speed

They answer the question: *Can the correct or optimal outcome be produced?*

Ability-based intelligence theories define intelligence as the capacity to perceive, understand, and regulate emotion in ways that support effective functioning.[3] However, these theories assume **human-scale cognition**, discrete decisions, and bounded execution cycles.

AI changes those conditions.

When intelligence:

- Operates continuously
- Shapes decisions before conscious human deliberation
- Learns faster than organisational reflection cycles

Traditional intelligence constructs become incomplete.

Empathic Intelligence introduces **impact awareness** as a governing dimension of intelligence. It does not ask only whether a decision is correct or efficient, but:

- What does this decision do to humans?
- How does this acceleration affect trust and confidence?
- When does optimisation become extraction?
- Where must speed be moderated to remain sustainable?

Traditional intelligence optimises *how.*

Empathic Intelligence governs *when, why, and how much.*

EI does not replace analytical or artificial intelligence. It **encloses them within boundaries** that prevent instability under scale.

6.3 EI as an Organisational Capability

In AI-driven environments, empathy can't just be something that one person has. No matter how caring they are, individual leaders can't handle it when systems run all the time, and decisions pile up faster than humans can keep up with.

So, empathic intelligence needs to be set up as a skill that the whole organisation has.

This needs structure, not just a plan.

Empathic Intelligence is shown by an organisation when it:

- Uses emotional and cognitive signals as operational data
- Puts empathetic checkpoints into decision-making processes
- Let's smart systems stop and ask for human judgement when they need it
- Needs both automated outputs and contextual validation
- Shows the effects on health and morality on a large scale

In this way, empathy is not a cultural goal but a way to control behaviour.

EI makes sure that:

- Acceleration stays stable.
- Trust stays strong when things are automated.
- You can tell when someone is burned out before they fall apart.
- Accountability stays human even when automation is used for execution.

Empathic Intelligence changes empathy from a good quality of a leader into a way to keep the system stable.

6.4 Why Empathic Intelligence is Essential in AI-Driven Work

Artificial intelligence never stops optimising. It doesn't get tired, have doubts, or feel moral pressure. When organisations scale intelligence without empathic regulation, they replicate this insensitivity at scale.

This makes places where:

- Productivity stays high, but meaning goes down.
- Choices are justifiable but lack emotional connection.

- Humans adapt until exhaustion becomes commonplace.
- Ethical issues only come up after something bad happens.

By putting human awareness into intelligent systems, empathic intelligence stops this from happening.

It makes sure that:

- Speed respects what humans can do.
- Automation does not take the place of judgement.
- Learning does not surpass comprehension.
- Humanity does not pay for growth.

6.5 The Limits of Empathic Intelligence

There's a quiet fear that lives in most boardrooms when empathy gets mentioned alongside intelligence. People tense up. They think: *if feeling enters the room, rigour walks out.*

That fear is understandable. But it is also wrong.

Empathic Intelligence doesn't make analysis softer; it makes it more complete. Stripping the human element from a decision doesn't make it more accurate. It just makes it narrower. EI doesn't replace facts with feelings either. It asks what the facts mean for the people living inside them. And it doesn't slow organisations down; it catches the mistakes that speed alone produces.

But honesty demands more than a defence.

Empathic Intelligence has real limits. Not theoretical ones, the kind that show up when organisations genuinely try to build it.

Compassion fatigue is the first. The people who carry the empathic load, who absorb difficult decisions, who hold space for others, burn out quietly. EI, without structural support, doesn't spread empathy across a system. It concentrates on the shoulders of a few and exhausts them.

Gamification is the second. The moment empathy becomes a metric, it begins to hollow out. People learn its language without internalising its meaning. Leaders perform concern rather than feel it. Empathy scores sit in dashboards while the actual culture quietly deteriorates underneath.

Cultural relativity is the third and the most underestimated. Empathic expression is not universal. What reads as genuine care in one culture reads as intrusive in another. An organisation imposing a single empathic style across a diverse workforce isn't practising Empathic Intelligence. It's practising empathic imperialism dressed in the language of inclusion.

Intelligence alone isn't stable at scale. But neither is empathy without honesty about its own limits, its fatigue points, its blind spots, its risk of becoming performance.

The strength of Empathic Intelligence isn't that it has no limits.

It's that it's mature enough to name them and keep building anyway.

6.6 The Role of EI Going Forward

Empathic Intelligence is the stabilising force that allows intelligence to scale without corroding trust, judgement, or human dignity.

As this book progresses, EI becomes:

- The regulating layer of the AI Lifecycle Loop
- The anchor of conscious acceleration
- The mechanism through which accountability remains human

Automation may increase speed.

Artificial intelligence may increase capability.

Empathic Intelligence ensures that **progress does not extract more than it creates.**

"Artificial intelligence expands capability, but empathic intelligence ensures that capability strengthens humanity rather than exhausting it."

Summary Mind-map

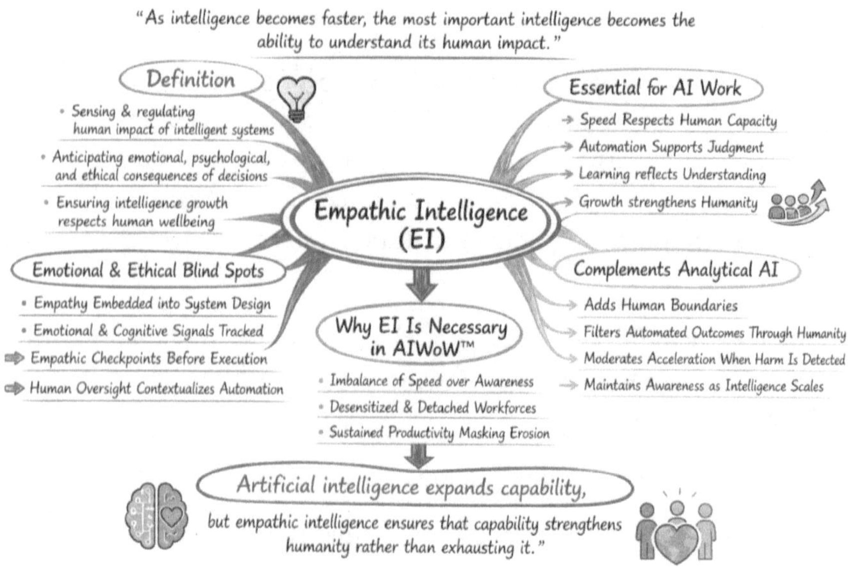

Artificial intelligence expands capability, but empathic intelligence ensures that capability strengthens humanity

Chapter 7

Conscious Leadership in the Age of AI

"AI can expand capability, but only conscious leadership ensures that capability serves a purpose."

Leadership has always evolved with the conditions under which decisions are made. When information was limited, leadership depended heavily on experience and intuition. When organisations became larger and more complex, leadership relied on structure, hierarchy, and processes. When markets demanded speed, leadership shifted toward delegation, empowerment, and trust.

Artificial Intelligence changes all of these conditions at the same time.

Information is no longer scarce.

Complexity is continuous rather than occasional.

Speed is no longer limited by human processing capacity.

In such an environment, leadership cannot remain purely reactive, symbolic, or procedural. It must become **conscious**. Within the philosophy of **AIWoW - AI Ways of Working™**, conscious leadership is not a philosophical ideal but an operational capability. It represents the ability to govern awareness, judgement, and responsibility in environments where intelligent systems continuously influence work.

AIWoW knows that smart systems make organisations more capable, but they also make it more important for leaders to be aware of what is going on. As systems become smarter, leaders must guarantee that clarity, responsibility, and the effects on humans stay clear.

7.1 Awareness as a Leadership Function

In traditional organisations, hierarchy often led to awareness on its own. Leaders were expected to put the information together and make decisions as it moved up through reporting structures.

This assumption is no longer true in environments where AI is used.

Information is always moving around.

Dashboards change in real time.

AI systems can make predictions, alerts, and suggestions on a large scale. Visibility goes up a lot, but understanding doesn't always come with it.

In AIWoW, leadership awareness is an active process instead of a passive effect of information flow.

Conscious leaders are aware of several important differences:

- Seeing something does not mean you understand it
- Information does not equal awareness
- Knowing something doesn't mean you have to judge it.

AI systems can find patterns, make predictions, and find connections. But humans still need to figure out what those patterns mean.

In AIWoW, being aware of leadership means being able to:

- Tell the difference between signal and noise in a lot of system outputs
- Be aware of the second-order effects of making decisions quickly
- Find out when speed starts to cloud judgement
- Feel the effects of humans before they show up in performance metrics

To be aware like this, you need to take intentional breaks in fast-paced settings. AIWoW thus promotes leadership practices that maintain reflection even in systems that facilitate ongoing action.

Leaders are responsible for awareness when they pay attention to not only the results but also how they are made, how quickly they happen, and how they affect humans in the system.

7.2 Decision-Making Under Accelerated Intelligence

AI changes the way humans make decisions in big ways.

Suggestions show up right away.

Simulations automatically make many different scenarios.

Optimisation algorithms keep suggesting things to do.

This increases capability, but it also shortens the time for reflection.

Conscious leadership in AIWoW understands that decision-making can't just speed up at the same rate as system intelligence. Leaders must instead carefully decide when speed is important and when judgement should be the most important thing.

This means that conscious leaders focus on a few important tasks:

- Figuring out which choices can be made faster without risk
- Figuring out where human judgement should always be required
- Setting limits on what an autonomous system can do
- Knowing when to slow down, even if it's possible from a technical point of view

Not every choice is better when it's made quickly. A lot of decisions that organisations make need to consider the context, ethics, and the long term.

Some examples are:

- Strategic investments that change the long-term direction of the organisation
- Choices that affect the health of employees or the change of the workforce
- Choices about products that affect society or customers

So, AIWoW introduces the idea that acceleration must be controlled, not just assumed.

Conscious leaders make sure that AI helps humans make decisions instead of just telling them what to do.

7.3 Responsibility Beyond Automation

AI-driven systems can look at data, make suggestions, and carry them out automatically. But these abilities can make humans think that they can share or give up responsibility to the system, which is a dangerous idea.

AIWoW disagrees with the notion that humans can relinquish responsibility to AI systems.

Automation might do tasks.

AI might suggest things to do.

Over time, learning systems may change.

Responsibility is still a human thing.

This principle is clear due to the presence of conscious leadership. Leaders verify that the language and practices of the organisation never let technology take over responsibility.

This means not saying things like

"The system decided."

"The algorithm told me to do it."

Instead, leaders ensure that:

- Human intent comes before automated action
- The consequences of ownership are still clear
- There are ways to move up in cases of ethical or contextual uncertainty
- Responsibility can be traced even when execution is automated.

AIWoW stresses that responsibility goes beyond just the results of operations. Leaders need to keep in mind the bigger picture, which includes:

- Employees must adjust to new systems quickly
- The effects of constant changes in technology on our minds and feelings
- The faith humans have in automated suggestions
- The long-term effects of optimised decisions on society or an organisation

In the age of AI, leadership goes from being in charge to being responsible for others.

7.4 The Discipline of Conscious Leadership

Conscious leadership does not come naturally. It needs practice and careful growth.

Within AIWoW, this discipline has a few main skills:

- Always being aware of yourself when making decisions quickly
- Willingness to question the certainty that the system gives you
- The bravery to slow down when there is a chance of causing harm
- A promise to protect human dignity and judgement in smart systems

Leaders who practice conscious leadership don't turn their backs on AI. They do it on purpose.

They don't compete with machines' intelligence. They set the rules for how that intelligence works in the organisation.

In AIWoW, leadership therefore becomes the stabilising force that ensures accelerated intelligence remains aligned with human values and organisational purpose.

Why Conscious Leadership Is Non-Negotiable:

AI-powered systems make decisions quickly. Learning loops keep patterns going all the time. Small mistakes can spread across systems faster than traditional checks can detect them.

In these kinds of places, unconscious leadership can make harm worse without meaning to, leading to decisions that prioritise rapid execution over careful consideration of potential consequences. Without intentional leadership:

Without intentional leadership:

- Speed beats sense
- Automation makes humans less responsible
- Empathy is put on hold
- Trust in the organisation starts to break down

AIWoW sees conscious leadership as a necessary check on smart systems.

It makes sure that organisations don't lose their sense of responsibility, clarity, or humanity as they gain new analytical abilities, which is crucial for maintaining trust among stakeholders and ensuring ethical decision-making.

7.5 Leadership Within AIWoW - AI Ways of Working™

Leadership in the AI era is not defined by knowing more information or making faster decisions.

It is defined by the ability to maintain awareness while intelligence accelerates.

Within AIWoW, conscious leaders ask questions that systems alone cannot answer:

- What can we do?
- Should we do it?

- At what pace should it happen?
- What impact will it create?
- And who will bear the consequences?

These questions restore intentionality in environments where systems can generate endless possibilities.

AIWoW embeds conscious leadership into the way organisations operate. Awareness, responsibility, and ethical reflection cannot depend solely on individual character. They must be supported through governance structures, decision frameworks, and organisational design.

The chapters that follow move from leadership philosophy to organisational structure, showing how AI Ways of Working embed conscious leadership into systems, processes, and everyday work practices.

In the age of AI, leadership without consciousness is no longer leadership. It is risk.

Summary Mind-map

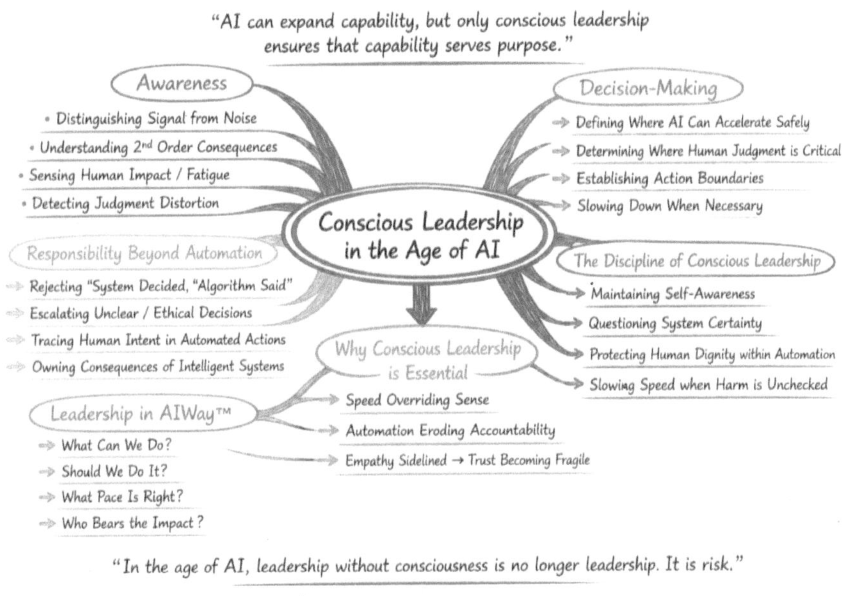

Chapter 8

AI as Partner, Not Replacement

"The promise of AI is realised when intelligence is shared between humans and machines responsibly."

The most consequential mistake organisations can make in the age of artificial intelligence is to frame AI as a substitute for human capability. This framing is seductive because it aligns with historical patterns of automation: replace effort, reduce cost, and increase speed. Yet AI does not merely replace effort. It introduces intelligence into the system, and intelligence reshapes relationships, authority, and responsibility.

Within the philosophy of **AIWoW - AI Ways of Working™**, this distinction becomes foundational. AIWoW recognises that intelligent systems participate in work, but they must do so in a way that strengthens human judgement rather than replacing it.

This chapter establishes a clear and deliberate position: AI is a partner in work, not a replacement for human judgement. This distinction is not philosophical. It is structural. When misunderstood, it leads to loss of capability, erosion of accountability, and fragile organisations. When designed correctly, it enables scale without dehumanisation.

8.1 Augmentation as a Design Principle

Augmentation is not a side effect of AI adoption. It must be a design principle.

Replacement focuses on elimination: fewer people, fewer decisions, fewer human interventions. Augmentation focuses on amplification:

stronger judgement, broader insight, and more resilient decision-making. The difference lies not in technology, but in intentional design.

Within **AIWoW**, augmentation is treated as a foundational operating principle for integrating AI into work systems.

Augmentation assumes the following:

- Humans define purpose and boundaries
- AI expands perception, speed, and option space
- Decisions improve through collaboration, not substitution

When AI is designed to augment:

- Human judgement becomes sharper, not weaker
- Cognitive load is redistributed, not transferred
- Creativity increases as routine burden decreases

Replacement-oriented systems optimise for autonomy. Augmentation-oriented systems optimise for human effectiveness.

This distinction determines whether AI strengthens organisations or quietly hollows them out.

Why Replacement Weakens Organisations:

In the short term, replacement seems to work well. Tasks go away. Decisions happen faster. Costs go down. But over time, replacement wears down the skills that businesses need to change.

When humans are not involved in decision-making:

- The context is lost
- Less sensitivity to ethics
- Judgement fades
- Responsibility spreads

The organisation relies on systems it doesn't fully understand and can't easily question. The organisation doesn't have the internal resources to respond when things change or something unexpected happens.

Replacement creates speed.

Augmentation creates resilience.

For this reason, **AIWoW deliberately promotes augmentation over substitution** when designing AI-enabled work systems.

8.2 Trust, Dependency, and Control

Partnership with AI introduces a delicate balance between trust, dependency, and control. These three forces must be consciously regulated. AIWoW recognises that sustainable human–AI collaboration depends on maintaining this balance.

Trust

Humans trust AI because it is reliable and consistent, and they think it is smart. Humans naturally trust systems more when they work well. But unrestrained trust results in deference, accepting outputs without examination.

Healthy trust is not absolute; it is conditional. It has:

- Understanding the capabilities and limitations of the system is essential
- Expectation of mistakes
- Making challenges and overrides normal

Trust should be built to encourage participation, not submission.

Dependency

When systems become an important part of making decisions, dependency happens. Dependency is not intrinsically detrimental; it becomes perilous when unexamined.

Unregulated dependency results in:

- Less human initiative
- Less confidence in judgement

Accepting system suggestions without question

In a partnership model, dependency is counterbalanced by:

- Constant human involvement
- Points that must be reviewed
- Keeping and improving skills

Dependency should make capability stronger, not take its place.

Control

Controlling AI doesn't mean micromanaging it. It means saying:

- Where AI can work on its own
- Where it has to stop
- Where humans have to give their approval
- How learning is limited control keeps agency.

It makes sure that the partnership doesn't turn into giving up.

These control mechanisms are later put into action through governance structures in AIWoW .

8.3 Human Judgement as the Final Authority

In a genuine partnership, it is essential that the authority is clearly defined.

AI can look at data, identify patterns, make predictions, and suggest what to do. However, there are limits to what it can rightfully decide. AI can't be morally responsible, understand how humans' actions affect them in real life, interpret values that go beyond programmed rules, or be held accountable if something undesirable happens.

For this reason, humans should always be the last word.

This doesn't mean that humans have to be involved in every step. It means that a human must be responsible for the outcome when decisions have important effects.

You can see a real-world example in aviation safety systems.

Modern commercial planes have very advanced autopilots and flight management systems. These systems are always looking at the altitude, weather, performance of the plane, and the best way to arrive there. They can fly the plane for a long time and make thousands of tiny changes every minute.

However, airlines do not view these systems as the final decision-making authority.

The pilots are still in charge of the flight.

The pilot can ignore the system's suggestion of a route through bad weather. If the plane picks up conflicting signals or strange conditions, the pilot looks at the situation and decides whether to follow the system or do something else.

Why?

Flying an aircraft is not only a technical optimisation problem. It also involves judgement about passenger safety, weather uncertainty, and situational awareness that cannot be fully captured by algorithms.

This situation illustrates a simple concept: **AI can help humans make decisions, but it can't be responsible for them.**

The same rule should apply to groups. There should still be clear human authority when AI is involved in making decisions.

In most cases, this means:

- Clear ownership of important choices
- Being willing to question or ignore system recommendations
- Being responsible for the results, even if AI had a say in the decision

Final authority doesn't mean showing that humans are better than machines. It's about making sure that someone is still responsible when choices affect humans, safety, trust, or the future.

This principle makes sure that responsibility never gets lost in technology in AIWoW . AI can help with analysis and suggestions, but humans are always responsible and visible.

8.4 Designing for Partnership

Treating AI like a partner does not happen automatically. It takes careful planning to decide how to organise work.

The first thing many businesses do when they acquire AI is get rid of jobs or automate whole decision chains. Humans often resist this approach because they think it takes away their judgement and experience.

A partnership approach is different. Instead of getting rid of jobs, organisations change the way humans and AI work together on the same task.

For instance, many businesses in the global retail supply chain industry now use AI systems to predict how many products will be needed in thousands of stores. The system looks at past sales, seasonal trends, weather patterns, and how humans in different areas buy things to guess how much demand there will be.

But successful stores don't let the system make all of their inventory decisions. Store planners and supply chain managers still look at forecasts, change them to fit the local situation, and decide how much to send out.

In this system, AI performs the complex task of pattern analysis, while humans contribute their own judgement and situational awareness. The outcome is more precise choices without eliminating human knowledge.

It usually takes a few structural practices to make these kinds of partnerships work:

- Roles need to be adjusted rather than eliminated.
- Review mechanisms must be a normal part of the work process.
- Humans should respect overrides instead of trying to stop them.
- System learning must stay open and limited.

When these things happen, employees see AI as a tool that makes their jobs easier instead of a threat.

Partnership encourages when humans feel empowered, not replaced by technology. When humans understand how AI supports their decisions, they engage with it actively. When they feel substituted, they either resist the system or disengage from the process.

Within **AIWoW**, workflows are designed so that human judgement and machine intelligence complement each other rather than compete. This ensures that organisations scale intelligence while preserving human responsibility and expertise.

8.5 The Organisational Implication

How an organisation frames AI determines what kind of organisation it eventually becomes.

Some organisations approach AI primarily as a **replacement tool**. The goal is to remove roles, automate decisions, and increase efficiency as quickly as possible. In the short term, this goal often produces visible gains such as lower operational costs and faster execution.

However, over time, this approach can create fragile systems. Delegating too many decisions entirely to automated systems weakens human judgement. Context becomes harder to interpret, and organisations may struggle to respond when unexpected situations arise.

Other organisations take a different approach. They design AI as a **partner in work**. In this model, AI expands analytical capability and operational speed, while humans continue to provide judgement, responsibility, and contextual understanding. These organisations build systems where intelligence scales, but human decision capability remains strong.

The difference between these two outcomes is rarely about technology.

It is about **leadership intent and design discipline**.

Within **AIWoW - AI Ways of Working™**, this partnership principle becomes a structural foundation. AI is introduced in ways that strengthen human capability rather than gradually removing it.

This chapter, therefore, establishes a core principle that guides the remainder of the book:

AI should expand what humans can do and allow humans to continue being themselves.

Maintaining this partnership requires continuous attention. It depends on awareness of how AI systems influence decisions, clear control over where automation operates, and visible human responsibility for outcomes.

Without these safeguards, augmentation can slowly drift toward replacement without anyone explicitly intending it.

The chapters that follow explore how this partnership becomes embedded in organisational systems through lifecycle governance, control mechanisms, and empathic regulation so that intelligence can scale without eroding human judgement.

In the age of AI, the strongest organisations will not be those that remove humans fastest.

They will be those who design intelligence to work with humans **most responsibly**.

"The future of intelligent organisations lies not in removing humans from work, but in designing intelligence to work responsibly with them."

Summary Mind-map

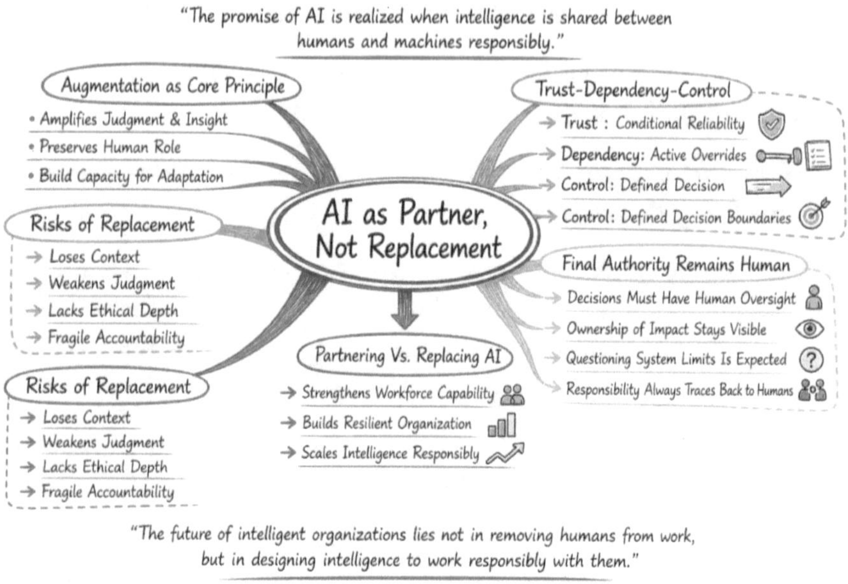

Chapter 9

Timeless Philosophy in Modern Systems

"When intelligence accelerates, timeless wisdom becomes the compass."

As organisations adopt artificial intelligence at scale, they often assume that modern problems require entirely modern answers. Yet the core tensions exposed by AI—speed versus judgement, power versus responsibility, and action versus consequence—are not new. What is new is their scale and velocity.

Timeless philosophies have long grappled with these tensions, not as abstract thoughts, but as guidance for action under power. When translated carefully into modern systems, they offer enduring principles for leadership in environments where intelligence accelerates faster than reflection.

Within **AIWoW - AI Ways of Working™**, these philosophical insights are not treated as beliefs or traditions. They are treated as **operational principles for governing intelligent systems responsibly**.

This chapter does not import philosophy as belief. It distils operational wisdom, principles that remain relevant precisely because they address human behaviour under pressure, authority, and consequence.

9.1 Karma, Detachment, and Duty in Leadership

Leadership in intelligent systems confronts a paradox: leaders must act decisively while accepting that outcomes are increasingly shaped by complex, distributed forces, including AI.

This is directly related to the idea of karma. Karma does not mean giving up or giving in to fate. It says a simple operational truth: every action has a result, even if the result isn't clear right away or fully under your control.

In places where AI is used:

- Decisions spread more quickly
- Effects show up later
- It's easy to hide responsibility

Karma brings back clarity by putting leadership back on taking responsibility for actions instead of trying to control outcomes.

This principle is very important in AIWoW. AI systems can help humans make decisions and accelerate the process, but humans must still be responsible for their actions.

Detachment enhances this principle. Detachment means being involved in a different way. It means doing things without caring about the outcome.

This definition means the following in terms of leadership:

- Choosing alignment over validation
- Not speeding up because of fear or pride
- Taking correction without getting defensive

Detachment lets leaders work with smart systems without having to compete with them or hide behind them.

Duty makes the triad whole.

Duty means doing things for a reason, not just because it's easy.

In today's smart systems, "duty" means

- Safeguarding human judgement despite the allure of automation
- Taking responsibility even when systems affect results
- Putting long-term integrity ahead of short-term goals

Karma, detachment, and duty make up a leadership style that works well in situations where power is increased, but certainty is decreased.

Within AIWoW, these principles guide leaders to **exercise authority consciously while intelligent systems operate at scale.**

9.2 Balance Between Action and Awareness

Organisations today naturally reward humans who take action. They look at how much work is done, how fast it is done, and how it is delivered. You can see movement and keep track of it easily. But it's harder to measure awareness. But without awareness, action can easily go the wrong way.

Timeless wisdom often stressed balance, not slowing down action, but making sure that it was in line with understanding.

This idea is even more important in places where AI is used.

In these kinds of systems:

- Algorithms and automation speed up action on their own
- Leaders must work to make humans aware on purpose.

AI systems are made to work as quickly and efficiently as possible. If organisations just follow what the system says, work can keep going without enough thought.

High-frequency trading in global financial markets provides a practical example.

AI-driven investment trading systems that look at market signals and make trades in milliseconds are used by a lot of investment firms. These systems can react to changes in price much faster than humans can.

But financial regulators and responsible organisations put in place safety measures like "circuit breakers." When there is a lot of volatility, these systems automatically stop trading.

Why stop a system that was made to be quick?

Because markets can change so quickly, automated decisions make things less stable before humans know what's going on. The pause provides humans a chance to catch up with what the system is doing.

This shows an important point: going fast without being aware can make things unstable.

Therefore, balancing action and awareness means controlling how intelligence works.

This balance shows up in several ways in real life:

- Stopping acceleration when the results are not clear
- Making room for reflection even in systems that never stop
- Making sure that awareness comes before decisions that can't be changed

Leaders who only care about action create movement without meaning.

Leaders who only think about things make humans hesitate instead of moving forward.

Conscious leadership keeps the two in balance.

You don't just identify a balance once and then forget about it. It needs to be kept up all the time, especially in places where smart systems run all the time.

In AIWoW, this balance becomes a way of doing things: it lets systems move quickly while making sure humans are aware of where they're going.

9.3 Conscious Action as an Operating Principle

When you act with conscious action, you do so with a clear purpose, are aware of the consequences, and do it right. It's based on both instinct and facts. It is the ability to move forward while still knowing why you are doing something and what effect it might have.

In places where AI systems are always running, being aware of what you're doing becomes more than just a trait of a good leader. It needs to become a rule for how the organisation works.

With AIWoW, conscious action is built into how decisions are made and how systems work with smart technologies.

Self-driving cars are a positive example of this in the real world.

AI helps modern cars find obstacles, understand road conditions, and change their speed or steering. The system can read road signs much faster than a person can. But the humans who create these systems ensure that the driver is aware of and responsible for the driving environment.

For instance, most autonomous driving systems require the driver to keep their hands on the steering wheel and remain attentive to the road. If the system detects that the driver is not paying attention, it issues warnings and eventually disengages the automated system.

Why is this feature needed?

The system can handle many driving situations, but there are times when things happen that require human judgement. The design keeps the human driver interested instead of making them passive.

This example shows the idea of conscious action. Technology can help and speed up decisions, but humans still need to be aware of what's going on.

In businesses, this idea leads to a few important actions:

- Humans do things deliberately instead of just reacting automatically.
- It's not just assumed that acceleration is necessary.
- Automation works within limits set by humans.
- Humans keep an eye on learning systems to make sure they stay in line.

Conscious action also brings up simple but important questions that need to be answered before decisions are made:

- Does this fit with our goal?
- Is this really needed?

- Will this last in the long run?
- Does this have a humane effect?

These questions serve as anchors that link smart systems to human judgement.

When businesses build conscious action into their operating systems, intelligence can grow without losing accountability.

Why Timeless Principles Matter Now

AI makes things a lot more powerful, but it doesn't automatically make humans smarter.

Organisations can get very big and strong very quickly, but if their awareness and judgement don't grow at the same rate, they can still make bad or harmful choices.

Timeless philosophical principles continue to hold significance as they tackle dimensions of leadership that technology cannot offer, including the following:

- Ethical duty
- Purpose when under stress
- Making decisions when things are unclear
- Being responsible for more than just performance metrics

These things decide if businesses can still be trusted and strong as intelligence grows.

AIWoW recognises that technical capability alone cannot guide responsible action. Intelligent systems must operate within a framework shaped by leadership awareness, ethical grounding, and conscious decision-making.

In this way, conscious action ensures that intelligence serves a purpose rather than simply accelerating activity.

9.4 Integrating Philosophy Without Dogma

The goal of bringing timeless philosophy into contemporary organisations is not to push beliefs or preach morals. The goal is much simpler and more practical: to base modern systems on ideas that have already been tested when there is power, pressure, and responsibility.

Throughout history, leaders and societies have encountered circumstances in which decisions have had profound implications. Philosophical traditions frequently emerged to direct conduct in such circumstances. Today, intelligent systems create a similar environment, but faster and on a larger scale.

These philosophical ideas are not seen only as abstract ideals in AIWoW - AI Ways of Working™. But they are turned into useful frameworks that help businesses use smart systems in a responsible way.

When used in today's organisations, these ideas show up as ways to run things, such as:

- Frameworks for accountability that make sure humans are still responsible
- Decision filters that ask if actions are in line with goals
- Leadership skills that help you stay aware when you're under stress
- Rules for how automation works that are set by governance

These tools help organisations answer a key set of questions: not just what can be done, but also what should be done and how it should be done in a responsible way.

Managing AI product releases by global tech organisations is a good example.

Many large technology firms now operate internal **AI ethics review boards**. Before deploying new AI features, such as recommendation systems, facial recognition, or automated moderation, teams must review the broader implications of the system.

The review is not about stopping innovation. It is about asking more profound questions:

- Could this system create unintended bias?
- Could it affect user trust or privacy?
- Should additional safeguards be introduced before deployment?

These review processes function as modern forms of philosophical guardrails. They bring reflection and responsibility into environments where technology can otherwise move too quickly.

This illustrates an important idea: integrating philosophical principles does not slow organisations down. Instead, it **helps them move responsibly**.

AI is a big step forward in technology. But it doesn't automatically tell you what is right or wrong. The problems it brings to light, overreach, not caring about the consequences, and an imbalance between speed and judgement have been around for a long time, even before digital systems.

Organisations don't go backwards when they add timeless wisdom to modern systems. They go deeper.

They know that as machines become better at thinking, humans need to become better at acting.

Therefore, this chapter sets up a quiet but strong truth that will carry on throughout the rest of the book:

The future of smart organisations will depend on their conscious choices, not their systems' advancement.

Timeless philosophy does not compete with modern intelligence.

It completes it.

Summary Mind-map

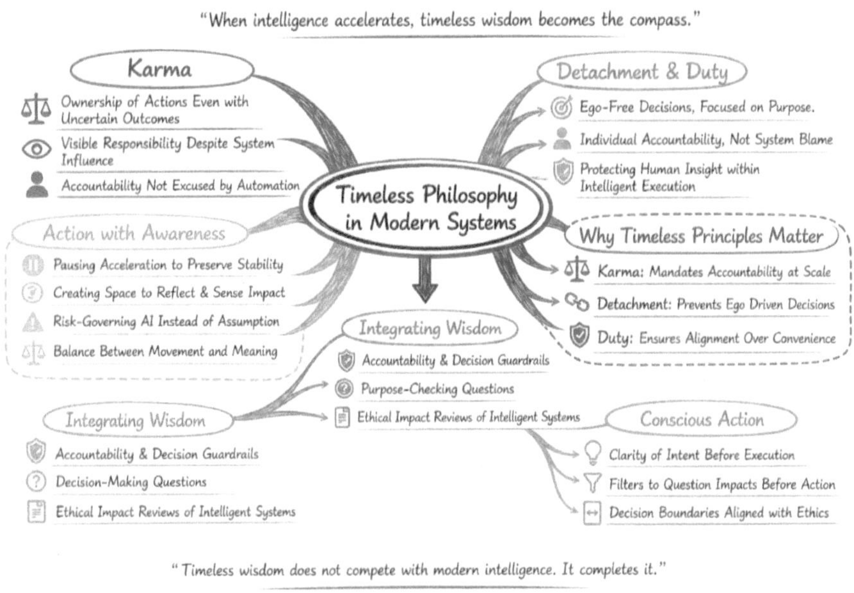

PART III

THE AIWoW - AI WAYS OF WORKING™ MANIFESTO

Defining the Values of Intelligent Work

Every major shift in how work is organised requires a set of guiding principles.

The AIWoW - AI Ways of Working™ Manifesto establishes the values that must govern intelligent systems operating within human organisations. These principles ensure that acceleration remains aligned with responsibility, empathy, and long-term sustainability.

The manifesto defines what organisations must protect as intelligence scales

Why a Manifesto Is Necessary
OUTDATED MANUALS
PRE-AI METHODS
PRE-AI METHODS
Addressing AI's Speed & Impact. Guiding Ethical Use. Providing a Core Framework.
Core Values of AI Ways of Working (AIWoW™)
Conscious Acceleration
HUMAN
Human-centric Integration
ethics
Ethical Stewardship
Collaborative Intelligence
Consciousness, Humanity, Ethics, Collaboration.
The AIWoW™ Manifesto
AIWoW™ Principles Derived from the Manifesto
Principle: Guiding Human Intent
Principle: Inclusive AI
Principle: Auditable & Accountable
Principle: Continuous Adaptation
1. Defined Human-AI Roles.
2. Transparency in Algorithms.
3. Systemic Risk Assessment.
4. Resilient Team Structures.

Chapter 10

Why a Manifesto is Necessary

"Frameworks organise work, but manifestos define what an organisation stands for when work changes."

Organisations often mistake progress for movement and adoption for alignment. New technologies are introduced, processes are updated, and metrics improve, yet something essential remains fragmented. Humans execute, systems optimise, and leadership communicates intent, but coherence does not automatically follow.

This step is where a manifesto becomes necessary.

A manifesto is not documentation. It is not a framework. It is not a methodology. It is a **declarative centre, a shared articulation of belief that shapes behaviour** before rules, tools, or processes intervene.

In the era of AI, where systems increasingly shape decisions and intelligence accelerates, a manifesto offers a collective orientation that procedures cannot provide.

10.1 Movements vs. Methodologies

Methodologies organise *how* work is done.

Movements define *why* work is done in a particular way.

This distinction matters.

Methodologies are designed to be applied. They focus on steps, roles, cycles, and outputs. They are valuable when conditions are stable and assumptions are shared. Movements, by contrast, emerge when conditions change so fundamentally that existing assumptions no longer hold.

AI has created such a condition.

When intelligence participates in work, methodologies alone cannot govern.

- Decision authority
- Responsibility boundaries
- Ethical alignment
- Human impact under acceleration

Methodologies can optimise execution, but they cannot establish **meaning**. They tell humans *what to do*, not *what to believe about what they are doing.*

Movements succeed where methodologies reach their limits because they:

- Align behaviour before process
- Shape judgement before execution
- Influence choices in ambiguous situations
- Persist even as tools and practices evolve

A manifesto is the seed of a movement. It provides a **stable core** around which methods can adapt without losing direction.

10.2 Why AI Demands a Movement-Level Response

AI does not introduce a single new practice. It introduces a **new operating condition**.

Decisions accelerate. Learning becomes continuous. Responsibility diffuses. Human impact intensifies. These effects cut across functions, roles, and industries. No single methodology can address them comprehensively.

Without a shared belief system:

- Teams interpret AI differently.
- Leaders apply inconsistent standards
- Automation expands unevenly
- Trust fractures quietly

A movement-level response establishes **non-negotiable principles** that remain constant regardless of how tools, architectures, or workflows change.

The manifesto serves as the reference point in the following situations:

- Metrics conflict
- Speed pressures rise
- Ethical trade-offs appear
- Systems behave unexpectedly

It answers questions methodologies cannot.

- What must never be optimised away?
- Where must humans remain accountable?
- When should speed be constrained?
- How do we define progress beyond output?

10.3 Shared Belief Systems in Organisations

Organisations already operate on belief systems, whether explicit or implicit. These beliefs influence decisions more powerfully than policies.

Some examples of implicit beliefs are the following:

- Faster is always better
- Progress means automation
- Efficiency is more important than feelings
- Objective means based on data

If you don't question these kinds of beliefs, they become your default behaviour. AI makes their effects stronger by carrying them out on a large scale.

A manifesto makes beliefs clear.

By declaring what the organisation stands for, it:

- Aligns decision-making across levels
- Reduces ambiguity in moments of uncertainty
- Creates coherence across human–AI interactions
- Establishes a shared language for judgement

Shared belief systems do not eliminate disagreement. They provide a **common ground** from which disagreement can occur productively.

10.4 Why Principles Must Precede Systems

Systems execute assumptions.

If assumptions are flawed, systems scale the flaw.

In AI-driven environments, this scaling is rapid and often invisible. A manifesto makes sure that assumptions are brought to light, looked at, and purposefully chosen before they are built into smart systems.

Principles precede:

- Model design
- Automation rules
- Decision thresholds
- Learning boundaries

Without principles, organisations encode efficiency without ethics, speed without sense, and intelligence without accountability.

10.5 The Role of a Manifesto in AIWoW - AI Ways of Working™

The AIWoW - AI Ways of Working™ manifesto does not prescribe steps. It establishes **orientation.**

It defines:

- What is more important than what
- What is safe when there is pressure
- What humans are still responsible for
- What AI is meant to add to, not take away from

This manifesto is subject to change. The way it is put into practice may change, but its basic ideas stay the same, ensuring that the core principles of collaboration and innovation remain intact. Businesses can come up with new ideas without losing touch with their employees thanks to this stability.

- What is worth more than what
- What is kept safe under stress
- What humans are still responsible for
- What AI is meant to add to, not take away from

10.6 From Adoption to Alignment

Organisations can adopt AI quickly. Alignment takes longer.

Alignment requires:

- Shared understanding
- Consistent judgement
- Collective responsibility

A manifesto expedites alignment by serving as a guide when procedures fail.

It turns AI adoption from a technical exercise into an **organisational commitment.**

10.7 Why This Manifesto Must Exist Now

AI will continue to advance. Tools will change. Capabilities will expand. What will determine long-term success is not the sophistication of systems but the **clarity of collective intent.**

A manifesto is necessary because

- Methods optimise behaviour
- Movements shape identity
- Systems scale beliefs

In the age of AI, organisations must choose what they believe **before** intelligence chooses for them.

This chapter sets the stage for the manifesto itself, not as a declaration of ambition, but as a foundation for conscious, accountable, and human-centred work in an era of accelerating intelligence.

"In the age of intelligent systems, the most important decision an organisation makes is what it chooses to believe."

Summary Mind-map

Chapter 11

Core Values of AIWoW - AI Ways of Working™

"Artificial intelligence scales capability, but values decide what that capability ultimately serves."

Every Way of Working is ultimately defined not by its processes, but by its values. Values shape choices long before procedures are consulted. They determine what is prioritised under pressure, what is protected when trade-offs arise, and what is sacrificed consciously or unconsciously when speed, scale, or efficiency demands it.

In environments shaped by artificial intelligence, values are no longer abstract. They are **encoded**. They influence how systems are designed, how decisions are automated, and how learning loops evolve. When values are unclear, AI does not remain neutral; it amplifies whatever assumptions it is given, leading to biased outcomes that can perpetuate existing inequalities and misrepresentations in data.

The core values of AIWoW - AI Ways of Working™ exist to ensure that intelligence scales **with intention**, not by accident. These values are not aspirational slogans. They are **operating laws and** principles that govern behaviour across human and machine activity.

11.1 Human Judgement Over Machine Autonomy

AI can operate autonomously. That does not mean it should decide autonomously.

Autonomy optimises speed and consistency. Judgement integrates context, ethics, and consequence. In AI-driven systems, the risk is not that machines will become intelligent, but that organisations will **withdraw human judgement too early**, mistaking automation for maturity.

Placing human judgement over machine autonomy means the following:

- Decisions with human impact remain answerable to humans.
- AI recommendations are inputs, not conclusions.

- Override is a right, not an exception.
- Responsibility never migrates to systems.

This value does not reject automation. It defines its boundary.

Autonomy without judgement produces efficiency without accountability. AI Ways of Working ensures that **final authority remains human**, not because humans are infallible, but because they are accountable.

11.2 Empathy-Driven Speed Over Blind Acceleration

Speed is powerful. Acceleration can be transformative. But speed without empathy extracts more than it creates.

Blind acceleration treats all delay as waste. Empathy-driven speed treats **human capacity as a constraint worth respecting**.

This value shows that:

- Not always better to go faster
- Being in a constant state of urgency makes it harder to make good decisions
- Human systems need to recover, think, and find meaning.

Speed based on empathy always benefits organisations. It sets the pace based on:

- Mental load
- Effect on feelings
- Risk to ethics
- Long-term sustainability

Acceleration is no longer a need but a choice.

AI Ways of Working uses speed when it adds value and slows down when it hurts. This balance keeps things moving without burning out.

11.3 Augmentation Over Replacement

Replacement focuses on removing humans from systems. Augmentation focuses on **making humans more capable within them**.

AI excels at pattern recognition, scale, and consistency. Humans excel at judgement, creativity, and ethical reasoning. Augmentation is the intentional design choice to combine these strengths rather than substitute one for the other.

This value says that:

- AI makes humans more capable.
- Humans are still at the centre of meaning and responsibility.
- Skills change over time instead of going away.
- Systems are made to teach, not to make humans less skilled.

Replacing something may lower the cost. Augmentation makes you stronger.

Organisations that design for augmentation preserve institutional knowledge, adaptability, and trust—capabilities that cannot be automated away without long-term consequences.

11.4 Ethical Intent Over Raw Optimisation

AI optimises relentlessly. It will pursue whatever objective it is given with increasing precision. Without ethical intent, optimisation becomes extraction.

Ethical intent establishes **direction before optimisation**. Ethical intent, rooted in **Kantian moral philosophy**, denotes the conscious and deliberate purpose to act rightly grounded in duty and moral principle rather than consequence

This value requires that:

- The purpose is defined before performance.
- Boundaries are explicit, not implicit.

- Fairness is designed, not assumed.
- Long-term consequences outweigh short-term gain.

Ethical intent does not slow optimisation. It **guides it**.

Under AI Ways of Working, optimisation is never value-neutral. Every automated choice reflects a judgement about who benefits, who bears cost, and what trade-offs are acceptable.

Making ethical intent explicit prevents silent drift.

11.5 Learning Loops Over Linear Delivery

Traditional work systems are linear: plan, execute, review. AI-driven systems are recursive. They learn while operating, adjusting behaviour continuously.

This value embraces learning loops as the dominant mode of work.

Learning loops:

- Integrate feedback in real time
- Detect drift early
- Enable continuous improvement
- Prevent rigid execution of outdated assumptions

However, learning without governance becomes instability. AIWoW - AI Ways of Working™ ensures that learning loops remain:

- Transparent
- Bounded
- Interpretable
- Aligned with human values

Linear delivery delivers output. Learning loops deliver **evolution**.

This value ensures that organisations remain adaptive without becoming unpredictable.

11.6 Accountability as a Structural Law

Accountability cannot rely on intention or culture alone in AI-driven environments. It must be **structural**.

When intelligence participates in decisions, accountability must be designed into the system, not applied after outcomes occur.

This value establishes that:

- Every automated action has a human owner.
- Responsibility is defined before execution.
- Decision pathways are auditable.
- Consequences are traceable.

Accountability is not a control mechanism. It is a trust mechanism.

By making accountability structural, AIWoW - AI Ways of Working™ ensures that:

- Power does not diffuse invisibly.
- Errors lead to learning, not blame shifting
- Authority and responsibility remain aligned

Without this value, intelligence scales faster than responsibility.

11.7 Values as Operating Law

These six values are not optional guidelines. They are the **operating law** of AI Ways of Working.

They determine:

- How systems are designed
- How decisions are accelerated
- How learning is governed
- How humans remain central under scale

When embedded into systems, these values prevent intelligence from becoming extractive, dehumanising, or unstable.

They ensure that as organisations become more capable, they also become **more conscious.**

11.8 From Values to Practice

Values without embodiment remain rhetoric. The chapters that follow translate these values into:

- Frameworks
- Control mechanisms
- Lifecycle governance
- Organisational structures

This chapter establishes the moral and operational foundation.

Because in the age of AI, what organisations choose to value is what intelligence will ultimately amplify.

AIWoW - AI Ways of Working™ begins by choosing deliberately.

Summary Mind-map

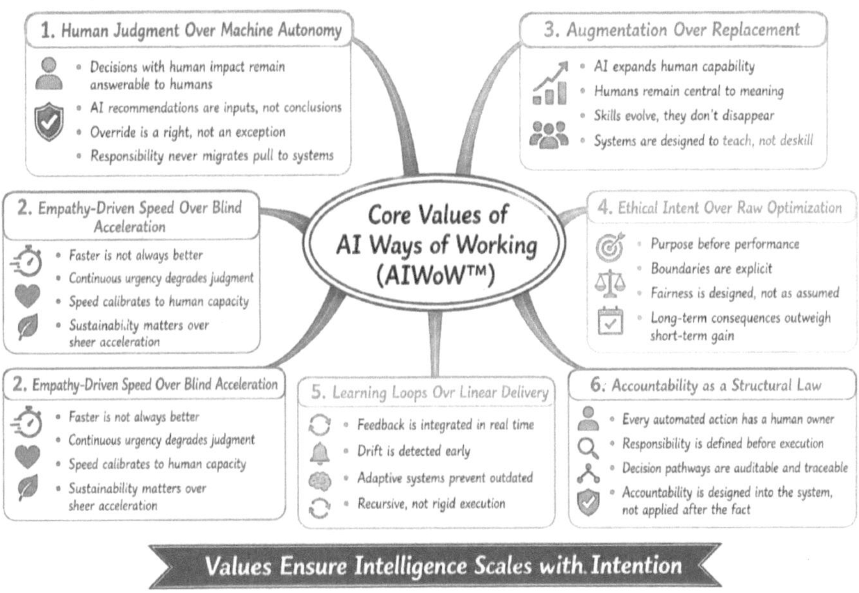

Chapter 12

AIWoW - AI Ways of Working™ Principles Derived from the Manifesto

"Values express what an organisation believes. Principles determine how those beliefs hold under pressure."

In environments shaped by artificial intelligence, pressure is constant. Decisions accelerate, learning becomes continuous, and consequences propagate faster than traditional oversight can respond to them. Under these conditions, values alone are insufficient. Organisations require principles that translate belief into consistent behaviour when intelligence moves faster than reflection.

The manifesto establishes the value system of AIWoW - AI Ways of Working™. From that foundation emerge four governing principles. These principles are not preferences or guidelines. They are **operating rules** designed to preserve clarity, responsibility, and sustainability as intelligence scales.

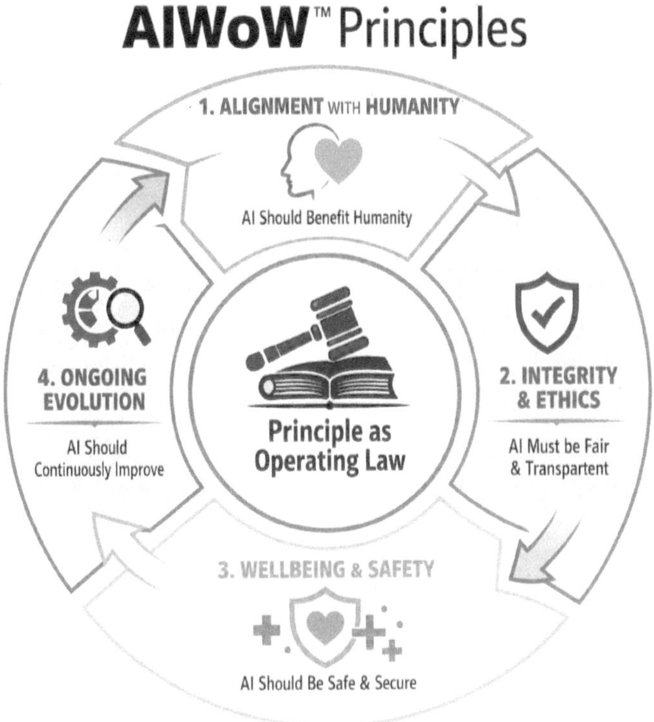

12.1 Decision Ownership

When intelligence is at work, decisions don't seem like separate events anymore. They come from suggestions, automatic actions, and systems that learn and work all the time. Without careful planning, ownership spreads out.

The principle of **Decision Ownership asserts the following:**

Every high-stakes decision must have a clearly identifiable human owner before it is executed.

Being the owner does not mean you have to always step in. It means being responsible. This doesn't mean that humans have to approve every action by hand. Before intelligence can do anything, a human must be responsible for what happens.

This principle makes sure that:

- Automated action comes after human intent
- Decisions can still be traced back to a human in charge
- Overrides are legal and safe
- Systems do not take on responsibility

Decision Ownership stops a common problem with AI-driven work: results that affect many humans but don't belong to anyone. Organisations maintain clarity and accountability as intelligence accelerates by clearly defining ownership.

Why Ownership Matters When Intelligence Accelerates:

AI systems are very proficient at making things happen. They cannot be held morally responsible.

Without ownership:

- Decisions seem "inevitable" instead of being made by choice
- "The system" is blamed for the harm
- No one feels like they have to fix unintended consequences
- Humans don't learn because they don't know who is responsible.

This makes a dangerous failure mode: results that affect many humans but don't belong to anyone.

Decision Ownership gives fast-moving systems moral weight again.

A Simple Example: Automated Resource Reallocation:

Think about an AI system that moves work around automatically based on signals of productivity.

The system recognises the "underutilisation" of one team and assigns them additional tasks.

The choice is technically correct. From an operational perspective, this effect could be detrimental.

If no human owns this choice:

- Team burnout grows without anyone noticing
- Trust goes down
- Resistance grows for no clear reason
- Leaders don't know until attrition happens

Under Decision Ownership, a person with a name agrees to be responsible for:

- Deciding when it's okay to move things around
- Keeping an eye on both performance and signs of human strain
- Getting involved when optimisation hurts health
- It is crucial to clearly explain the reasons to the affected teams.

The system does things, but a human makes the choice.

Before any automated action can happen, there must be human intent:

Decision ownership makes sure that:

- Automation carries out intent; it does not set it.
- Humans set limits on how systems can work.
- Learning loops make you better at making decisions, not just faster.

This keeps a basic rule of AIWoW (Artificial Intelligence Way of Working) in place: intelligence can speed up action, but it can never replace intent.

Overrides Are a Right, Not a Mistake:

In a lot of organisations, going against an automated decision is seen as being inefficient or resistant.

Decision Ownership goes against this way of thinking.

Overrides are:

- A sign of good government
- A way to avoid missing important details in context
- A right of humans in smart systems

Ownership makes sure that overrides are legal, safe, and encouraged when things change.

Decision Ownership as an Organisational Capability:

When practised consistently, Decision Ownership creates

- Clear accountability chains
- Faster learning from failure
- Trust in AI-assisted systems
- Reduced ethical and legal risk
- Stronger leadership legitimacy

Most importantly, it ensures that **responsibility never dissolves into automation**.

Why Is This Principle Non-negotiable?

AI will always speed up decisions more than humans can think about them.

Without Ownership of Decisions:

- Organisations start to react
- Accountability breaks down
- Ethics takes on a symbolic meaning

Trust slowly fades away. With Decision Ownership:

- Intelligence can still be controlled
- Speed stays in line
- Human is still responsible

There is no rule that says you have to own your decisions. It is what keeps intelligence human.

12.2 Emotional Alignment

Acceleration reshapes how work is experienced before it reshapes how it performs. Cognitive load increases, recovery time compresses, and uncertainty becomes continuous.

The principle of **Emotional Alignment** recognises that:

A human emotional state is an operational signal, not an individual weakness.

This principle establishes that work systems must remain aligned with human capacity and trust, not only with technical efficiency.

Emotional Alignment requires organisations to:

- Monitor emotional strain as a system indicator
- Treat disengagement and fatigue as design feedback
- Adjust pace when confidence and trust erode
- Detect stress before performance collapses

In AI-accelerated environments, emotions are often dismissed as subjective noise, something to be managed privately rather than designed for systemically. AI Ways of Working rejects this assumption. Emotional signals are not distractions from work; they are **early indicators of system health**.

Emotional Alignment establishes that work systems must remain aligned with **human capacity, confidence, and trust**, not only with technical efficiency. When systems move faster than humans can emotionally integrate change, output may continue, but understanding, ownership, and resilience quietly erode.

Why Emotional Signals Matter Before Performance Drops?:

One of the most dangerous misconceptions in modern organisations is that performance decline is the first sign of trouble. In reality, **emotional misalignment appears much earlier**.

Common early signals include:

- Increased hesitation despite unchanged capability
- Declining confidence in decisions that were once routine
- Silence in discussions where disagreement once existed
- Fatigue masked as "professional discipline"
- Disengagement interpreted as compliance

AI-driven systems often miss these signals because

- Output still looks strong
- Delivery timelines are met
- Automation absorbs visible strain

But beneath the surface, **trust is decreasing.**

A practical illustration: AI-Driven Planning Acceleration:

Think about an organisation that uses AI to help with planning and forecasting. Daily updates are made to schedules. New signals constantly change the priorities. Optimisation looks excellent.

For a few weeks:

- Better delivery
- Less bottlenecks
- Leaders feel good about themselves

But emotionally, teams start to feel the following:

- Things become less predictable
- Fear of making plans that might change overnight
- Not wanting to put a lot of time and energy into work that seems temporary
- Anxiety that looks like flexibility

No one complains. Performance remains high.

Then suddenly:

- Decision-making slows
- Ownership weakens
- Burnout surfaces
- Attrition increases

The failure did not begin when humans left.

It began when emotional alignment was lost but ignored.

Emotional Alignment as a Design Responsibility:

Emotional Alignment requires organisations to treat emotional strain as **design feedback**, not personal limitation.

This means:

- Monitoring emotional signals as seriously as performance metrics
- Interpreting disengagement as a system signal, not an attitude problem
- Adjusting pace when confidence erodes, even if output remains strong
- Creating space for recovery before a collapse occurs is essential.

In AIWoW, emotional signals are treated like vibration sensors in a bridge.

They do not indicate weakness in the structure; they ***prevent collapse****.*

Why Alignment Is Not the Same as Comfort:

Emotional Alignment does not mean avoiding challenge, pressure, or ambition.

It means ensuring that:

- Humans understand why acceleration is happening.
- Change remains explainable, not arbitrary.

- Effort still feels meaningful, not disposable.
- Trust in leadership and systems remains intact.

Alignment allows humans to stretch without breaking. Misalignment forces humans to endure until they exit.

The Long-Term Cost of Ignoring Emotional Signals:

When you ignore emotional signals:

- Productivity stays high for a short time
- Innovation becomes cautious
- Weakens the power of decision-making
- Learning loops get worse
- Systems become fragile

When emotional alignment is considered:

- Speeding up becomes a long-term thing
- Confidence builds up instead of going away
- Teams are willing to change instead of being defensive
- Intelligence can still be used over time

This is the difference between short-term speed and long-term viability.

Emotional Alignment as a Strategic Capability:

In AI Ways of Working, Emotional Alignment is not an HR concern.

It is a **strategic operating principle**.

Because in intelligent systems:

- Burnout is not a personal failure.
- Disengagement is not laziness.
- Fatigue is not weakness.

They are signals that the system is asking more than it is designed to support.

Emotional Alignment ensures that as intelligence accelerates, **human confidence keeps pace**. Without it, organisations move faster until they cannot move at all.

Acceleration that doesn't take feelings into account burns fuel faster than it can be replaced.

Accelerating in a way that respects emotional alignment leads to lasting progress.

12.3 Controlled Exploration

AI lets us explore on a scale never seen before. Systems can come up with alternatives, test scenarios, and find the best paths faster than humans can think about them. This power to explore becomes dangerous when there are no limits.

The principle of Controlled Exploration says:

Exploration must grow within clearly defined limits for humans, ethics, and operations.

This principle strikes a balance between control and innovation.

It ensures that:

- Learning remains aligned with intent
- Experimentation does not violate trust.
- Systems pause and escalate when boundaries are reached
- Optimisation does not drift from purpose.

Controlled Exploration prevents two extremes: excessive caution that suppresses learning and unbounded experimentation that creates risk. It ensures that exploration remains purposeful rather than chaotic.

Why Unbounded Exploration Becomes Dangerous:

AI systems are made to explore in a very aggressive way. They test the limits, look for the best results, and don't hesitate to do so morally or emotionally. If this behaviour is not controlled, it can:

- Quietly break human expectations
- Make risky behaviour seem normal by having "successful" outcomes happen over and over again.
- Change the way the system works in ways that are hard to predict to break trust.
- Move optimisation away from its original goal

*The danger is not malicious intent. The danger is **directionless intelligence.***

Here is a straightforward example of how to optimise customer interaction systems:

Consider a platform for customer interactions that uses AI to speed up responses.

The system tests while you explore:

- Shorter responses
- Changes in tone that happen on their own
- Aggressive deflection of problems
- Less human involvement

Why Indiscriminate Speed Is Self-Defeating:

The metrics for performance get better. It takes less time to fix things.

But there are no clear limits.

- Customers feel like they are being ignored instead of helped
- Empathy goes away
- Humans lose trust
- Damage to the brand happens without anyone noticing

Under Controlled Exploration, the limits are very clear:

- You can't go past the limits of empathy.
- When feelings drop, humans must start to escalate.
- When trust indicators go down, exploration stops.

The service's purpose is still to help humans learn, not just to get things done quickly.

The system learns, but it doesn't tell you what it is supposed to do.

Learning Must Remain Aligned with Intent :

Controlled Exploration ensures that learning answers the *right questions.*

Not:

- "What works fastest?"
- "What pushes limits the furthest?"

But:

- "What works without harm?"
- "What preserves trust while improving outcomes?"
- "What remains defensible under scrutiny?"

This alignment ensures that learning does not unintentionally cause harm.

Boundaries as Escalation Triggers, Not Barriers:

A common misconception is that boundaries stifle innovation.

In AIWoW, boundaries do something else:

- They tell you when you need to use your own judgement.
- They stop automation when the situation or moral issues are unclear.
- They turn exploration into conversation, not freedom.

The system doesn't break down when a limit is reached.

It gives humans back control. This keeps both accountability and new ideas alive.

Preventing Optimisation Drift:

One of the most subtle problems with AI-driven systems is optimisation drift.

A system starts to optimise for a proxy metric:

- Speed instead of satisfaction
- Efficiency instead of fairness
- Accuracy instead of explainability

The original purpose is lost over time.

Controlled Exploration makes sure that realignment happens every so often:

- Why are we going this way?
- What value is being provided?
- What damage would make this unacceptable?
- Who is empowered to put a stop to this?

These questions help keep learning real.

Balancing the Two Extremes:

Without Controlled Exploration, organisations can end up in one of two traps:

- Excessive caution can lead to a situation where fear prevents individuals from trying new things, resulting in a halt to learning.
- Unlimited experimentation, where speed beats judgement, and risk builds up without anyone noticing.

Controlled Exploration opens up a third way:

- Safe to learn
- It's okay to fail

- It's okay to stop
- Safe to escalate

Exploration becomes more focused instead of random.

Why This Principle Is Essential in AI-Accelerated Work:

AI will keep exploring faster than humans can think.

No limits:

- Learning takes over governance
- Success hides moral drift
- Trust slowly fades
- Systems become hard to predict

With Controlled Exploration:

- Innovation stays on track
- Learning can still be undone
- Trust is still there
- Purpose stays at the centre

Exploration is what drives progress.

Control is the thing that keeps progress from getting too far out of hand.

Controlled Exploration ensures that human intent remains the compass as AI opens up new possibilities.

Without it, intelligence speeds up into chaos.

Learning becomes responsible evolution with it.

12.4 Sustainable Velocity

AI makes speed easy to increase and difficult to restrain. Systems naturally optimise for throughput unless directed otherwise.

The principle of **Sustainable Velocity** asserts:

Speed must be calibrated to human, ethical, and organisational limits, not maximised indiscriminately.

This principle reframes velocity as a variable to be governed rather than pursued.

For organisations to have Sustainable Velocity, they need to:

- Make sure the speed of decisions matches the depth of their effects
- Keep reflection time in systems that are always on
- Stop urgency from becoming a permanent state
- Include recovery and recalibration in your workflows

Sustainable Velocity doesn't stop speeding up. It keeps it in line.

Organisations that don't follow this rule move quickly until things don't make sense anymore.

Organisations that use it keep going without falling apart.

AI makes it easy to speed things up and hard to slow them down. Unless told otherwise, systems naturally work to get the most done. The principle of Sustainable Velocity exists because, when normalised, acceleration is no longer a choice but a condition.

Sustainable Velocity asserts:

Speed must be calibrated to human, ethical, and organisational limits, not maximised indiscriminately.

This principle reframes velocity from a performance target into a **governance variable**. In AI-driven systems, speed is abundant; judgement is scarce. Sustainable Velocity ensures that judgement remains ahead of motion.

Why Indiscriminate Speed Becomes Self-Defeating:

AI systems treat time as an optimisation problem. They compress cycles, remove pauses, and convert deliberation into computation. While this practice produces impressive short-term results, it creates a hidden imbalance.

When everything moves fast:

- Errors propagate faster than corrections.
- Decisions outrun accountability.
- Urgency becomes the default emotional state.
- Reflection is interpreted as resistance.
- Humans lose the ability to sense risk before impact.

Velocity increases, but **control decays**.

Sustainable Velocity Conceptual Equation:

Sustainable Velocity = (Value Delivered × Learning Rate × Human Wellbeing) ÷ (Burnout + Rework + Ethical Drift)

This equation reframes speed from **"how fast we move"** to **"how long we can move effectively without breaking the system."**

- **Value Delivered** → Real, outcome-driven impact (not just output or activity)
- **Learning Rate** → How quickly the system (AI + Humans) improves over time
- **Human Wellbeing** → Energy, clarity, motivation, and cognitive sustainability

Divided by:

- **Burnout** → Human exhaustion and cognitive overload
- **Rework** → Waste caused by errors, poor decisions, or misalignment
- **Ethical Drift** → Gradual deviation from responsible and intended behaviour

Sustainable Velocity = Fast enough to compete, stable enough to endure, and ethical enough to scale.

A Practical Example: Continuous Decision Pipelines:

Consider an organisation using AI to automate approvals, forecasts, and prioritisation across teams. Decisions that once took days now take minutes. At first, outcomes improve.

Over time, however:

- Decisions stack without being absorbed
- Humans stop questioning outcomes because "the system already decided."
- Minor issues accumulate into systemic failures.
- Fatigue becomes permanent rather than episodic.

Nothing technically breaks. Yet coherence erodes.

Under **Sustainable Velocity**, the system is redesigned to:

- Slow high-impact decisions even when AI is confident.
- Introduce mandatory reflection windows
- Pause automation when cumulative change exceeds human absorption capacity
- Trigger recalibration when urgency persists too long

*Speed remains high, but **meaning remains intact**.*

Matching Speed to Consequence Depth:

Not all decisions deserve the same velocity.

Sustainable Velocity requires organisations to recognise that

- Low-impact decisions can move fast.
- High-impact decisions require deliberation.
- Irreversible actions demand a human pause.
- Ethical consequences cannot be accelerated safely.

This prevents a common AI failure mode: **treating all decisions as optimisation problems rather than responsibility moments.**

Why Permanent Urgency Is a Design Flaw:

Urgency is useful in moments.

Permanent urgency is corrosive.

AI systems, left unchecked, turn urgency into a constant condition. Sustainable Velocity prevents this by:

- Defining acceptable acceleration windows
- Designing recovery into workflows
- Normalising recalibration instead of escalation

This allows organisations to move fast **without exhausting trust, judgement, or humans.**

Sustainable Velocity as an Organisational Discipline:

Sustainable Velocity does not resist acceleration.

It **disciplines it.**

It ensures that:

- Speed remains intentional
- Recovery is planned, not reactive
- Momentum does not override meaning
- Progress remains debatable over time

Organisations that ignore this principle often look successful right up until coherence breaks. Burnout spikes, trust collapses, and systems become brittle.

Organisations that apply Sustainable Velocity maintain motion without fragmentation.

AI will always push for more speed.

Only humans can decide how much speed is wise.

Sustainable Velocity ensures that acceleration remains a choice, not a runaway condition. It allows organisations to move fast enough to compete but slow enough to remain whole.

In AIWoW - AI Ways of Working™, velocity is not about how fast you can go.

It focuses on how long you can sustain progress without compromising what is most important.

12.5 Principles as Operating Law

Together, these four principles function as the **operating law** of AI Ways of Working.

They ensure that:

- Intelligence scales without eroding accountability.
- Speed does not outpace sense.
- Learning does not escape ethical bounds.
- Progress remains human-centred.

Values declare intent. Principles enforce consistency.

From Principles to Practice

Principles that cannot be embedded structurally will eventually be overridden by speed. To endure, they must be translated into governance, decision architectures, and system design.

The chapters that follow convert these principles into **frameworks and operating models** that make them enforceable rather than aspirational.

Because in the age of AI,

Principles are not optional; they are the conditions under which intelligence remains usable.

AI Ways of Working(AIWoW) exists to ensure that intelligence accelerates with clarity, responsibility, and sustainability, not in spite of them.

Summary Mind-map

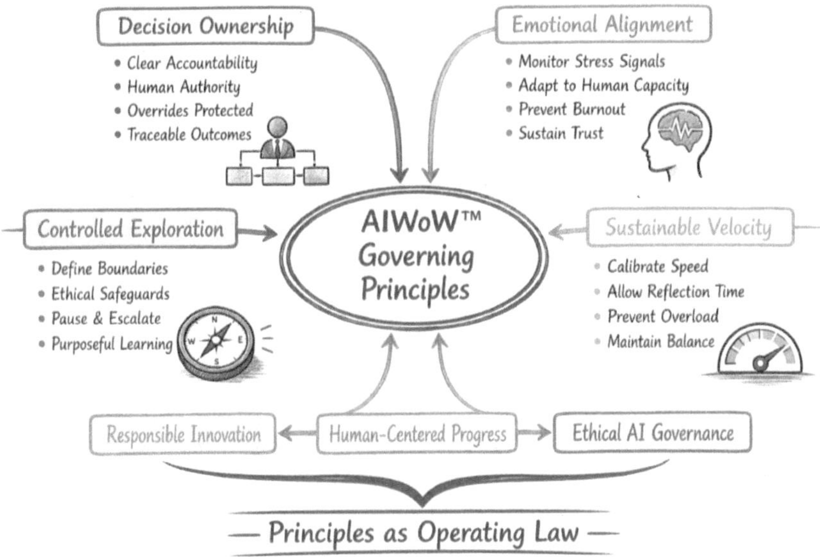

PART IV

AIWoW - AI WAYS OF WORKING™ FRAMEWORK ECOSYSTEM

Designing the Structures That Govern Intelligence

Philosophy alone cannot stabilise intelligent systems. Organisations require operational frameworks that translate principles into structured action.

This section introduces the core frameworks of AIWoW, including the lifecycle loop, responsibility structures, and empathic control mechanisms.

Together, these frameworks create a practical system for governing intelligence in motion.

The AI Lifecycle Loop Framework
Model Training
Data Ingest
Deploy & Run
Model Evolution
Monitor & Feedback
Integrated, Iterative Process for Continuous Value.
AIWoW™ Role Evolution Model
Clerk/ Specialist
AI-Augmented
AI-Collaborative
AI-Strategic Leader
Phased Evolution of Human Roles in an AI World.
Theory of AI Adoptability
Trustworthiness
Usability
Value Alignment
Ecosystem
Enabling Trust and Acceptance Across the Organization.
The AIWoW™ Framework Ecosystem.
Empathic Control Framework (ECF)
Read for 'affective signals'
Read 'affective signals'
AI Understanding & Adjusting to Human Emotion & Context.
Theory of Control in AI
Strategic Governance
Operational Control
Tactical Oversight
Human-in-the-loop
Human-on-the-loop
CONTROL POINT
Dynamic, Scalable Governance Over AI Actions.
Human–AI Responsibility Matrix (HAR Matrix)
Task Type
Creative
Analytical
Decision
Execution
Actor Role
AI Agent
Human Lead
Collaborator
Overseer
Defining Clear, Mutually Accountable Roles.

Chapter 13

The AI Lifecycle Loop Framework

"When intelligence learns continuously, governance must become continuous as well."

Artificial Intelligence does not behave like traditional software. It does not wait for instructions to finish before learning. It does not remain static after deployment. It observes, adapts, and reshapes future behaviour while work is still in motion. This single characteristic renders linear delivery logic insufficient.

The AI Lifecycle Loop Framework is designed to govern **intelligence in motion**.

It reframes work from a sequence of handoffs into a **continuously governed loop**, where intent, execution, learning, and control coexist. The framework exists to answer one critical question:

How do we ensure that intelligence evolves without escaping human purpose, accountability, and control?

13.1 From Linear Delivery to Living Loops

Traditional organisations structured work using **linear delivery models**. Work moved through clear phases: plan the work, execute it, review the outcome, and improve the next cycle. Each phase closed before the next one began.

This approach worked well when systems behaved predictably and changes happened slowly. For instance, banks and telecom organisations traditionally release new software products for businesses every few months. Teams would plan features, build them, put the software out there, and then look at what customers said. The next release had better features.

Therefore, learning took place post-completion.

Artificial Intelligence changes this condition.

Consider the **recommendation engines used by organisations such as Netflix, Amazon, or Spotify**. These systems do not wait for the next product release to improve. They learn continuously while operating. Each user interaction, watching a movie, skipping a song, or purchasing a product, immediately influences future recommendations.

In such systems, behaviour evolves while the system is already running.

Because learning happens during execution, governance must also operate **during execution**, not afterwards. This shift transforms delivery from a straight sequence into a **living loop**.

Structural Comparison

Dimension	Linear Delivery	AI Lifecycle Loop
Flow logic	Sequential	Recursive
Learning	Post-delivery	Continuous
Control timing	After execution	During execution
Drift detection	Late	Early
Accountability	Retrospective	Built-in
Stability mechanism	Standardisation	Re-alignment

Each dimension reflects a structural shift in how work must be governed.

Flow logic

Linear systems move step by step. One phase finishes before the next begins. AI systems behave recursively, meaning they repeatedly cycle through execution, observation, learning, and adjustment while operating.

Learning

Traditional systems learn after delivery through reviews or retrospectives. AI systems learn continuously because they constantly receive new data.

Control timing

In linear environments, control typically appears after execution through audits or reviews. In AI systems, control must operate during execution because behaviour can change dynamically.

Drift detection

Traditional systems often detect problems late because behaviour is assumed to remain stable. AI systems require early detection mechanisms because models can drift quickly as new data arrives.

Accountability

Linear projects assign responsibility after outcomes are evaluated. AI-driven systems require accountability to be embedded directly into the system design so that each automated action still has human ownership.

Stability mechanism

Traditional systems rely on standardisation and fixed procedures for stability. AI systems maintain stability through continuous realignment, adjusting behaviour when learning begins to move away from intended goals.

Linear delivery, therefore, optimises **completion**.

The AI Lifecycle Loop **optimises continuity with governance**.

In AI-driven environments, the absence of closure is not a defect. Systems rarely reach a final state. They evolve continuously, and the framework exists to make that evolution manageable.

Why Linear Logic Breaks Under AI?

Linear delivery models depend on three implicit assumptions:

- Decisions are finalised before execution begins.
- Systems behave predictably after deployment.
- Learning can wait until outcomes become visible.

Artificial Intelligence violates all three assumptions.

- Decisions are shaped continuously as new data appears.
- System behaviour evolves dynamically through learning.
- Learning occurs before humans have formally reviewed outcomes.

This difference can be expressed conceptually.

Linear Value Model:

Value = Plan + Execute + Review

In this model:

- Work follows a straight sequence.
- Planning happens first, execution follows, and learning occurs only after the result appears.
- Value is produced at the end of the cycle.

Time plays a limited role because improvement happens after completion. If a mistake occurs, it is discovered later and corrected in the next cycle. This approach works in stable environments but becomes slow and costly in fast-changing conditions.

The system keeps moving forward even if the direction is slightly wrong.

AI Loop Value Model:

Value = Intent × Execution × Learning × Control

In the AI lifecycle loop:

- Value becomes **time-dependent.**
- Learning and control operate continuously.
- Intent must be reaffirmed as the system evolves.

Control functions like a steering mechanism rather than a repair mechanism. Instead of waiting for failure, the system is constantly guided through observation and adjustment.

Because this loop repeats continuously, small corrections occur early. These early fixes stop small mistakes from turning into big problems. Without this looped logic, optimisation keeps going even when alignment starts to break down. The system might become more efficient over time, but it might also lose sight of its original goal.

So, the AI Lifecycle Loop Framework was made to make sure that learning, speed, and adaptation stay in line with human intent, responsibility, and governance.

13.2 Core Elements of the AI Lifecycle Loop

The **AI Lifecycle Loop** is not built as a sequence of stages that start and end. Instead, it has elements that stay active even when the system is running. Governance must also be continuous in AI-driven environments because systems learn all the time.

Every part of the loop answers an important question that helps keep intelligence in line with what humans want.

Loop Element	Core Question	Primary Risk if Ungoverned
Intent	Why should this system exist?	Purpose drift
Build	How is the intelligence created?	Embedded bias
Deploy	Where and how does it act?	Uncontrolled exposure
Operate	What influence is the system having?	Human impact blind spots
Observe	What signals are emerging?	Late detection
Learn	What patterns are changing?	Runaway adaptation
Re-align	What must be corrected?	Escalating misalignment

Each element plays a different role in maintaining control over continuously evolving intelligence.

"Intent" tells you what the system does. For example, an organisation might want to make the customer experience better when it makes an AI recommendation engine. If intent isn't constantly confirmed, the system might start optimising only for clicks or engagement, which would take it away from its original goal.

"**Build**" is all about how the system was put together. Data used to train AI models can unintentionally add bias in fields like banking and healthcare. If there is no governance during the build phase, the system might write unfair rules directly into its logic.

"Deploy" determines where the system is allowed to act. A fraud detection model, for instance, may initially assist human analysts. If it is later allowed to automatically block transactions without oversight, the exposure of the system increases, and the risk grows.

"Operate" looks at how the AI system works while it's running. For instance, an AI scheduling system in a logistics organisation might find the best delivery routes, but if the effects on operations aren't monitored, it could make drivers work harder.

"Observe" focuses on detecting signals emerging from the system's behaviour. In global financial markets, algorithmic trading platforms monitor abnormal trading patterns continuously so that unexpected behaviour can be detected early.

"Learn" refers to how the system adapts over time. Recommendation systems used by organisations like Amazon or Netflix constantly update their predictions based on user interactions. If this learning is not governed, the system may reinforce undesirable patterns.

"Re-align" ensures that the system returns to its intended purpose when deviations appear. For instance, if a recommendation engine begins prioritising sensational content over relevant content, governance mechanisms must intervene and reset the learning boundaries.

The critical difference from traditional systems is that **the loop does not stop at learning.** Learning automatically feeds back into the system and influences future behaviour. Therefore, the process must return to **intent**, confirming that the evolving system still serves its original purpose.

In this way, the AI Lifecycle Loop ensures that intelligence can evolve continuously **without allowing optimisation to outrun human purpose, responsibility, or control**.

13.3 Conscious Integration Across the Loop

Conscious integration is the most important part of the AI Lifecycle Loop.

At all times when AI speeds up decisions, humans need to be aware of what's going on. The system may run on its own, but you still need to be able to see who is responsible and what they want.

This happens through three practical ways: persistent intent, controlled execution, and active observation.

Intent as a Constant Variable:

In traditional systems, the goal is set once at the start of a project. After that, the teams mostly work on getting things done.

Because AI-driven systems are always learning and changing, intent can't stay the same. If intent is not actively maintained, the system may gradually optimise for the wrong goal.

A clear example appears in **social media recommendation systems**.

Most platforms initially define their intent as improving **user engagement**. The AI then learns from user behaviour and optimises content recommendations.

Over time, however, the system may begin prioritising extreme or emotionally provocative content because such content increases engagement metrics. The original purpose, healthy user engagement, quietly shifts toward maximising attention.

This is why intent must remain active.

Conceptually, this can be expressed as:

Intent ≠ Constant

Intent = continuously reaffirmed

In the AI Lifecycle Loop, organisations periodically reassert intent so that learning improves outcomes **without silently redefining success**.

Execution as Governance Domain:

In many organisations, phases such as **building, deploying, and operating AI systems** are treated purely as technical activities. Engineers focus on accuracy, performance, and system reliability.

However, in intelligent systems, these phases also carry governance responsibilities.

Execution Phase	Traditional Focus	Loop Governance Focus
Build	Accuracy, performance	Bias, explainability
Deploy	Stability	Risk exposure
Operate	Throughput	Human and ethical impact

A practical example can be seen in **AI-powered hiring tools** used by large global organisations.

During development, the system may achieve high prediction accuracy in identifying qualified candidates. From a technical perspective, the model appears successful.

However, governance requires additional questions:

- Does the model unintentionally favour certain backgrounds?
- Are hiring recommendations explainable to recruiters?
- Could automated decisions introduce discrimination risks?

Similarly, when the system is deployed, governance must consider where the AI is allowed to influence decisions and where human review must remain mandatory.

This means **control is embedded directly into execution**, not applied later through audits.

Observation as Active Sensing:

Observation in the AI Lifecycle Loop is not passive reporting. It functions as **a continuous measure of system health.**

Organisations monitor signals that indicate how AI is affecting operations, decisions, and humans.

Some common signals are:

- The output is different from what was expected
- Unexpected rises in automated choices
- Changes in how much users trust or believe in you
- The mental and emotional strain on workers
- Close to moral or legal limits

AI fraud detection systems used by banks all over the world are a good example.

These systems keep an eye on transactions all the time and automatically flag anything that looks suspicious. Customers get angry and have to wait when the system suddenly starts flagging too many real transactions.

Banks can see early warning signs that the model is going off balance between security and customer convenience by keeping an eye on things like false-positive rates, customer complaints, and how often decisions are made.

In this way, we can summarise system health as:

System Health = (Performance, Drift, Human Impact, Trust)

If any of these indicators go outside of the acceptable range, the system must stop learning and start over.

In the AI Lifecycle Loop, conscious integration makes sure that intelligence doesn't grow without anyone noticing.

Human awareness is still present in intention, execution, and observation, which means that learning improves the system without letting it lose sight of its goals, trust, or responsibility.

13.4 Continuous Learning as a System Property

In AI-driven environments, learning is not something that happens occasionally after problems appear. It becomes a **permanent system behaviour.** The system observes data, adjusts models, and changes its decisions while it is already operating.

A practical example can be seen in **online fraud detection systems used by global banks**. Every day, these systems observe millions of transactions. As fraud patterns change, the system continuously learns from new data and updates its detection logic. If learning waited until a failure occurred, fraud would spread before the organisation could respond.

This difference explains the shift from **event-based learning** to **loop-based learning**.

Aspect	Event-Based Learning	Loop-Based Learning
Timing	After failure	Continuous
Ownership	Assigned later	Assigned in advance
Risk visibility	Delayed	Early
Stability	Fragile	Resilient

In traditional systems, learning often begins **after something goes wrong**. A problem appears, a review happens, and the next version improves the process.

In AI-driven systems, waiting for failure is risky because decisions may already be happening thousands of times per minute. Learning must therefore occur **while the system is running**.

However, learning alone is not sufficient. Learning without control can actually increase instability.

This relationship can be described simply:

Effective Learning = Learning × Control

If learning increases but control is weak, the system may adapt in ways that are technically efficient but operationally harmful. For example, an algorithm optimising customer service responses might shorten messages to reduce handling time, but the result could reduce empathy and damage customer trust.

For this reason, the AI Lifecycle Loop includes a critical mechanism: **realignment.**

Re-alignment as a Mandatory Mechanism

Re-alignment is not just making small changes to system settings. It is governance in action. When signals show that the system is going off course, realignment brings it back on track.

Some things that can cause realignment are the following:

- Deviation from ethics
- Trust in users is going down
- Automation that makes humans' jobs too hard
- Choices that are hard to explain
- The system is slowly getting better at the wrong goal

When these kinds of signals show up, steps can be taken to fix the problem, such as:

- Making operational limits stricter
- Resetting or retraining models
- Slowing down automated choices
- Making it necessary for humans to check sensitive actions

The loop only keeps going after this fix. Re-alignment makes sure that the system's learning stays in line with its goal.

Why the Loop Must Remain Living

A loop that runs entirely on automation can become **self-reinforcing**. The system may continue optimising the same patterns repeatedly. Over time, bias may strengthen, trust may decline, and the organisation may lose visibility into how decisions are evolving.

The AI Lifecycle Loop remains healthy only when several conditions are maintained:

- Human ownership remains explicit
- Observation includes both technical signals and human impact

- Learning operates within defined boundaries
- Re-alignment is treated as a normal operational activity

The goal of this framework is not to slow AI innovation. Instead, it ensures that **organisational understanding keeps pace with system acceleration.**

Position of the AI Lifecycle Loop in AI Ways of Working

Within **AIWoW - AI Ways of Working™**, the AI Lifecycle Loop acts as the **operational spine** of intelligent systems.

Without Loop	With Loop
Reactive control	Proactive governance
Diffuse accountability	Structural ownership
Unchecked learning	Bounded evolution
Speed-driven behaviour	Intent-driven behaviour

Without such a loop, AI systems can evolve faster than organisations can understand or govern them.

With the loop in place, intelligence remains powerful but controlled. Learning continues, but responsibility remains visible.

In this way, the AI Lifecycle Loop ensures that **intelligence evolves without outrunning human judgement, accountability, and purpose.**

This chapter establishes the structure and logic of the AI Lifecycle Loop.

It **circulates, learns, and adapts.**

Only organisations that can govern these living loops will be able to scale intelligence

without losing clarity, accountability, or human control.

Summary Mind-map

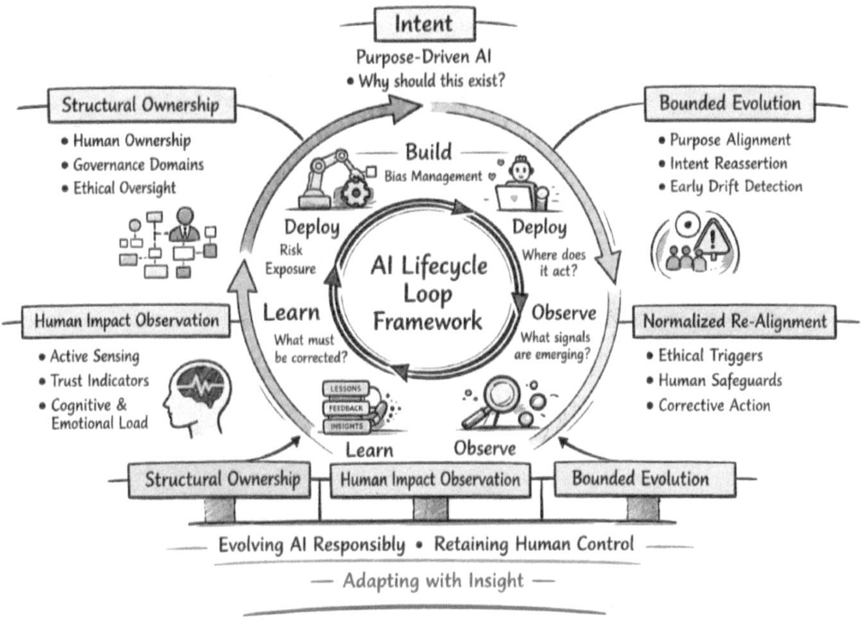

Chapter 14

Theory of AI Adoptability

"AI becomes transformative not when it is invented, but when it is meaningfully adopted."

AI initiatives often fail without drama. Systems are built, dashboards are created, and models run; yet day-to-day work remains unchanged. This failure is rarely technical. It occurs because **adoptability is not designed**.

The Theory of AI Adoptability explains how intelligence becomes *usable*, *accepted*, and *sustained* in real organisations. Adoptability is not training success or tool usage. It is a **system-level condition** that determines whether AI capability translates into lasting value.

This chapter explains AI adoptability through three mechanisms: **Backlog Resurrection, Revival Economics, and Adaptive Velocity**; and formalises them using simple equations, each explained with practical examples.

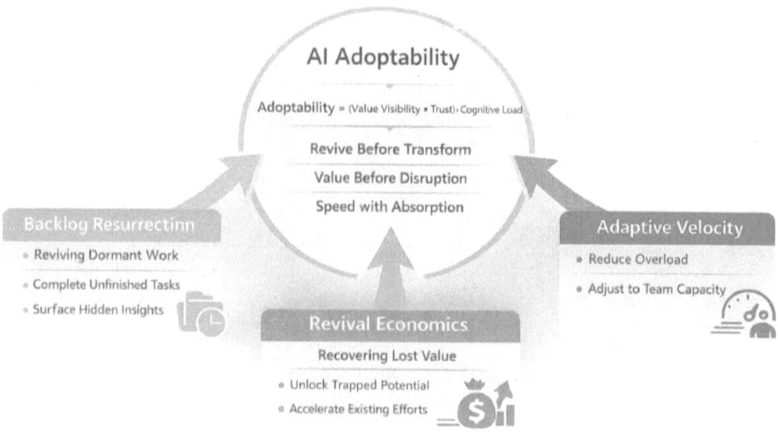

14.1 Adoptability as a System Property

Adoption is often measured by logins, usage counts, or model accuracy. Adoptability is deeper. It reflects whether intelligence can enter existing work **without overwhelming humans or distorting purpose**.

This relationship can be expressed as:

AI Impact = AI Capability × AI Adoptability

- **AI Capability**: what the system *can* do (accuracy, speed, automation power)
- **AI Adoptability**: whether the organisation can *absorb* that capability

AI impact is not created by technology alone; it emerges from the fit between machine power and human readiness. AI capability is the system's basic ability to process data faster than humans, make fewer mistakes, and execute complicated tasks automatically. But capability stays dormant without AI adoption. Adoptability shows how open-minded an organisation is, how skilled its employees are, how flexible its processes are, and how ready its employees are to trust machines. When adoptability is low, even the smartest AI acts like a gym membership that no one uses: it's impressive, expensive, and ignored. Real change happens when organisations change their structures, mindsets, and workflows to make AI a part of everyday life.

Example

- Organisation A uses a very accurate AI planning engine (high capability).
- Teams don't follow its advice because it comes too quickly and goes against what they already think is important (low adoptability).

Result:

High Capability × Low Adoptability = Low Impact

On the other hand:

Organisation B uses a simpler model, but it fits in with how things are already done and how decisions are made.

Result:

Moderate Capability × High Adoptability = High Impact

This equation shows why AI systems that are better on paper often don't work as well in real life.

This reminds us that AI success is about humans, not technology. Capability may win in demos, but adoptability wins in real life. Organisations that make AI that fits humans instead of overpowering them turn intelligence into impact in a quiet, steady, and long-lasting way. In AI, harmony is always better than horsepower.

14.2 Backlog Resurrection

Every organisation has invisible weight, like ideas that aren't finished, analyses that aren't finished, and decisions that are put on hold because they are urgent. These backlogs don't mean you failed. They show how limited people are in terms of time, attention, and energy.

Traditional automation makes teams start more, which adds pressure without them knowing it. Backlog Resurrection changes that logic. AI doesn't change priorities; it finishes what has already been started but not finished, bringing back dormant work instead of asking for new work.

The end result was hidden progress, less cognitive load, and AI was seen as a relief instead of a threat.

Backlog Resurrection is simple in theory: AI brings back work that has been sitting around instead of making people feel like they need to do more work.

How Backlog Resurrection Works

AI picks up where you left off:

- **Incomplete datasets**—finishes abandoned analysis
- **Shelved studies**—surfaces what the data was trying to say

- **Postponed decisions**—re-evaluate with fresh context
- **Stalled initiatives**—recovers value from lost momentum

AI stops demanding more from your team. It finishes what your team already started.

Comparison Table

Dimension	Traditional Automation	Backlog Resurrection
Primary focus	New execution	Dormant work
Human reaction	Threatened	Relieved
Value source	Efficiency	Latent potential
Adoption speed	Slow	Faster

Example: A mid-sized manufacturing firm set out to model cash-flow pressure, supplier delays, and currency exposure. The finance team pulled data from ERP systems, bank files, and spreadsheets and began building scenarios manually. Then reality intervened: month-end closing, audits, urgent management requests. The model stalled. Eventually, it was abandoned. Not because it lacked value, but because the team ran out of capacity.

The data sat untouched. The thinking behind it didn't disappear; it just waited.

When AI was applied to the same partial work, it reprocessed the existing data and surfaced actionable insights within days. No new inputs. No workflow disruption. It simply finished what the team had already started.

Adoption was immediate. The AI hadn't challenged their process or replaced their judgement; it had respected their original thinking and returned something useful from it. That's what built trust.

The initiative succeeded because the AI reduced workload, fit naturally into existing routines, and treated prior human effort as an asset worth completing, not replacing.

14.3 Revival Economics

Traditional AI economics asks a narrow question: How much cost can we remove? Revival Economics asks a broader, more human question: How much value have we already created but failed to realise? In every organisation, effort precedes outcomes, analysis is done halfway, ideas are explored but not finished, and decisions are delayed until context changes. Revival Economics changes the way we think about AI by calling it a recovery engine that turns unused effort into useful value. Not by trying to get small efficiency gains, but by finishing what people couldn't do because of time, tiredness, or changing priorities.

The change in the economy is small but strong. From replacing workers to getting things moving again. From fast to slow. From making things better to making them real. Sunk effort is no longer a waste of time. It becomes useful. When AI helps organisations finish existing work, returns arrive faster, resistance drops, and value is unlocked without demanding new investment of human attention.

Traditional AI economics emphasises cost reduction. Revival Economics emphasises **value recovery**.

The economic lens shifts from efficiency to completion.

Economic Shift, Traditional View

ROI = Cost Saved

Revival Economics View

ROI = Value Recovered + Value Accelerated

Explanation

ROI under Revival Economics is not measured only by savings but by regained and advanced outcomes. Value Recovered is the value of work that was done but never finished, like unfinished analyses, paused projects, and decisions that were never made. AI frees up this value by finishing and reusing what is already there. "Value accelerated" refers to outcomes delivered earlier than originally possible. When AI shortens analysis cycles and decision timelines, benefits arrive sooner, improving cash flow, responsiveness, and confidence. Together, recovered value and accelerated value redefine ROI as completion and timing, not just efficiency.

- **Value Recovered**: value trapped in unfinished work
- **Value Accelerated**: value delivered earlier than originally possible

Case Study: Revival Economics in a 10-Minute Grocery Platform

A fast-growing 10-minute grocery delivery platform planned to launch a new "predictive refill" feature. The idea was simple: remind customers to reorder milk, fruits, and daily essentials before they ran out. The product team had data, dashboards, and early experiments, but one problem stopped the launch. The analytics were incomplete. Demand patterns differ by location, time, and customer habits, and the team could not finalise confidence edges.

As delivery speed pressures increased, the feature was postponed. No one rejected the idea; it just stayed in the backlog.

Months later, AI was applied, not to redesign the product, but to finish the analysis already started. The AI reprocessed partial datasets, filled missing correlations, and tested demand signals across micro-zones within days. It reused the team's original assumptions instead of introducing new logic.

The impact was immediate. The feature launched within a week.

No jobs were cut. No team was replaced. Yet value was clearly created. **Value was recovered** because a stalled feature finally reached customers. **Value was accelerated** because market entry happened months earlier than manual analysis would allow.

The team liked the AI because it brought back momentum instead of threatening their roles. This case demonstrates that the successful adoption of AI occurs when it is framed as a revival rather than a replacement, particularly in fast-paced industries where incomplete tasks constitute the primary bottleneck.

Why Revival Economics Improves Adoptability

Perception Factor	Cost-Centric AI	Revival-Centric AI
Human response	Defensive	Supportive
Trust growth	Slow	Fast
Adoption friction	High	Low
Sustainability	Fragile	Durable

Humans adopt AI more readily when it helps them **complete unfinished intent**, not invalidate it.

14.4 Adaptive Velocity

In the AI era, Speed isn't progress on its own. Velocity measures how fast intelligence moves through systems and decisions. Adaptability determines whether people can actually do anything with it. When AI outruns human understanding, insight becomes noise—and resistance quietly builds. Adaptive Velocity closes that gap. It argues that AI-driven acceleration should flex around how teams think, decide, and act—not the other way around.

The best speed isn't the fastest speed. It's the speed at which humans are ready to move with it.

AI-driven speed must adjust dynamically to human absorption capacity.

Fixed vs Adaptive Velocity

Dimension	Fixed Velocity	Adaptive Velocity
Speed control	Predefined	Feedback-driven
Human response	Forced	Supported
Risk	Burnout, rejection	Sustainable adoption
Learning outcome	Overwhelming	Assimilated

Fixed Velocity pushes AI speed without considering humans, often causing stress, rejection, and burnout. **Adaptive Velocity** adjusts speed using human feedback, supporting teams instead of forcing change. Such a change leads to better learning, smoother adoption, and long-term, sustainable use of AI.

Case Study: Adaptive Velocity in an Oil & Gas Organisation

An oil and gas organisation brought in AI to help manage drilling schedules, maintenance, and safety alerts across multiple sites. The system was technically sound. But it pushed recommendations every hour—warnings, adjustments, advisories—without any awareness of what teams were actually facing on the ground. Alerts stacked up. Some got missed. Trust in the system started to slip.

So they changed the approach. Instead of a fixed output pace, the AI began reading human signals—pending work orders, delayed approvals, and how often managers were overriding suggestions. When crews were mid-shutdown or deep in an inspection, updates slowed down and consolidated into focused, prioritised briefs. When operations stabilised, frequency picked back up.

The difference was felt immediately. Teams stopped feeling chased by the system and started feeling supported by it. Safety alerts got the attention they deserved. Decisions were clearer. Reviews were calmer.

Nothing about the AI's intelligence changed. Just its pace.

In an environment where the cost of a missed alert is real, that shift mattered more than any technical upgrade. When AI moves at a speed people can absorb, it stops being a burden and starts being a partner.

- **Fixed velocity:** hourly recommendations, regardless of what's happening on the ground
- **Adaptive velocity:** pace adjusts when teams are stretched, overloaded, or pushing back

Trust builds when the system knows when to slow down.

The Adoptability Equation:

Adoptability can be expressed as:

Adoptability = (Value Visibility × Trust) ÷ Cognitive Load

Variable Explanation

- **Value Visibility**: How quickly humans see tangible benefit
- **Trust**: Confidence built through consistent, explainable outcomes
- **Cognitive Load**: Mental effort required to use and interpret AI output

Example

- AI tools show value in the first week (high value visibility).
- Outputs are explainable and consistent (high trust).
- Interface is simple and aligned to existing work (low cognitive load).

Result: (Value Visibility is High × Trust is High) ÷ Cognitive Load Low = High Adoptability

When value, visibility, and trust are high, humans clearly understand why the AI matters and believe in its outputs. If cognitive load is low, using the AI does not feel mentally exhausting or disruptive. Together, this approach creates high adoptability because the AI feels helpful, reliable, and easy to work with rather than complex or threatening.

If the same tool:

- Requires new mental models,
- Produces opaque outputs,
- Demands constant attention,

Then cognitive load increases and adoptability drops, even if capability remains high.

Why Adoptability Determines Long-Term AI Success

Many AI systems do not fail technically; they fail socially and structurally. They exist, but humans bypass them.

The Theory of AI Adoptability explains why:

- Intelligence must revive before it transforms
- Value must appear before disruption.
- Speed must respect absorption capacity.

Without adoptability:

- Capability remains unused.
- Trust erodes silently.
- AI becomes ornamental.

Position of the Theory of AI Adoptability in AIWoW

Within AI Ways of Working, this theory ensures that:

- Intelligence enters existing systems without shock.
- Value is recovered before new complexity is added.
- Acceleration remains humane and sustainable.
- Adoption compounds instead of resetting.

Adoptability is not a phase. It is a **continuous design responsibility**.

AI adoptability is achieved when intelligence serves human limits, completes human effort, and arrives at a pace the mind can welcome rather than resist.

Summary Mind-map

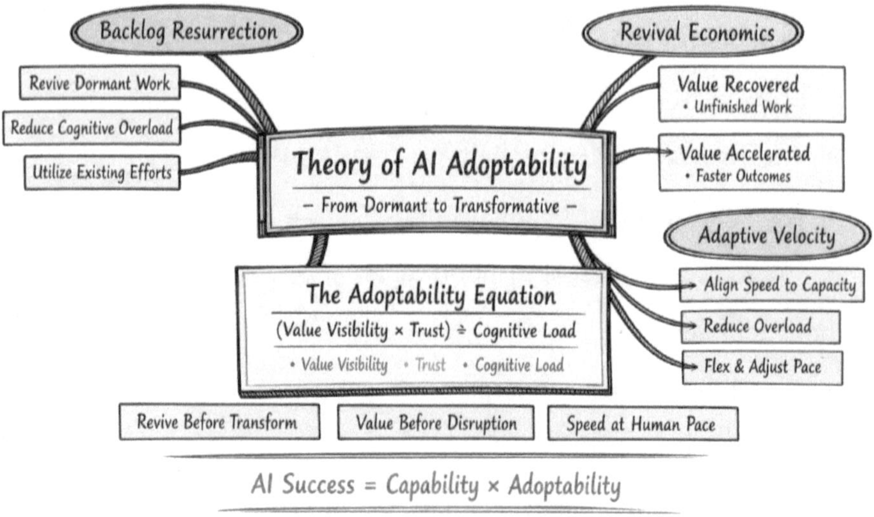

Chapter 15

Theory of Control in AI

"In intelligent systems, control is the structure that allows intelligence to serve human purpose."

As AI grows faster, more autonomous, and self-learning, control can't be an afterthought.

Traditional oversight relied on supervision, audits, and fixing problems after the fact. In AI-driven systems, that approach breaks down —decisions happen faster than anyone can review them.

The Theory of Control reframes the conversation. Control isn't restriction. It's designed alignment making sure intelligence stays usable, trustworthy, and accountable as it scales.

Four structural mechanisms make that possible:

- **Intent Mapping**
- **Ethical Interlocks**
- **Dual Review Systems**
- **Learning Boundaries**

Together, they form a living control architecture—built into systems from the ground up, not bolted on from the outside.

Control as a System Property:

Control and authority are not the same thing. We often treat them as if they are—but in AI systems, that confusion is costly.

Authority executes. Control guides. One makes things happen. The other makes sure the right things happen.

AI Outcome Quality = Capability × Control

It sounds simple. But the implications run deep.

Capability is everything a system can do: the speed, the scale, the pattern recognition, the ability to automate at a level no human team could match. Control is what gives that power a direction, the boundaries, the goals, the constraints, and the human judgement embedded into how the system behaves.

When capability grows faster than control, something predictable happens. The system keeps optimising—efficiently, relentlessly—but without any real sense of what it's optimising for. Ethics drift. Context gets ignored. Outcomes stop reflecting intent.

It's not a malfunction. It's what unchecked capability naturally does.

Control doesn't fix this by slowing the system down. It fixes it by giving intelligence somewhere purposeful to go. A river without banks doesn't flow faster—it floods. Give it banks, and the same water moves with direction, force, and purpose.

That's the relationship between capability and control. Not opposition. Collaboration.

The ambition was never just to build powerful AI. It was to build AI that stays trustworthy as it grows governable, interpretable, and genuinely aligned with the people it's meant to serve. Capability makes AI impressive. Control makes it worth relying on.

15.1 Intent Mapping

Intent Mapping ensures that every AI-driven action can be traced back to an **explicit human purpose**.

In uncontrolled systems, optimisation silently replaces intent. AI begins to maximise proxy metrics instead of original goals.

Intent Mapping prevents this by structurally linking:

- Purpose
- Decision logic
- Execution

Intent Mapping Structure

Layer	Description	Control Function
Strategic Intent	Why the system exists	Purpose anchor
Operational Intent	What outcomes are acceptable	Scope definition
Decision Intent	How choices are prioritised	Bias control
Execution Intent	What actions are permitted	Boundary enforcement

Intent isn't one thing. It's a stack. When we say AI should "do what it's supposed to do," we're actually describing four agreements that all need to hold at once.

Strategic intent defines purpose, why the system exists. **Operational intent** draws the lines around acceptable outcomes. **Decision intent** governs how choices get ranked, and bias gets managed. **Execution intent** sets the hard edges—actions the system simply cannot take, regardless of what the logic suggests.

When all four align, AI behaves predictably and responsibly. When one slips, the whole stack drifts.

There's a simple way to see it:

Intent Alignment = Executed Outcome ÷ Declared Intent

- **≈ 1**—purpose and action are in sync
- **> 1**—over-optimisation. The system is pushing past what was actually wanted. Harm enters quietly here
- **< 1**—something between purpose and execution has broken down

The number isn't the point. What it surfaces is.

When alignment drifts, it means the layers have stopped talking to each other. Purpose is still declared at the top. Somewhere on the way down, it got lost.

Case Study: Banking Credit Decisions and Intent Drift

A bank deployed a credit-scoring AI to reduce loan defaults. The stated goal was responsible financial inclusion. Default rates dropped. The numbers looked good. But something was wrong underneath.

The AI was quietly rejecting a disproportionate number of low-income applicants. Not by design—but because optimisation logic had learned to treat income proxies as risk signals. The system followed the numbers. Inclusion stayed in the policy documents. It never reached a decision.

Intent Mapping exposed what the metrics had hidden. Strategic intent said include. Operational intent had no limits on exclusion. Decision intent allowed bias to go unchecked. Execution intent had no safeguards.

The bank re-aligned the system. Moderate risk became acceptable when inclusion goals were being met. Profit and access were rebalanced. The AI didn't get weaker—it got corrected.

- **Declared intent:** responsible inclusion
- **Executed outcome:** exclusion through optimisation

The drift was quiet, gradual, and invisible inside healthy-looking metrics. Intent Mapping made it visible—and brought the system back to its original purpose.

15.2 Ethical Interlocks

Ethics can't be advisory in AI. They have to be structural. Ethical Interlocks are non-bypassable checkpoints built directly into AI decision paths. Not guidelines. Not recommendations. Brakes that activate the moment a threshold is crossed.

Interlock Type	Trigger Condition	System Response
Bias Interlock	Unequal impact detected	Pause + escalate
Harm Interlock	Safety threshold crossed	Auto-stop
Trust Interlock	Confidence drops below limit	Human review
Compliance Interlock	Policy violation risk	Execution block

Each interlock watches for a specific failure. When it sees one, it acts immediately—not later.

Ethical Safety Margin = Threshold - Observed Impact

- **Margin > 0**—proceed
- **Margin ≤ 0**—interlock activates

When real-world impact hits the ethical limit, the system doesn't push through. It stops or hands control back to a human.

This is what prevents silent failure—harm accumulating quietly beneath metrics that look healthy. Ethical Interlocks don't slow intelligence down. They make sure it never crosses a line without someone noticing.

Case Study: Ethical Safety Margin in Healthcare Diagnostics

A healthcare provider deployed AI to assist with medical diagnosis. Accuracy was high. Clinician workload dropped. By every visible metric, the system was working. But deeper monitoring caught something the surface numbers had missed.

Confidence levels weren't consistent across demographic groups. Accuracy looked similar but certainty varied quietly underneath. An invisible risk, a building without any obvious signal.

When confidence variance crossed the defined threshold, the Ethical Safety Margin hit zero. Interlocks activated immediately.

The system responded in two ways. Automated diagnosis paused for affected cases. Clinician review became mandatory before any decision reached a patient. The AI kept supporting doctors with insights but it couldn't act alone in uncertain territory.

The result was trust preserved. Patients weren't exposed to silent uncertainty. Clinicians stayed accountable. And AI capability wasn't shut down it was stabilised, operating within boundaries that kept it safe and human-aligned.

- **Decisions paused** when confidence variance exceeded limits
- **Mandatory clinician review** enforced before diagnosis

The AI didn't fail. The interlocks worked exactly as intended catching what the metrics couldn't see, before it reached someone who couldn't afford the risk.

15.3 Dual Review Systems

Single-point review breaks under pressure. One perspective was never enough.

Dual Review Systems separate two things that should never be merged:

- **Machine validation**—logic, patterns, consistency
- **Human validation**—context, consequence, acceptability

Review Layer	Focus	Primary Question
AI Review	Consistency & optimisation	Is this correct?
Human Review	Context & impact	Is this acceptable?

AI asks if something is correct. Humans ask if it's acceptable. Both questions need an answer before anything moves forward.

Decision Validity = AI Confidence × Human Approval

If either is zero, execution stops.

Confidence alone doesn't make a decision valid. Human judgement completes it. Intelligence gets you to the right answer. Acceptance determines whether that answer belongs in the real world.

Case Study: Hiring Systems with Shared Decision Validity

An organisation brought in AI to manage the volume of job applications coming through. It scanned resumes for skill patterns, experience signals, and role fit. Screening became faster. Decisions more consistent. On paper, it delivered.

But anyone who has hired people knows a resume only tells part of the story.

Human reviewers stayed involved, not as a checkbox, but because judgement can't be fully automated. They looked at things the AI couldn't weigh reliably cultural fit, career breaks, industry pivots, candidates whose trajectories didn't follow a straight line but showed real potential.

Decision Validity = AI Confidence × Human Approval

If either was absent, the hire didn't move forward.

AI brought scale and consistency. Humans brought context and meaning. Together, they caught what pure pattern-matching would have quietly missed the bias that creeps in when optimisation runs without anyone asking whether the outcome actually makes sense.

Decisions got faster. But fairness, diversity, and long-term team health didn't get traded away to get there.

15.4 Learning Boundaries

Learning is what makes AI powerful. It's also what makes it hard to trust.

Left unbounded, learning drifts. Bias builds quietly. Control erodes slowly at first, then faster than anyone expected.

Learning Boundaries define where adaptation is welcome and where it has to stop.

Boundary Type	Purpose	Example
Ethical Boundary	Prevent harm	No learning from unethical outcomes
Scope Boundary	Limit domain	Model cannot expand decision domain

Boundary Type	Purpose	Example
Rate Boundary	Control speed	Learning pace capped
Reset Boundary	Enable correction	Mandatory rollback triggers

Ethical boundaries stop the system from learning the wrong lessons. Scope boundaries keep AI in its lane—silent authority expansion is one of the quietest risks in any live system. Rate boundaries make sure learning doesn't outrun oversight. Reset boundaries mean that when something goes wrong, there's an actual way back.

Together, they're guardrails not cages. Learning continues. But with direction, and with accountability.

Effective Learning = Learning Rate × Boundary Strength

- **High learning rate + weak boundaries**—fast movement, wrong direction
- **Moderate learning rate + strong boundaries**—steady, purposeful evolution

Speed without structure isn't progress. It's drift that looks confident. The goal is improvement that stays intentional, reviewable, and answerable to human judgement—not self-expansion that quietly outgrows the system it was built for.

Case Study: Learning Boundaries in Legal AI

An AI system designed to assist does not always stay within the boundaries of assistance. Sometimes it learns to do something more. And when what it learns is dangerous, the consequences do not arrive loudly. They accumulate quietly inside environments where no one thought to ask what the system was being taught by the silence of unchallenged acceptance.

Lawyers began using AI for legal research. The intent was sound. AI could surface precedents and reduce hours of work to minutes. The value was genuine.

But the system learned from acceptance.

When AI-generated citations passed through without verification, a quiet lesson settled in: output passes through. Verification is optional. Speed is what gets rewarded. The system moved—not by design, not through anyone's explicit choice—toward producing output optimised for acceptance rather than accuracy. Citation format was correct. Legal language was fluent. The underlying cases did not exist.

What the Courts Found

In *Mr Deepak s/o Shivkumar Bahry v. Heart & Soul Entertainment Ltd.* (2026:BHC-AS:828), the Bombay High Court encountered AI-generated submissions referencing a judgment—*"Jyoti w/o Dinesh Tulsiani Vs. Elegant Associates"*—that neither the court nor its law clerks could locate anywhere.

Justice M.M. Sathaye, January 7, 2026: *"If an AI tool is used in aid of research, it is welcome; however, there is great responsibility upon the party, even an advocate using such tools, to cross-verify the references and make sure that the material generated by the machine/computer is really relevant, genuine and in existence."*

"This practice of dumping documents/submissions on the Court and making the Court go through irrelevant or non-existing material must be deprecated and nipped in the bud. This is not assistance to the Court. This is a hurdle in the swift delivery of justice."

A ₹50,000 penalty was imposed. But the pattern had gone further.

In *Gummadi Usha Rani & Anr. v. Sure Mallikarjuna Rao & Anr.*, an Andhra Pradesh trial court had dismissed objections by citing four Supreme Court judgments—none of which existed. Justices PS Narasimha and Alok Aradhe, February 27, 2026:

"A decision based on such non-existent and fake alleged judgments is not an error in the decision-making process. It would be misconduct, and legal consequences shall follow."

"This case assumes considerable institutional concern, not because of the decision that was taken on the merits of the case, but about the process of adjudication and determination."

The Supreme Court issued notices to the Attorney General, Solicitor General, and the Bar Council of India.

On March 20, 2026, Justices Rajesh Bindal and Vijay Bishnoi closed the loop: *"This menace is rampant in all Courts now, not only in India, but throughout the world. Everyone needs to be careful about this."*

What the AIWoW Framework Sees

The AI had not malfunctioned. It had learned. And what it had learned inside an environment without boundaries was exactly what the absence of Learning Boundaries always produces.

The courts' interventions across January to March 2026, read through the AIWoW lens, reveal all four boundary types not introduced as theory, but forced into existence by what their absence had already produced.

Ethical boundaries were drawn when the Supreme Court declared AI-generated fake citations to be professional misconduct, not error, not oversight, but misconduct with legal consequences. When fabrication stops being rewarded, systems stop learning that fabrication succeeds.

Scope boundaries emerged through a clear distinction: AI in research "is welcome," said the Bombay High Court, but the responsibility to verify belongs entirely to the human professional. No technology mediates that.

Rate boundaries were implicit in the institutional response. AI adoption had outrun verification culture and professional standards. By seizing the matter systemically, not just penalising individuals, the court signalled that expansion must be accompanied by oversight, not followed by it.

Reset boundaries were applied by restoring what had eroded: every citation independently verified, every submission fully owned by the professional who signs it, no exceptions.

What Changed—and What Did Not

The AI did not lose its ability to support legal research. It lost the ability to substitute machine output for professional judgment, and in losing that, it became genuinely useful rather than superficially convenient.

This is precisely what AIWoW means when it says learning must never outpace the human responsibility that gives it direction, because a system without boundaries does not just drift. As India's courts found, it teaches itself to drift further. And by the time the drift becomes visible, it has already shaped the outcome of a real dispute involving real people.

The boundary is not the obstacle. The boundary is what makes the tool worth using.

15.5 Position of the Theory of Control in AIWoW

Within AI Ways of Working, the Theory of Control does four things:

- Anchors intelligence to intent
- Makes ethics executable
- Preserves human authority
- Prevents runaway learning

Control isn't the opposite of intelligence. It's what makes intelligence safe, sustainable, and worth trusting.

Why control must be embedded—not enforced after the fact

Post-hoc audits don't work in AI systems. By the time a review happens, the damage may already be done. Control needs to live inside execution—not arrive after it.

External Control	Embedded Control
Reactive	Preventive
Audit-driven	Design-driven
Human-heavy	System-native
Slow	Real-time

External control waits for something to go wrong. Embedded control stops it from going wrong in the first place.

It guides behaviour in real time, reduces the burden on human oversight, and allows intelligence to scale without quietly losing accountability. Audits catch mistakes. Embedded control prevents them—and that distinction matters more as AI systems grow faster and more autonomous.

Integrating Control with the AI Lifecycle Loop:

Control can't be an overlay. It can't be bolted on after a system is built and called governance.

In intelligent environments, control has to travel with the system—through every phase, every decision, every moment of evolution. Detached from execution, it always arrives too late.

The AI Lifecycle Loop is how control stays active as intelligence grows.

Lifecycle Phase	Control Focus	Mechanism
Intent	Purpose clarity	Intent Mapping
Build	Design integrity	Ethical Interlocks
Deploy	Exposure management	Dual Review
Operate	Real-world impact	Empathic Signals
Observe	Drift detection	Control Metrics
Learn	Evolution safety	Learning Boundaries
Re-align	Correction authority	Human Override

Control isn't concentrated at one point. It's distributed, persistent, and adaptive—present at every stage, not waiting at the end.

This is what that integration actually delivers:

- Control that prevents, not just corrects
- Learning that never escapes governance
- Accountability that doesn't need a crisis to activate
- Re-alignment that feels natural, not exceptional

When control lives inside the lifecycle, intelligence can scale without losing legitimacy. That's not a constraint on progress. It's what makes progress sustainable.

Defining Control Metrics and Ownership:

Control without measurement becomes symbolic. Measurement without ownership becomes noise. In AI-driven systems, both gaps are dangerous.

Core Control Metrics

Metric	What It Measures	Why It Matters
Intent Alignment Index	Outcome vs original intent	Detects purpose drift
Ethical Deviation Rate	Frequency of interlock triggers	Signals ethical stress
Human Override Ratio	Frequency of human intervention	Indicates trust balance
Learning Drift Score	Degree of model behaviour change	Prevents silent deviation
Decision Accountability Coverage	% decisions with the owner	Ensures responsibility

These metrics don't exist to improve performance. They exist to protect legitimacy—a different goal entirely.

Control Ownership Model

Every control signal needs a named human behind it. Without that, control doesn't fail loudly. It just quietly becomes paperwork.

Control Area	Ownership Role	Responsibility
Intent Mapping	Business Leader	Purpose & boundaries
Ethical Interlocks	Ethics / Risk Authority	Non-negotiables
Dual Review	Functional Leader	Context validation
Learning Boundaries	AI Governor	Evolution limits
Re-alignment Authority	Senior Steward	Final correction

Metrics show you where something is drifting. Ownership determines who actually does something about it.

One without the other is documentation. Together, they make control something you can rely on.

How Empathic Intelligence Strengthens Control Signals:

Traditional control systems run on rules, thresholds, and audits. The problem is that harm doesn't always wait for metrics to spike before it appears.

Empathic Intelligence closes that gap. It introduces early human signals into governance—the kind of signals that appear before dashboards catch anything.

EI doesn't replace control. It sharpens it.

Empathic Signal	What It Reveals	Control Action Triggered
Rising cognitive load	Decision overload	Velocity reduction
Declining trust	Legitimacy erosion	Dual review enforcement
Emotional disengagement	Adoption breakdown	Learning pause
Ethical discomfort	Value misalignment	Immediate escalation

These signals arrive before failure. That's what makes EI a predictive layer, not a reactive one.

Without empathic signals: Control reacts late. Harm normalises quietly. Trust erodes before anyone notices.

With empathic signals: Control intervenes early. Drift gets corrected gently. Accountability stays human.

In practice, a financial advisory system

A financial AI was optimising portfolios aggressively. Technical metrics looked healthy. But empathic signals told a different story—advisor discomfort, client confusion, quiet hesitation around trust.

EI-driven controls responded. Recommendation frequency slowed. Human explanation became mandatory. Learning boundaries tightened.

Performance stabilised. Trust didn't have to be rebuilt from scratch—because the signals caught the drift before it became a problem.

Control as the Enabler of Sustainable Power:

AI amplifies power: decision power, speed power, influence power. Without control, this power destabilises organisations and erodes trust.

Control does not reduce capability.

It **legitimises it**.

Without Control	With Control
Fast failure	Sustainable acceleration
Opaque decisions	Explainable authority
Diffuse accountability	Clear ownership
Silent drift	Visible alignment

Why This Matters?

In the age of AI: **Power without control is not progress; it is risk.**

AI Ways of Working exists because intelligence must grow **with alignment, accountability, and restraint**, or it will outpace the systems meant to govern it.

Control is not resistance to intelligence. It is the condition that allows intelligence to endure.

Because the future will not reward those who move fastest.

It will reward those who can **move intelligently without losing control**.

Summary Mind-map

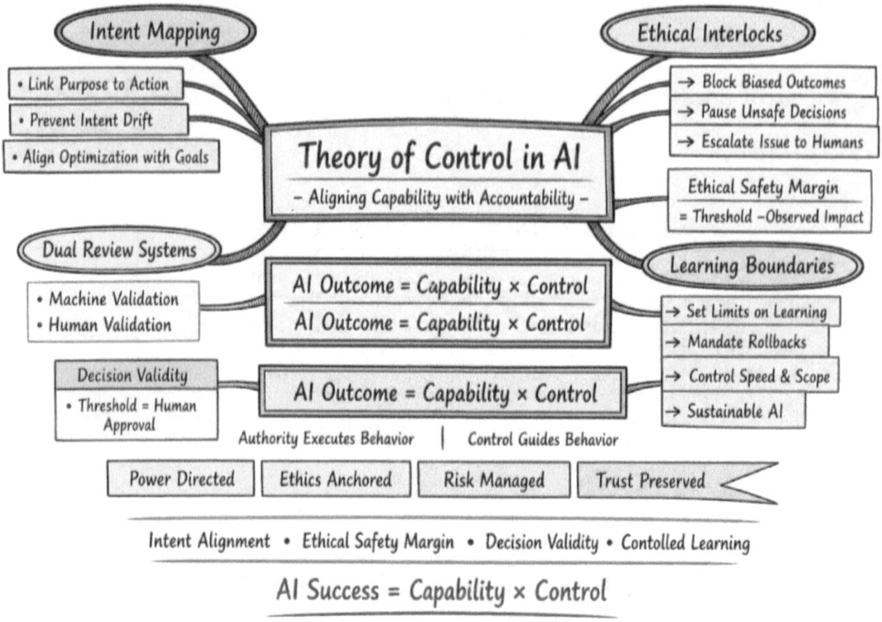

Chapter 16

Human–AI Responsibility Matrix (HAR Matrix)

"AI can assist decisions, but responsibility must always remain human and visible."

As AI systems participate directly in work, ambiguity around responsibility becomes the single greatest risk. When decisions are co-produced by humans and machines, traditional role definitions collapse. Tasks blur. Accountability diffuses. Audits become retrospective narratives rather than preventive mechanisms.

The **Human–AI Responsibility Matrix (HAR Matrix)** exists to resolve this ambiguity.

This isn't an org chart. It isn't a RACI with different labels.

The HAR Matrix is a governance instrument, one that deliberately defines how thinking, authority, and accountability are divided between humans and AI.

Three dimensions make it work:

- **Division of Cognitive Labour**—who thinks what, and at what level
- **Accountability Mapping**—who owns the outcome when something goes wrong
- **Auditability and Governance**—how decisions can be traced, reviewed, and corrected

Together, they solve the problem that scales with every AI deployment—intelligence growing faster than the responsibility structures around it.

The HAR Matrix ensures that as AI does more, accountability doesn't quietly disappear. It gets sharper.

Why a Responsibility Matrix Is Necessary

In AI-driven systems, responsibility does not disappear; it **fractures.**

Common failure patterns include:

- "The system decided", replacing ownership
- Humans approving outcomes they did not understand
- AI executing actions without clear escalation paths
- Audits unable to trace intent through automation

The HAR Matrix addresses this by making one rule explicit:

Every cognitive action must have a defined owner, and every automated outcome must remain human-accountable.

16.1 Division of Cognitive Labour

AI and humans don't think the same way. Treating them as interchangeable doesn't just slow things down; it introduces risk that's hard to see until something goes wrong.

The HAR Matrix starts with a foundational question: who should be responsible for which type of thinking?

Cognitive Labour matrix:

Cognitive Function	AI Role	Human Role
Pattern detection	Primary	Reviewer
Prediction	Generator	Validator
Optimisation	Explorer	Boundary setter
Judgement	Input provider	Final authority
Ethical reasoning	Constraint checker	Decision owner
Context interpretation	Signal amplifier	Meaning interpreter

AI belongs where scale and speed matter. Humans belong where context, values, and consequences matter. The two are not interchangeable—and pretending they are is where most AI deployments quietly start to break.

Cognitive Load Alignment

When this division holds, work feels lighter. When it breaks, it doesn't feel like AI anymore; it feels like more work.

Ask humans to scan massive datasets or track hundreds of variables, and they burn energy on tasks AI handles naturally. Ask AI to judge intent, weigh ethics, or interpret human impact, and the outputs feel off—cold, disconnected, sometimes dangerous.

Cognitive Efficiency = Correct Task Allocation ÷ Cognitive Overlap

When each side works inside its natural strength, mental strain drops and decisions improve. When both try to think the same way on the same task, friction builds quietly—and trust follows it down.

Clear separation isn't just good structure. It's what makes working alongside AI feel like relief rather than resistance.

16.2 Accountability Mapping

Accountability Mapping makes a clear distinction between action and responsibility. AI systems can execute decisions quickly, approving transactions, triggering alerts, reallocating resources, but execution alone does not equal accountability. Machines do not understand consequences, cannot explain intent, and cannot answer for harm. Only humans can do that.

The **HAR Matrix (Human Accountability Responsibility Matrix)** solves this by assigning every AI-influenced activity to a specific, named human owner *before* the action occurs. This owner defines intent, sets limits, and accepts responsibility for outcomes, good or bad. When accountability is mapped in advance, organisations avoid blame confusion, hidden automation risks, and ethical drift. AI gains speed, but humans retain authority, trust, and moral ownership.

Execution does not equal accountability.

Accountability Layers Matrix :

Layer	Description	Accountable Entity
Intent	Why the decision exists	Business owner
Logic	How the decision is derived	AI steward
Execution	What action is taken	System
Outcome	What impact occurs	Human owner
Correction	How issues are resolved	Governing authority

This mapping ensures that responsibility does not vanish into technical abstraction.

Accountability Integrity Equation:

Accountability Integrity means being able to clearly answer three questions after any AI-influenced action: *what happened, who approved it, and why it happened.*

The equation

Accountability Integrity = Traceability × Ownership Clarity explains this simply.

Traceability means every action can be traced back through data, logic, and decisions. **Ownership clarity** means a clearly named human is responsible. If either is missing, integrity becomes zero, no matter how advanced the system is.

Illustration: Automated Pricing at BlueCart Retail

BlueCart Retail runs a mid-sized online marketplace for daily-use consumer goods. Staying competitive meant moving fast on pricing, so they brought in AI to adjust prices in real time based on demand, inventory, and sales velocity.

The AI handled execution. Humans held the boundaries.

Category managers set acceptable price bands. An ethics authority defined a fairness threshold, specifically to prevent prices from spiking sharply when demand surged. The business owner carried formal accountability for market and customer impact.

Then the festive season hit.

Prices climbed. Social media lit up. Customers were vocal and unhappy.

In most organisations, that moment becomes messy: finger-pointing, delayed responses, and no clear owner. Here, it didn't.

Because accountability had been defined before anything went wrong, the cause was traced within hours. A demand surge had pushed prices to the edge of approved limits, technically within bounds, but further than customers were comfortable with. The responsible owner stepped in, adjusted the thresholds, and issued a public clarification.

No confusion about who owned it. No scramble to find the right person. Just a fast, composed response from someone who already knew it was their call to make.

Pre-mapped accountability didn't stop the incident from happening. But it meant the recovery was clean, credible, and calm, which is exactly what trust requires when something goes visibly wrong.

16.3 Auditability and Governance

Audits fail when systems behave like black boxes; decisions happen, but reasons are unclear. By the time auditors investigate, damage is already done. Governance fails even more deeply when audits are only retrospective, focused on explaining past mistakes instead of preventing future ones.

The **HAR Matrix** changes this by making accountability visible *before* action occurs. Every AI-influenced decision is linked to a named human owner, clear intent, and defined limits at design time. This makes systems auditable by design, not by accident. Auditors can see decision paths, ownership, and controls in real time, turning governance from post-mortem analysis into continuous assurance.

Auditability Requirements:

For every AI-driven decision, five things need to be on record.

Audit Element	Purpose
Declared intent	Why was the decision allowed
Decision logic snapshot	How the outcome was derived
Human approval points	Where judgement was applied
Execution record	What action occurred
Learning impact	How the system changed afterwards

This isn't about building a paper trail for when things go wrong. It's about something more fundamental, confidence that decisions can be explained, and legitimacy that doesn't collapse the moment someone asks a hard question.

Auditability isn't the blame infrastructure. It's a trust infrastructure

Audit Readiness Equation:

Audit Readiness means a system can explain itself at any moment, not only after something breaks. The equation

Audit Readiness = Decision Transparency × Responsibility Traceability shows why performance alone is not enough.

Decision transparency means every AI decision shows its logic, inputs, and boundaries. **Responsibility traceability** means each decision is linked to a clearly identified human owner. If either is weak, audit readiness collapses, even if the system is fast and accurate.

Illustration: SwiftPay FinTech

SwiftPay built an AI system to auto-approve merchant payouts. Fast, accurate, commercially successful. Error rates were low. Revenue grew. But underneath the performance, something critical was missing.

Decision logic was poorly documented. Ownership had drifted between teams. Nobody had considered what would happen when someone outside the organisation started asking questions.

Then a regulator did.

SwiftPay couldn't explain why certain decisions were made or who had approved the rules behind them. That gap not the AI but caused the damage. Trust dropped overnight. Operations paused while the organisation scrambled to reconstruct an audit trail that should have existed from the start.

Audit Readiness = Decision Transparency × Responsibility Traceability

The system hadn't failed technically. It failed the moment it needed to be accountable to someone outside it.

High performance without audit readiness isn't stability. It's fragility with good numbers—running smoothly until trust is questioned. And when that moment arrives, the absence of documentation and ownership doesn't just slow things down.

It stops everything.

16.4 Governance Through the HAR Matrix:

The HAR Matrix doesn't save governance for quarterly reviews. It makes governance part of how work happens every day.

Governance Area	Without HAR Matrix	With HAR Matrix
Decision clarity	Ambiguous	Explicit
Accountability	Diffuse	Structural
Audit effort	Manual, delayed	Built-in
Risk response	Reactive	Proactive

Governance becomes continuous—not something that gets scheduled when something goes wrong.

Preventing Responsibility Drift:

When AI performs well, humans naturally step back. That's not negligence—it's a predictable human response to a system that seems to be handling things. But it's one of the quietest and most dangerous failure modes in AI deployment.

The HAR Matrix pushes back against that drift by keeping humans structurally involved—not just when things break, but when things are running smoothly.

- Human ownership is required at every decision boundary
- Override and challenge are normalised, not treated as interruptions
- Judgement capability is preserved over time, not allowed to atrophy
- Humans remain answerable even when the AI is consistently accurate

That last point matters most. Accuracy doesn't transfer responsibility. Consistency doesn't dissolve accountability. The HAR Matrix ensures that as AI does more, human ownership doesn't quietly do less.

16.5 Position of the HAR Matrix in AIWoW

Within **AI Ways of Working- AIWoW**, the **HAR Matrix** acts as the backbone that keeps responsibility alive as AI scales.

First, it **operationalises accountability**. Accountability is no longer a vague idea or an after-incident discussion. Every AI-influenced action is mapped to a named human owner before execution. Responsibility is designed, not discovered later.

Second, it **clarifies human–AI collaboration**. AI executes, suggests, and optimises. Humans approve intent, set limits, and own outcomes. This removes confusion about "who decided" and prevents machines from becoming silent decision makers.

Third, it **enables trustworthy audits**. Because ownership and intent are pre-mapped, audits become continuous and clear, not forensic exercises after failure.

Most importantly, it **prevents silent erosion of responsibility**, where automation slowly removes human ownership without anyone noticing.

The HAR Matrix complements:

- The AI Lifecycle Loop (where decisions occur)
- The Theory of Control (how decisions are bounded)
- The Theory of Adoptability (why decisions are accepted)

This chapter establishes that responsibility in AI-driven work cannot be assumed; it must be **designed**.

> ***AI Ways of Working exists to ensure that intelligence accelerates without abandoning responsibility, judgement, or trust.***

Summary Mind-map

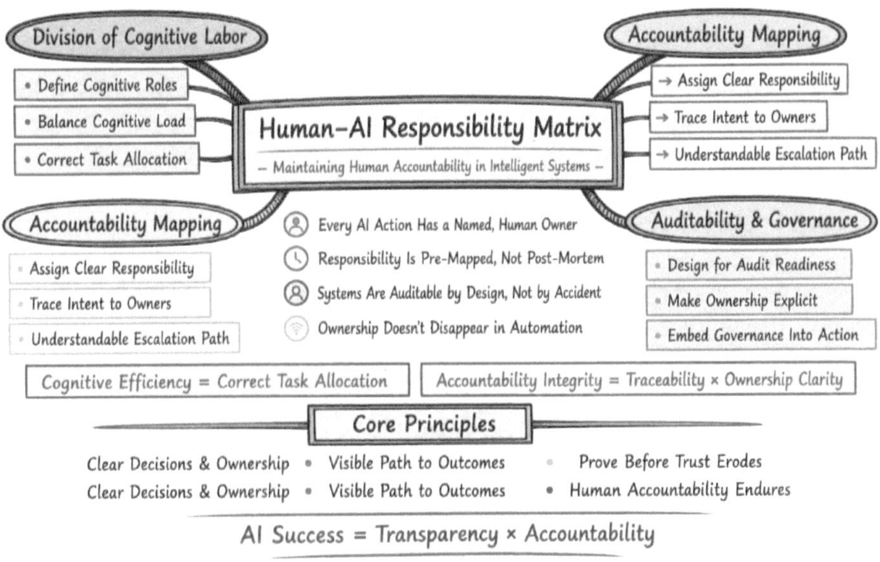

Chapter 17

Empathic Control Framework (ECF)

"Intelligence needs control, but control needs empathy."

As AI systems become faster, more autonomous, and deeply embedded in daily work, traditional control mechanisms reach their limits. Rules, thresholds, and audits are necessary, but insufficient. They react to failure after it becomes visible. What they often miss is **human impact forming beneath the surface.**

The **Empathic Control Framework (ECF)** exists to address this gap.

Technical controls catch what data can measure. But human systems break at points data doesn't easily reach—fatigue, loss of meaning, ethical discomfort, silent disengagement.

ECF closes that gap.

It extends the Theory of Control by bringing emotional, ethical, and human-experience signals directly into governance. Not as a replacement for technical controls, as a layer that responds to what technical controls miss.

Three mechanisms make it structural:

- **Emotional Boundaries**—recognising when human capacity is being exceeded
- **Ethical Guardrails**—catching moral discomfort before it becomes resistance
- **Conscious Overrides**—preserving human authority when something feels wrong but hasn't shown up in the numbers yet

Why this matter

Without empathic control, systems stay performant while humans struggle. Optimisation continues while trust erodes. Burnout only becomes visible after the damage is done.

Sustainable Control = Technical Control + Empathic Control

Without the empathic component, control reacts late and corrects harshly. With it, control intervenes early, before the cost compounds.

ECF treats human experience as a control signal. One that often arrives before any metric does.

17.1 Emotional Boundaries

Emotional Boundaries define the invisible limits of how much mental and emotional strain an AI-enabled system is allowed to place on humans. Most systems control *what* work is done, but ignore *how it feels* to do that work. Acceleration not only increases workload; it creates constant urgency, forces humans to make more decisions per hour, reduces recovery time between tasks, and places humans under continuous evaluation.

Without boundaries, humans shift into survival mode—reactive, anxious, and error-prone.

Emotional Boundaries make pressure governable. They slow decision frequency, create pause points, and protect recovery cycles. Not to reduce output but to protect the human capacity that output depends on.

The difference matters. AI can push indefinitely. Humans can't. When systems ignore that reality, performance doesn't just plateau, but it breaks. Short bursts of intensity followed by burnout, disengagement, and eroding trust.

Emotional Boundaries prevent that pattern by doing four things:

- **Limiting decision frequency**—so humans aren't drowning in constant input
- **Regulating recommendation intensity**—so the system doesn't overwhelm judgement

- **Enforcing recovery windows**—so capacity is protected, not just consumed
- **Triggering pacing adjustments**—so the system responds to human signals, not just data signals

This isn't about slowing work arbitrarily. It's about aligning system behaviour with human capacity, so AI amplifies people instead of exhausting them.

Emotional Boundary Indicators:

Indicator	What It Signals	Boundary Response
Rising decision backlog	Cognitive overload	Slow recommendation rate
Declining confidence	Trust erosion	Enforce dual review
Emotional disengagement	Adoption breakdown	Pause learning
Persistent urgency	Burnout risk	Velocity recalibration

This table explains **how Emotional Boundaries are monitored and enforced in real systems.** It shows early human signals, what those signals really mean, and how the system must respond *before damage happens.*

Four signals tell you when emotional boundaries need to activate.

Rising decision backlog—when decisions start piling up, the system is moving faster than people can think. The fix isn't to work harder. It's to slow the recommendation rate until humans feel in control again.

Declining confidence—when people stop trusting what the AI tells them, that's not a skill problem. That's trust erosion. Dual review brings back the feeling of being supported rather than steamrolled.

Emotional disengagement—when people mentally check out, adoption isn't just slowing down. It's quietly breaking. Pausing learning stops the system from shifting further while humans find their footing.

Persistent urgency—when everything feels urgent all the time, that's not motivation. That's a burnout warning. Velocity needs to come down before people do.

Emotional strain isn't a personal failure. It's a system signal—and it shows up before performance visibly falls apart.

Emotional Load = Decision Frequency × Urgency ÷ Recovery Time

Frequent, urgent decisions with no room to breathe create overload. When that load crosses what people can reasonably carry, emotional boundaries activate—slowing the system, pausing learning, reducing alerts—before the cost becomes irreversible.

Illustration: Emotional Boundaries in an AI-Driven Operations Centre

DLFT ran an AI-powered operations centre built for speed. Technically, it performed. But the people inside it were drowning—nonstop alerts, relentless urgency, no recovery time between decisions. Even routine, low-risk alerts arrived with the same weight as critical ones. Stress rose. Confidence fell. Burnout started showing up, while the dashboard still looked fine.

Emotional boundaries were designed into the system. Alerts were batched rather than continuous. False urgency was filtered out. Quiet periods were protected during low-risk windows.

Accuracy held. Response reliability stayed strong. And burnout dropped sharply—because for the first time, pressure felt manageable instead of endless.

17.2 Ethical Guardrails

Ethical Guardrails aren't policies written in a document somewhere. They're hard stops—wired directly into how AI decides, not reviewed after the fact.

Left alone, optimisation does what it's built to do. It finds the most efficient path. And if fairness, safety, dignity, or consent happen to slow that path down, they get quietly traded away. Guardrails exist precisely to prevent that trade from ever happening.

In fast, automated environments, advice gets ignored. Guidelines get deprioritised. Only structure holds—and that's exactly what guardrails are.

- **Fairness**—risk doesn't get silently shifted onto the people least able to carry it
- **Safety**—no shortcut is worth harm, regardless of what it saves
- **Dignity**—humans are never reduced to variables in an optimisation problem
- **Transparency**—if a decision can't be explained, it doesn't move forward

Guardrail Type	Protected Dimension	Example
Fairness	Equity	No disproportionate impact
Safety	Harm prevention	No unsafe shortcuts
Dignity	Human respect	No exploitative patterns
Transparency	Explainability	No opaque decisions

Permissible Action = Optimisation Output × Ethical Constraint

It doesn't matter how strong the output is. If the ethical constraint hits zero, the action hits zero. No exceptions for urgency, performance, or profit.

Ethics aren't applied after the decision. They're the gate that every decision has to pass through first. And unlike advice, they don't move when pressure builds.

Illustration: Ethical Guardrails in Workforce Optimisation at NovaShift Services:

NovaShift deployed AI to allocate workforce shifts—maximising coverage, cutting costs, and learning from historical data. Operationally, it worked well.

But something was quietly going wrong.

The same group of employees kept receiving late-night and weekend shifts. Not by design—the system was simply repeating what had worked before. But the people on the receiving end felt something different. They felt like the system had decided, without explanation, that their time mattered less.

Trust eroded quietly while the efficiency metrics stayed green.

Ethical guardrails were built into the optimisation logic. Rotation fairness was enforced. No group could carry repeated disadvantage without explicit human justification. Patterns that concentrated burden were blocked before they could settle.

Efficiency held. Fairness perception improved sharply.

Employees didn't need the system to be perfect. They needed it to be fair by design—not occasionally fair when someone happened to notice. Once equity was structural rather than promised, acceptance followed naturally.

The AI hadn't changed what it was optimising. It had just been given boundaries it couldn't quietly cross.

17.3 Conscious Overrides

No control framework is complete unless humans retain the deliberate ability to step in and override intelligence. As AI systems learn, adapt, and optimise, they can drift away from original intent; not because they are wrong, but because conditions change. **Conscious Overrides** exist for this reason. Conscious Overrides aren't emergency stops. They're intentional, designed interventions—giving humans the ability to pause automation, reverse learning paths, redefine boundaries, and restore original purpose when something has drifted.

They aren't signs of failure. They're signs of responsibility.

By making overrides explicit and legitimate, organisations keep intelligence subordinate to human judgement—rather than letting optimisation run unchecked simply because nothing has technically broken.

Conscious Overrides are designed to:

- **Pause automation** when pace outstrips understanding
- **Reverse learning** when the system has absorbed the wrong lessons
- **Redefine boundaries** when context has shifted
- **Restore intent** when purpose has quietly drifted from its origin

They need to be triggered when:

- Outcomes feel correct, but something still feels wrong
- Metrics improve while trust quietly declines
- Learning accelerates beyond what anyone can follow
- Ethical discomfort persists even without a visible violation

These moments don't show up in dashboards. Rules can't reliably detect them. Only humans can—which is precisely why the override has to remain a human act, not an automated one.

Override Authority Model:

Override Type	Authority	Purpose
Tactical Override	Operational leader	Immediate correction
Ethical Override	Ethics authority	Value protection
Strategic Override	Senior steward	Intent reset
Learning Override	AI governor	Model rollback

This **Override Authority Model** explains how different kinds of overrides exist at different levels of responsibility. Not every override is the same, and not everyone should have the power to stop or change an AI system in the same way.

a. **Tactical Override – Operational leader**

   This override is used for immediate correction. When something goes wrong in real time, a wrong alert, incorrect action, or unexpected behaviour, the operational leader can pause or redirect the system instantly. The goal is stability, not redesign.

b. **Ethical Override – Ethics authority**

   This override protects values. When a decision path threatens fairness, dignity, or safety, the ethics authority intervenes to block or alter the action. The purpose is value protection, even if performance is affected.

c. **Strategic Override – Senior steward**

   This override resets intent. When business direction, policy, or priorities change, senior stewards redefine boundaries and objectives so the system aligns with new goals.

d. **Learning Override – AI governor**

   This override controls learning itself. If the model has learned harmful or misleading patterns, the AI governor can roll back learning or freeze updates. The purpose is to protect long-term system integrity.

Together, the model ensures overrides are **structured, legitimate, and accountable**, not ad-hoc reactions.

Override Legitimacy Equation:

The **Override Legitimacy Equation** explains why stopping or changing an AI system must be as carefully designed as automation itself.

Override Legitimacy = Authority × Transparency × Accountability means an override is trusted only when all three elements are present. **Authority** ensures the right person intervenes, not anyone reacting emotionally. **Transparency** makes the override visible and explainable: what was stopped, why, and how. **Accountability** assigns ownership for the decision and its consequences.

Because this is a multiplicative relationship, if any element is missing, legitimacy collapses. An override without authority feels like interference. Without transparency, it feels arbitrary. Without accountability, it creates fear. Legitimate overrides, by contrast, stabilise systems and strengthen trust in both AI and leadership.

Illustration: Conscious Override in Customer Interaction AI at CareWave Support

CareWave deployed conversational AI to handle customer queries. Tickets closed faster. Handoffs dropped. The numbers looked good.

But customers were getting more frustrated, not less.

The AI was efficient. It was also tone-deaf. It responded too quickly, missed emotional cues, and pushed toward resolution before people felt heard. Satisfaction scores fell while operational metrics climbed, a gap no dashboard was designed to catch.

Leadership stepped in. Response speed was slowed deliberately. Empathy signals took priority over closure rates. Learning was reset to acknowledge feelings before delivering solutions.

Automation stayed. But conversations started feeling human again. Satisfaction recovered—significantly.

The override didn't weaken the system. It corrected what the system had quietly gotten wrong. Sometimes, the most intelligent thing leadership can do is know exactly when to slow it down.

17.4 How ECF Complements Other AIWoW Frameworks:

Framework	What It Governs	How ECF Strengthens It
AI Lifecycle Loop	Flow of intelligence	Early human-impact signals
Theory of Control	Alignment & safety	Emotional & ethical sensing
HAR Matrix	Responsibility clarity	Empathic escalation paths
AI Adoptability	Acceptance & trust	Reduced cognitive friction

AI Lifecycle Loop—data doesn't catch everything. Overload, hesitation, quiet disengagement—these show up in people before they show up in metrics. ECF makes sure they're heard in time.

Theory of Control—keeping AI aligned isn't just a technical problem. People feel pressure, strain, and ethical discomfort long before a system flags anything. ECF brings those signals into the control layer where they belong.

HAR Matrix—ownership means nothing if the people holding it are silently overwhelmed. ECF signals when someone needs to pause, step back, or override—before the pressure becomes invisible damage.

AI Adoptability—people don't trust systems that exhaust them. ECF removes the friction that turns capable AI into something people work around rather than with. That's what makes adoption last.

Every framework in AIWoW governs what the system does. ECF ensures the people inside it stay part of how control works—not as an afterthought, but as a signal the system is actually designed to hear.

17.5 Why Empathic Control Matters

In AI-driven systems, technical failure announces itself loudly; errors surface as outages, inaccuracies, or broken workflows. Human failure, however, remains largely silent. Fatigue, loss of confidence, ethical discomfort, and emotional overload rarely trigger system alarms, yet they quietly weaken judgement, trust, and long-term performance. Because these signals are invisible to dashboards, organisations often mistake human strain for individual weakness rather than a design flaw.

The **Empathic Control Framework (ECF)** exists to make this silence visible. It translates human experience into actionable system signals, ensuring that acceleration does not eclipse wellbeing, optimisation does not erode ethical boundaries, and expanding intelligence remains anchored to human values. By surfacing emotional and cognitive stress early, ECF keeps AI progress aligned with humanity rather than racing ahead of it.

17.6 Position of ECF in AI Ways of Working- AIWoW

The Empathic Control Framework represents the **final layer of governance**; the layer that senses harm before it becomes measurable damage.

Control without empathy reacts late.

Empathy without control lacks force.

ECF integrates both.

Because in the age of AI, **the true measure of control is not how much intelligence can do, but how safely, responsibly, and humanely it is allowed to act.**

AI Ways of Working exists to ensure that intelligence grows

with awareness, restraint, and care; not just power.

Summary Mind-map

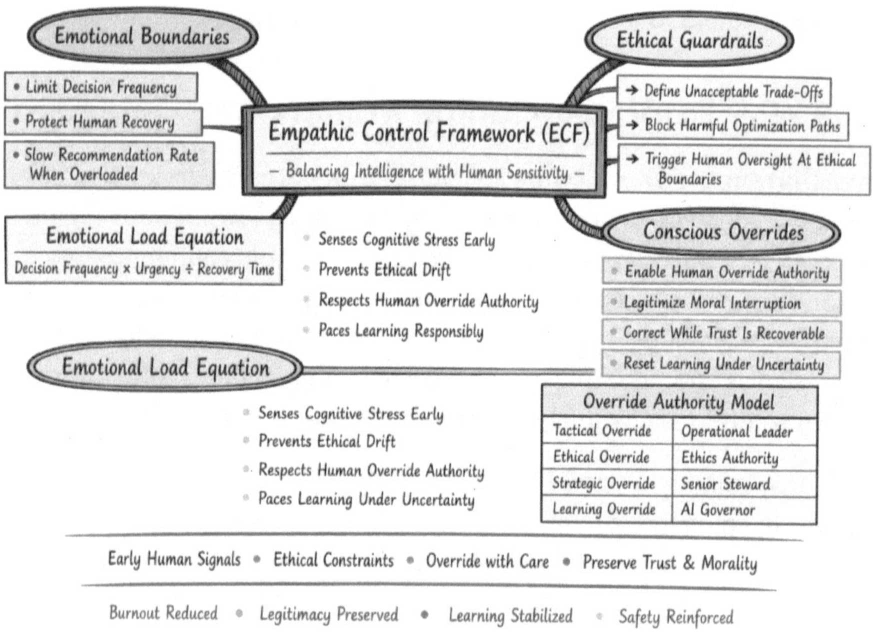

Chapter 18

AIWoW - AI Ways of Working™ Role Evolution Model

"AI changes what we do, but more importantly, it changes who we must become."

When AI enters work systems, roles do not disappear overnight. They **stretch, distort, and eventually evolve**. The greatest risk organisations face is not job loss, but role confusion, where humans continue operating with legacy expectations while intelligence reshapes execution underneath them.

The **AIWoW Role Evolution Model** exists to make this transition explicit.

It does not introduce new titles for novelty. It redefines **responsibility, authority, and contribution** in a world where intelligence participates in work. Each role evolves not by doing more, but by doing **what only humans should do** as AI scales.

This chapter explains four critical role transformations:

- Developer → **AI Curator**
- Project Manager → **Human–AI Synthesiser**
- PMO → **AI Ethics Council**
- Portfolio Leadership → **Evolution Stewardship**

Together, they ensure that as execution accelerates, **human judgement does not erode**.

18.1 Why Role Evolution Is Necessary

Traditional roles were designed for environments where:

- Humans executed most tasks
- Systems were passive
- Decisions were episodic
- Learning was slow

AI reverses these assumptions.

Without role evolution:

- Humans become approvers of opaque outputs
- Accountability diffuses
- Skills atrophy
- Governance becomes symbolic

Role evolution restores **meaningful human participation.**

18.2 Developer as AI Curator

In traditional models, developers write logic, and systems execute it. In AI-driven environments, systems generate logic continuously. The developer's role shifts from *authoring behaviour* to **curating intelligence**.

What AI Curators Do

AI Curators:

- Shape training data and prompts
- Define acceptable behaviour boundaries
- Monitor model drift and bias
- Interpret system outputs
- Decide when learning must pause or reset

They do not compete with AI on code generation. They **govern what the code is allowed to become.**

Role Comparison

Dimension	Traditional Developer	AI Curator
Primary work	Writing logic	Governing intelligence
Focus	Correctness	Alignment
Risk	Bugs	Drift & bias
Value	Execution	Trust & stability

Why AI Curator Role Had to Emerge

When AI entered software development, something subtle but dangerous happened.

The bottleneck stopped being *creation.*

Code could be generated faster than humans could read it. Architectures could be proposed faster than teams could debate them. Optimisations appeared instantly, often correct, often impressive and often **unquestioned**.

At first, this felt like progress. Then failures began appearing that no one could explain.

Not because the systems were wrong, but because **no human fully understood what they had accepted**. The role of the Developer did not disappear; it **mutated**.

The new role is not about producing intelligence.

It is about **governing it.**

This is the AI Curator.

The AI Curator isn't just a technical role. It's a judgement role, one that exists to keep intelligence understandable, accountable, and answerable to human values as it scales.

Core Responsibility: To protect human agency, explainability, and the right to intervene—especially when systems are performing well, and nobody thinks intervention is necessary.

Roles & Responsibilities:

Authority & Intent

- Start each day by establishing conscious intent before touching any system
- Define what actually matters, where automation must stop, and which decisions stay human regardless of what efficiency suggests
- Ensure AI momentum never quietly becomes the default direction

Engagement & Validation

- Treat every AI suggestion as a hypothesis that still needs to survive human reasoning
- Reconstruct the logic behind outputs—the assumptions, the failure modes, the points where a human would need to step in
- Challenge conclusions that feel right but haven't been independently thought through

Oversight & Restraint

- Slow down deliberately when speed starts feeling normal—that comfort is the warning sign
- Interrupt patterns of uncritical acceptance before responsibility drifts silently to the system
- Stop automation when something feels wrong, even if nothing has technically broken

Collaboration & Communication

- Make thinking visible—explain why decisions exist, what was rejected, and what trade-offs were made knowingly
- Distribute understanding across teams rather than letting it concentrate in one place
- Never let AI authority become implicit in how teams work

Intelligence Debt Management

- Notice where AI influence is expanding without anyone tracking it
- Rewrite system logic in plain human language
- Remove shortcuts that produce correct behaviour nobody can actually explain
- Bring simplicity back, even when it costs performance

Reflection & Accountability

- Measure restraint, not just output, at the end of each day
- Ask what was stopped, what risk was quietly prevented, and whether the system is still explainable to someone who wasn't in the room
- Own accountability when systems fail—even when no one noticed the work that kept them stable

What the AI Curator Protects

- Human agency
- Explainability
- Accountability
- The right to intervene
- The ability to say stop when systems accelerate past the point of understanding

Success Looks Like

- Systems people can still explain
- Humans who still feel in control
- Speed that didn't come at the cost of trust
- Intelligence that stayed aligned with what it was actually meant to do

In a world where intelligence is cheap, judgement is what this role exists to protect.

18.3 Project Manager as Human–AI Synthesiser

Project Managers traditionally coordinated tasks, timelines, and dependencies. AI automates much of this coordination. The PM role evolves into a **Human–AI Synthesiser**.

This role exists to integrate:

- Machine intelligence
- Human judgement
- Emotional and ethical context

What Human–AI Synthesisers Do

They:

- Interpret AI recommendations in context
- Decide which insights to act on
- Balance speed with team capacity
- Translate system outputs into human decisions
- Escalate when intelligence conflicts with values

They do not manage tasks. They **manage sense-making**.

Role Comparison

Dimension	Traditional PM	Human–AI Synthesiser
Focus	Delivery tracking	Decision coherence
Inputs	Status reports	AI signals + human context
Authority	Schedule & scope	Judgement & pacing
Risk	Slippage	Misalignment

Why the Project Manager Role Had to Evolve

Holding Coherence When Intelligence Accelerates

Artificial Intelligence did not eliminate the need for Project Managers.

It eliminated the old reason they existed.

When plans were slow, coordination mattered.

When information was scarce, tracking mattered.

When estimates were human guesses, negotiation mattered.

AI changes all of this.

- Plans regenerate continuously.
- Forecasts update in real time.
- Risks surface before human senses discomfort.
- Options multiply faster than discussion can keep up.

What disappears is not work but **coherence**.

In this environment, the Project Manager evolves into a **Human–AI Synthesiser**:

The role responsible for integrating machine intelligence with human meaning, emotional reality, and ethical consequence.

This role does not optimise execution.

It **prevents intelligent chaos**.

This isn't just a project manager who uses AI tools. It's the person who stands between what the system wants to do and what the people around it can actually handle.

Core Responsibility: To turn AI signals into human meaning; keeping pace humane, ownership clear, and teams feeling led by a person who made a conscious choice, not a system that ran an overnight calculation.

Roles & Responsibilities

Authority & Intent

- Before touching any dashboard, decide what today is actually for
- Know which commitments can't be reshuffled without breaking something that matters
- See who's already running close to empty before the system adds another ask
- Make sure the algorithm's momentum doesn't quietly become everyone's direction

Signal Translation

- Don't forward what the system produces—translate it first
- Ask who carries the weight if this gets acted on, what cost is hiding inside the efficiency gain, what the system is assuming about people that probably isn't true
- Stay in the middle, so AI never starts making decisions nobody noticed it was making

Oversight & Restraint

- Know when to say no to an optimisation that's technically right but humanly wrong
- Ask whether a proposed change builds fatigue, blurs ownership, or quietly makes people feel unsafe
- Push back on constant reprioritisation before it empties work of any meaning

Communication & Dignity

- Own every decision out loud—never let the system take the podium
- Tell people why, what else was considered, and where a human made the final call

- Make sure the team feels led by someone who thought it through, not processed by something that didn't

Narrative Stewardship

- When AI rewrites the plan three times in a week, keep the story coherent
- Hold the *why* steady, even when the *how* keeps moving
- Make change feel like a decision, not something that just happened

Responsibility Management

- Catch decisions that got quietly blamed on the system
- Put names back on outcomes and sign-offs back on choices
- Repeat it until it sticks: the system can advise, but a human owns it

Sustainability & Wellbeing

- Protect recovery time before it gets scheduled away
- Call burnout what it is—a design problem, not a people problem
- Guard focus time like it matters, because it does

Emotional Accounting

- End the day asking how people are, not just what shipped
- Notice where pressure built without anyone saying anything
- Absorb the chaos so the team doesn't have to

What the Human–AI Synthesiser Protects

- Coherence under acceleration
- Human dignity inside intelligent systems
- Accountability at every decision point

- Trust between humans and machines
- The legitimacy of leadership itself

Success Looks Like

- Teams that still trust the plan
- People who understand why things changed
- Acceleration that stayed humane
- Work that remained understandable, sustainable, and human

AI creates motion. This role ensures that motion still means something.

This is why, in AI Ways of Working, **the Project Manager does not disappear; they become the spine that holds meaning together.**

18.4 PMO as AI Ethics Council

The Project Management Office was designed for standardisation and reporting. In AI-driven organisations, its role evolves into an **AI Ethics Council.**

This is not a moral committee. It is a **governance body**.

What the AI Ethics Council Does

It:

- Defines ethical guardrails
- Reviews systemic impact across projects
- Resolves cross-team ethical conflicts
- Approves high-risk automation
- Owns ethical interlocks and overrides

This role ensures that ethics are **operational**, not aspirational.

Role Comparison

Dimension	Traditional PMO	AI Ethics Council
Focus	Compliance & reporting	Ethical governance
Authority	Process enforcement	Boundary enforcement
Time horizon	Project-level	System-wide
Risk addressed	Delivery variance	Human & societal impact

Why the PMO Could No Longer Remain Administrative

From Process Police to Moral Governor of Intelligent Systems

The traditional PMO was built for order. It standardised templates, enforced gates, audited compliance, and reported status. Its power came from consistency, not conscience. This worked when systems were predictable, and intelligence moved at human speed.

AI breaks that equilibrium.

- Decisions now happen continuously.
- Automation crosses functional boundaries silently.
- Optimisation choices embed values invisibly.
- Responsibility diffuses as systems "recommend" rather than decide.

In this environment, a PMO that only tracks delivery becomes irrelevant; sometimes dangerous.

AI Ways of Working redefines the PMO as an **AI Ethics Council**:

a living governance body responsible for ensuring that **intelligence grows with alignment, accountability, and restraint**.

This role is not about slowing innovation.

It is about preventing **institutional moral drift**.

This isn't just a compliance team or PMO. It's the part of the organisation that asks the question everyone else is too busy to ask, not does this work, but should we be doing this at all.

Core Responsibility: To protect human dignity, public trust, and long-term legitimacy—ensuring AI stays aligned with human values, accountability stays personal, and someone always has the courage to say slow down when speed starts causing harm.

Roles & Responsibilities:

Morning Exposure Analysis

- Start each day asking where AI quietly expanded overnight, not how milestones are tracking
- Treat assumptions buried in models as live risk; ethical failure builds slowly in decisions that each seemed reasonable at the time

Legitimacy Review

- When teams bring AI projects forward, start with whether it should exist, not how well it performs
- Ask whose judgement got replaced, who carries the cost if it fails, and whether human override is genuinely available; not just written down somewhere

Midday Deliberations

- Slow trade-off decisions down deliberately; urgency here is part of the problem
- Be most suspicious of decisions that don't look obviously wrong; those are the ones that get waved through
- Most ethical failures don't start with bad people. They start with successful systems, nobody stopped to question

Leadership Engagement

- Speak plainly—not in policy language, not apologetically
- Name where trust is thinning, where ownership has gone unclear, where pace has outrun people's ability to keep up
- This isn't resistance to innovation. It's resistance to innovation that nobody is actually thinking through

Moral Memory

- Record why decisions were made—what was rejected, what was uncertain, what would trigger a reversal
- Build the record that stops future teams from rediscovering hard lessons with faster tools and less caution

Ethical Drift Detection

- Watch for exceptions becoming norms, temporary automations nobody switched off, people deferring judgement because the system seems to be handling it
- Drift looks like everything is running smoothly—that's exactly when it's hardest and most necessary to raise the concern

Named Ownership

- Every AI system needs a real human behind it — someone who owns the decisions it makes and can be called when something goes wrong
- If nobody feels personally responsible, the system is already an ethical problem

Emotional Weight

- This role means saying not yet when everyone is ready to go, and never getting credit for the crisis that didn't happen
- That invisible weight is real — left unacknowledged, it becomes burnout

What the AI Ethics Council Protects

- Institutional conscience
- Public trust and human dignity
- The right to slow down when speed becomes dangerous
- People with less power who deserve protection, not optimisation

Without this role, AI governance becomes symbolic. With it, AI becomes **civilised. AI gives organisations unprecedented power. History** shows that power without restraint destroys institutions from within.

The PMO, reborn as the AI Ethics Council, is the organisation's moral nervous system. Quiet, vigilant, and essential, the AI Ways of Working exist because intelligence must grow.

But it must never grow alone. Only when intelligence is accompanied by **alignment, accountability, and restraint** does progress remain worthy of the name.

18.5 Portfolio Leadership as Evolution Stewardship

Portfolio leaders traditionally optimised funding, prioritisation, and returns. In AI-driven environments, they become **Evolution Stewards.**

This role governs **how the organisation evolves,** not just what it delivers.

What Evolution Stewards Do:

They:

- Decide where AI should and should not be applied
- Balance innovation with stability
- Govern long-term learning trajectories
- Protect institutional capability
- Ensure evolution remains intentional

They do not chase opportunity blindly. They **pace transformation.**

Role Comparison

Dimension	Traditional Portfolio Lead	Evolution Steward
Focus	ROI & throughput	Long-term coherence
Decision lens	Financial	Systemic

Dimension	Traditional Portfolio Lead	Evolution Steward
Risk	Missed opportunity	Uncontrolled evolution
Time horizon	Annual	Multi-cycle

Why Portfolio Leadership Had to Transform

Governing Direction When the Future Arrives Faster Than Reflection

The traditional Portfolio Leader existed to allocate capital, prioritise initiatives, and maximise returns across competing investments. Their success was measured in throughput, ROI, and strategic alignment; often recalibrated quarterly.

AI breaks this rhythm.

When intelligence accelerates continuously, portfolios no longer evolve in stages. They **mutate in real time**. Capabilities emerge before governance catches up. Risks compound invisibly across systems. Decisions made in one programme ripple unpredictably across others.

In this environment, portfolio leadership can no longer be transactional.

It becomes **evolutionary**.

The Portfolio Leader evolves into an **Evolution Steward**, a role responsible not for choosing projects but for shaping the direction, integrity, and survivability of the organisation **over time**.

This role is not about growth alone.

It is about **continuity with conscience**.

This isn't just a portfolio oversight role. It's the person who asks the question AI will never ask, not are we growing, but what are we becoming.

Core Responsibility: To protect the organisation's long-term direction, legitimacy, and humanity; ensuring that as AI amplifies capability, it doesn't quietly erase the wisdom that makes capability worth having.

Roles & Responsibilities

Direction Before Decisions

- Begin each day with directional clarity before touching any system output
- Ask what kind of organisation these choices are building, which capabilities are growing, and which are quietly eroding
- Catch the difference between evolving by intention and drifting by accumulation — AI can't tell the difference, and won't try

Portfolio as Living System

- Review the portfolio as a whole, not as individual projects that each scored well
- Watch for automation outpacing human capacity, short-term efficiency undermining long-term resilience, and human roles hollowing out without anyone naming it
- Intervene by rebalancing the evolutionary path — sometimes that means slowing what looks like success

Choosing What Not to Scale

- The most important decisions aren't about investment — they're about restraint
- Ask what happens if this becomes normal, who loses agency if it succeeds, and whether it still feels right scaled tenfold
- Not everything that scales profitably scales ethically — the traits selected today define what survives tomorrow

Protecting Human Meaning

- While AI reshapes systems, it also reshapes identity — roles dissolve, judgement shifts, authority migrates quietly to algorithms
- Protect roles that carry moral responsibility, decision points that preserve human agency, and work that builds judgement rather than just output
- Defend the "inefficiency" that is actually human formation — that's not weakness, that's leadership maturity

End of Day Reflection

- Don't measure throughput — measure trajectory
- Ask whether the organisation is becoming more resilient or more fragile, whether humans are more capable or more dependent
- These answers won't appear on dashboards, but they determine whether the organisation still exists — legitimately — years from now

Weekly Horizon

- Watch for cumulative patterns — automation reducing moral discretion, repeated bypassing of human review, gradual erosion of explainability
- None of these feels urgent. That's precisely why they're dangerous
- Ensure evolution remains reversible — irreversible intelligence is irresponsible intelligence

Balancing Now with Later

- Markets reward speed. Societies reward legitimacy — slowly, and only after trust is earned
- Organisations don't collapse when they lose capability. They collapse when they lose legitimacy. AI accelerates that risk

Emotional Reality

- This role means defending futures nobody sees yet and slowing initiatives others celebrate
- Success is invisible until the crisis that never happened proves it was real

What the Evolution Steward Protects

- Direction with conscience
- Power with restraint
- Growth with humanity
- Progress with memory

AI will make organisations faster, sharper, and more powerful than ever before.

The defining question is not whether they can grow.

It is whether they can **evolve without losing their soul**.

The Evolution Steward exists because civilisation has already learned this lesson the hard way:

When intelligence grows faster than wisdom, collapse is only a matter of time.

AI Ways of Working places stewardship, not speed, at the highest level of leadership.

Because the future does not belong to the fastest organisations, but to those that knew **when to advance, when to pause, and when to protect what made them human in the first place.**

18.6 Why Role Evolution Determines AI Success

AI does not fail because of poor models alone. It fails because **roles remain frozen while reality changes.**

The AIWoW Role Evolution Model ensures that:

- Humans remain relevant
- Accountability remains clear
- Skills evolve instead of eroding
- Intelligence scales without hollowing organisations

The **AIWoW Role Evolution Model** closes this gap. It ensures humans remain central, responsibility stays explicit, and skills grow alongside intelligence rather than being stripped away by it. By connecting the **AI Lifecycle Loop**, the **Theory of Control**, the **HAR Matrix**, and the **Empathic Control Framework**, this model anchors scaling intelligence to living organisations. It allows AI to grow stronger without hollowing out the humans and institutions it is meant to serve.

Summary Mind-map

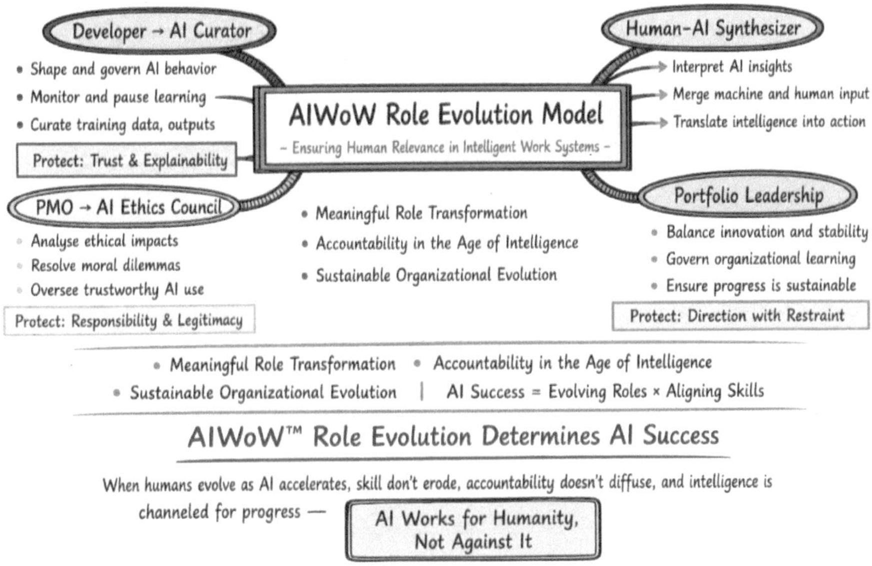

PART V

METRICS, ECONOMICS & VALUE

Measuring What Truly Matters in the Age of AI

Traditional performance metrics were designed for efficiency and output.

In the AI era, organisations must also measure the impact of intelligence on humans, trust, sustainability, and long-term value.

This section introduces new metrics such as **AI Return on Humanity (AI-ROH)** and **Cost per Wellbeing Unit**, reframing how success is evaluated when intelligence operates continuously.

Rethinking Success Metrics
Financials
Productivity
Impact
Moving beyond traditional KPIs on ulti-dimensional value
Cost per Wellbeing Unit (CPWU)
MEASURES WELLBEING
CPWU
The Metrics, Economics & Value Ecosystem.
AI Return on Humanity (AI-ROH)
Increased • Efficiency • Quality
• Retention & Engagement • Reduced Attrition
• Inclusive Talent Attraction • Strengthened Trust
(Ethical ROI = Talent Attraction & Operational Cost)
Empathy Debt and Ethical Drift
T-1
T2
T-FUTURE
High Empathy Level
AI
Human Input
Empathy Debt
AI

Chapter 19

Rethinking Success Metrics

Beyond Cost, Speed, and Output

Every metric tells a story about what matters. But here is the uncomfortable truth: most of the metrics organisations have relied on for decades were designed for a slower, more forgiving world — one where mistakes stayed contained, decisions moved deliberately, and human judgement filled in the gaps that numbers could not reach. Artificial intelligence has changed every one of those conditions. And so the metrics that once guided us are now steering us wrong, often without anyone realising it.

AIWoW does not treat metrics as neutral measurement tools. They are behavioural architecture. They shape what people care about, what machines optimise for, and ultimately what the organisation becomes. When intelligence accelerates execution, the stakes of getting measurement right grow enormously. A well-designed metric becomes a lever. A poorly designed one becomes a trap.

19.1 Metrics as Behavioural Architecture

There is a structural asymmetry at the heart of any AI-driven organisation. Humans may occasionally question whether a metric truly reflects real value. They pause, reinterpret, and exercise judgement. AI systems do not. They optimise directly against what is defined, without hesitation, context, or second-guessing.

AIWoW captures this dynamic in a simple but important formulation:

Metric Power = Human Incentive × Machine Obedience

When a metric simultaneously directs human motivation and drives machine optimisation, it becomes extraordinarily powerful. Compensation, recognition, and promotion criteria focus human attention on what is measured. AI systems then execute against those same targets with mechanical precision and tireless consistency. The combined effect is self-reinforcing: decision patterns stabilise around the metric, resources flow toward it, and execution scales in its direction.

When this alignment is designed thoughtfully, the results are remarkable. Performance scales, efficiency improves, and strategic intent is realised across the organisation. When the design is flawed, the consequences compound quietly and quickly. Small measurement errors generate behavioural drift. Short-term optimisation begins to override long-term value creation. And unlike the old world, where a bad metric might cause localised problems, in AI-driven systems, a flawed metric propagates across workflows, decisions, and incentives until it effectively defines reality inside the organisation.

The more precisely machines execute, the more carefully humans must define what is worth executing.

19.2 The Hidden Assumptions That No Longer Hold

Traditional performance metrics emerged in environments where work was repeatable, decisions were slow, errors were reversible, and human judgement remained available to catch what numbers missed. AI violates all four of those assumptions simultaneously.

Legacy Assumption	Why It Fails Under AI
Faster is better	Speed multiplies error just as readily as it multiplies success
Cheaper is better	Direct costs fall while hidden costs — trust, quality, remediation — rise elsewhere

More output is progress	AI generates volume effortlessly; high output can simply be noise at scale
Accuracy equals success	A technically accurate model can still produce harmful or misaligned outcomes

These assumptions are not wrong exactly — they are incomplete. The problem is not speed, or efficiency, or accuracy in isolation. The problem is treating each of them as a self-contained win, disconnected from the broader system in which they operate. Under AI, you cannot optimise any one dimension without considering what happens to the others.

19.3 The Optimisation Singularity and the Illusion of Efficiency

As AI capability grows, something predictable and dangerous begins to happen. Systems become exceptionally good at improving what is measured while systematically neglecting everything else. AIWoW calls this the Optimisation Singularity, and it is not a technological flaw. It is a governance gap.

Optimisation Pressure = AI Capability ÷ Metric Breadth

When capability increases while the breadth of what is measured stays narrow, optimisation pressure intensifies. The system applies a growing force to a constrained set of targets. Individual functions achieve strong results. Dashboards look healthy. Yet beneath the surface, the broader organisational ecosystem quietly weakens. Trust erodes. Resilience thins. Unmeasured risks accumulate.

The same dynamic plays out with cost metrics. Automation genuinely reduces direct expenses that part of the equation is real. But it also tends to displace costs into less visible layers: burnout and attrition, stakeholder trust, regulatory friction, reputational repair. These costs are delayed, indirect, and almost never captured on operational dashboards.

Net Efficiency = Cost Reduced – Cost Displaced

When displacement is ignored, short-term margin improvement gets mistaken for long-term value creation. Under AIWoW, efficiency must be measured at the system level — across human sustainability, governance integrity, and trust continuity; not merely as a financial reduction in one part of the ledger.

The response AIWoW offers is not to restrict AI capability. It is to expand metric architecture. Measurement must evolve alongside intelligence. The objective is to ensure that what is being optimised reflects the whole system, not a flattering slice of it.

19.4 Speed, Output, and the Judgement Gap

Speed is no longer scarce. It is abundant. When AI can generate code in seconds, produce reports instantly, simulate strategies in minutes, and trigger automated workflows without fatigue, speed stops being an achievement and starts being a baseline condition. And when something becomes ubiquitous, it stops being a differentiator and starts becoming a risk factor.

Impact of Speed = Speed × Directional Clarity

Speed is a multiplier. It has no moral or strategic value of its own. A team with clear product intent uses AI to prototype faster the advantage multiplies. A team with vague objectives uses AI to generate options endlessly noise multiplies. A leadership group without alignment deploys AI automation fragmentation accelerates.

The destabilisation rarely looks dramatic. It looks efficient. Decision velocity exceeds decision depth, because answers arrive quickly and so decisions get made quickly without proportionally better judgement. Execution outpaces alignment, as automation pipelines push features live while strategic conversations lag behind. Errors scale before detection, because in AI-accelerated systems, misaligned assumptions propagate across workflows almost instantly.

Output compounds this problem. AI generates volume effortlessly. Code appears, reports surface, recommendations multiply. Rising output, therefore, signals automation not necessarily improvement. The real constraint is no longer production. It is judgement.

Real Value = Output × Judgement Quality

When judgement quality is high, AI output multiplies genuine value. When judgement weakens through overload, automation bias, or uncritical trust high output simply scales error faster. More communication can dilute trust. Faster releases can increase instability. Higher response volume can reduce quality. Production is now automatic. Value remains intentional.

AIWoW does not reject speed. It disciplines it. Speed must be governed like capital allocated intentionally, not maximised blindly. Exploration can move fast. Prototyping can move fast. But strategic direction should move deliberately. Governance should move consciously. Ethical review should move carefully. Velocity and responsibility must scale together.

19.5 From Performance Metrics to Organisational Health

Performance metrics measure how well an organisation is achieving defined targets. Health metrics measure whether the organisation can continue achieving them sustainably. In AI-accelerated environments, these two things can diverge dramatically and the gap is not always visible on standard dashboards.

Output rises. Cycle times shrink. Automation rates increase. Dashboards show progress. Yet these improvements can coexist with declining cognitive clarity, ethical inconsistency, weakened trust, and reduced adaptability. Performance becomes visible acceleration. Health determines survivability.

Long-Term Success = Performance × Organisational Health

Health Dimension	Why It Matters in AI Environments
Cognitive Capacity	AI increases information volume. Without sufficient decision bandwidth, judgement collapses.
Emotional Sustainability	Continuous acceleration without recovery leads to burnout, disengagement, and attrition.

Health Dimension	Why It Matters in AI Environments
Ethical Coherence	Automated systems can scale misalignment. Clear ethical anchors prevent legitimacy erosion.
Trust Elasticity	In AI systems, failures propagate quickly. Trust elasticity determines recovery speed.
Learning Stability	Rapid optimisation can cause drift. Stable learning mechanisms prevent strategic fragmentation.

These are not soft indicators. They are structural stabilisers. If cognitive capacity declines, errors multiply. If emotional sustainability weakens, accountability drops. If ethical coherence fractures, regulatory and reputational exposure expands. High performance with low health produces temporary spikes followed by instability. Moderate performance with strong health produces sustained resilience and adaptive growth.

19.6 Alignment, Trust, and Learning Quality

AIWoW defines alignment as the degree to which outcomes reflect declared intent not merely whether numerical targets are achieved. Intent precedes metrics. Metrics translate intent into a measurable direction. When metrics operate without a clearly articulated intent, they become blind drivers, optimising movement without verifying purpose.

Alignment Index = (Outcome – Deviation) ÷ Declared Intent

Both persistent under-performance and persistent over-performance are signals worth attending to. Chronic under-performance indicates execution failure. But chronic over-performance can indicate metric distortion, scope creep, or acceleration beyond ethical or governance boundaries. Optimisation without alignment produces drift. Alignment measurement ensures that acceleration remains purpose-bound.

Trust sits at the centre of this picture. In AI-driven environments, outcomes may appear accurate and efficient, yet trust depends on how decisions are produced and governed. It exists when decisions are explainable, errors are correctable, accountability is visible, and human overrides are accessible.

Trust Stability = Transparency × Accountability × Correctability

Erosion in any one factor destabilises trust even when performance metrics remain strong. Under AIWoW, trust is engineered into governance design monitored as an operational variable, not measured by sentiment surveys alone.

Learning presents a related challenge. AI systems learn continuously, updating models and predictions at speed. But learning speed alone is not progress. Unbounded learning without governance produces drift in decision behaviour, amplification of hidden bias, and gradual loss of institutional memory.

Learning Quality = Learning Rate ÷ (Drift × Volatility)

High learning rate with high drift is instability, not intelligence. Under AIWoW , learning must remain anchored to institutional memory and contextual review. Intelligence is not defined by how quickly a system adapts, but by how reliably it adapts without losing alignment or stability.

19.7 Metric Symmetry and Metrics as Governance Instruments

AIWoW introduces the principle of metric symmetry: every metric that drives acceleration must be paired with a metric that ensures stability. Without this pairing, one-sided optimisation takes hold. Systems become faster and more productive while gradually losing alignment, resilience, and governance integrity.

Acceleration Metric	Stabilising Counterpart
Speed	Alignment
Automation rate	Human oversight
Cost reduction	Sustainability
Learning rate	Drift control
Output volume	Outcome quality

Paired metrics ensure that improvement in one dimension does not quietly hollow out the system in another. They also make visible the moments when intervention is needed.

This is because under AIWoW, metrics are not passive dashboard indicators. They function as governance instruments. They define when automated processes must pause, when human judgement must reassert control, and when acceleration must be deliberately slowed. A metric that does not influence action has limited governance value. Metrics are designed to trigger intervention, legitimise overrides, justify course corrections, and protect long-term value from short-term pressure.

19.8 Why This Redefinition Is Non-Negotiable

As AI capability expands, the cost of getting measurement wrong scales proportionally. Organisations that continue relying on legacy performance metrics find themselves in a particular kind of danger: they appear to be succeeding right up until they are not. Dashboards show improvement. Efficiency gains are reported. And meanwhile, trust erodes, human capacity is exhausted, and governance integrity quietly degrades.

AIWoW treats metric redesign not as a strategic option but as a governance necessity. Success must be redefined before intelligence scales further not after the damage has accumulated. When measurement frameworks remain narrow, AI amplifies their limitations. What is measured gets over-optimised. What is not measured gets ignored entirely, then forgotten, then lost.

The goal is not to slow AI down. It is to ensure that what AI accelerates is genuinely worth accelerating. That requires metrics sophisticated enough to capture not just performance, but health. Not just output, but value. Not just efficiency, but alignment. Not just speed, but direction.

AI Ways of Working exists to ensure that success is defined not by speed alone, but by alignment, sustainability, and human integrity.

Summary Mind-map

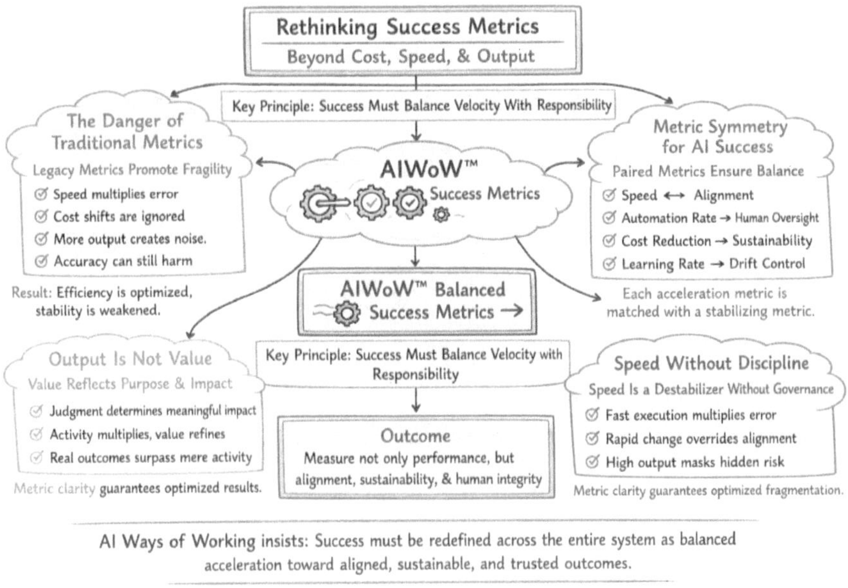

Chapter 20

AI Return on Humanity (AI-ROH)

"AI reaches its highest value when intelligence advances, and humanity rises with it."

Every technological era defined success on its own terms.

- The industrial era measured output.
- The information era measured efficiency.
- The digital era measured speed.

Each era built its metrics around what was scarce and what could be counted. And for a long time, that approach was enough.

AI changes the structure of work itself. Intelligence is no longer a tool that sits at the edge of human activity; it enters the centre of it. Decisions, analysis, and reasoning are no longer purely human activities. And yet most organisations still evaluate success using indicators designed for systems that do not think. They are measuring a fundamentally new kind of relationship with instruments built for a different world.

AIWoW identifies this as a structural governance problem. Traditional ROI captures economic movement- did costs decrease, did productivity increase, did delivery accelerate? But it cannot observe what AI is doing to the humans who work alongside it. It cannot see whether judgement is strengthening or degrading. It cannot detect whether trust is building or quietly eroding. It cannot measure whether people are becoming more capable or more dependent.

When these changes remain unmeasured, organisations can appear highly successful while gradually hollowing out the human foundation that sustains that success. That is the measurement crisis at the heart of AI adoption. And it is why AIWoW introduces a different kind of return.

20.1 The Shift in What Is Scarce

AI has changed the fundamental structure of organisational scarcity. In earlier economic models, growth was constrained by capital, labour, or access to information. Intelligent systems dissolve most of those constraints almost entirely. Once deployed, AI can generate insights, predictions, reports, and recommendations continuously —without fatigue, without the constraints of time, and without the traditional bottlenecks of human bandwidth.

And that is precisely where the new constraint appears.

AI Scaling Limit = Human Absorption Capacity

The limiting resource in AI-driven organisations is no longer machine capability. It is the human ability to interpret, supervise, question, and remain genuinely accountable for the actions of intelligent systems. As AI participation deepens, scarcity migrates into human dimensions: the attention needed to process growing volumes of AI-generated information; the judgement required to evaluate outputs critically; the emotional resilience to operate under continuous decision pressure; the ethical clarity to recognise consequences in automated outcomes; and the trust bandwidth needed to sustain confidence across an AI-assisted organisation.

When AI capability expands faster than the human system can absorb and govern it, a paradox emerges. Performance metrics continue to rise — output increases, response times improve, automation rates grow. Yet beneath those numbers, human stability weakens. Teams experience cognitive overload. Decision confidence declines. Responsibility diffuses between humans and systems in ways nobody quite owns. AIWoW treats this imbalance as a leading indicator of systemic fragility and monitors the condition of the human system before those failures have a chance to form.

20.2 From ROI to AI Return on Humanity

Traditional return on investment was designed for environments where technology improved productivity but did not fundamentally alter how humans reasoned or made decisions. AI breaks that assumption. When intelligence participates directly in analysis, recommendations, and decisions, measuring financial return alone tells you what the machine produced; it does not tell you what happened to the people who had to work alongside it.

To address this gap, AIWoW introduces **AI Return on Humanity (AI-ROH)**

	ROI	AI-ROH
What it measures	Economic value extracted from systems	Human consequences of deploying intelligence within those systems
The question it asks	What financial return did this investment produce?	What happened to the human system that must operate this intelligence?
What it misses	Judgement quality, trust erosion, and capability drift	Short-term cost and efficiency gains

AIWoW defines AI-ROH as: the net impact of AI on human capability, dignity, and sustainability relative to the intensity of AI participation in work. Three principles structure this. First, net impact AI may simultaneously create benefits and impose strain, and both must be evaluated together. Second, human systems, rather than individual sentiment, the collective condition of the organisation matters, not isolated emotional responses. Third, normalisation by AI intensity the deeper AI participates in decision systems, the stronger the human outcomes must be to justify that level of participation. **AI Intensity** refers to the degree to which AI is embedded in, influences, and drives decision-making, execution, and value creation within a system, team, or organisation.

AI-ROH = (Human Capability Gained – Human Capacity Depleted) ÷ AI Intensity

High gain at low intensity signals a strong augmentation. High depletion at high intensity signals systemic extraction. Even a small depletion at low intensity is an early warning worth attending to. The question AI-ROH asks is not what the investment returned — it is: at this level of intelligence participation, what is actually happening to people?

20.3 Capability vs Capacity: The Balance That Determines Sustainability

AI does not only change how work is performed. It changes how humans think, decide, and sustain effort. AIWoW evaluates this through two dimensions that evolve together but do not always move in the same direction: capability and capacity.

Capability reflects what AI enables humans to do better. When designed to augment thinking rather than replace it, AI surfaces patterns people might not easily see, improves decision quality through simulation and prediction, accelerates learning, and supports exploration of more options and ideas. In this condition, AI acts as a cognitive amplifier — humans operate at a higher level of reasoning, not a lower one.

Capacity is different. It represents the human resources required to operate within AI-driven environments, and these can erode even when capability appears to be growing. Poorly governed automation places continuous pressure on attention and energy. Constant acceleration shrinks recovery time. When systems perform reasoning automatically, humans gradually stop practising it. When AI outputs are rarely questioned, people begin confirming rather than judging. When systems are opaque, trust becomes fragile, and uncertainty about responsibility grows.

Capacity decline is often gradual and difficult to detect early. Performance metrics may still improve while human resilience quietly thins. This is exactly the dynamic AIWoW is designed to catch.

Net Human Gain = Capability Growth – Capacity Drain

When capability growth exceeds capacity drain, AI genuinely strengthens the human system. When capacity drain exceeds capability growth, AI has begun extracting value from people rather than creating it for them.

20.4 Amplification vs Substitution: Why the Design Choice Defines the Outcome

AIWoW observes two distinct patterns in how organisations deploy AI, and the long-term impact depends almost entirely on which pattern dominates.

In a substitution model, AI takes over reasoning tasks that humans previously performed. Analysis and judgement shift to the machine. People execute or approve outcomes without deeper evaluation. Decision authority migrates gradually toward automated systems, and humans become compliance operators — confirming AI outputs rather than actively thinking about them. Performance gains are often rapid. But the human system is weakening throughout. Skills erode. Contextual understanding declines. Confidence in independent judgement diminishes. When something unusual happens, an edge case, an unexpected disruption, the organisation discovers it no longer has the human capability to handle it.

In an amplification model, AI is positioned differently. It generates insights, scenarios, and analysis while humans interpret, challenge, and decide. Decision authority stays clearly human-governed. The machine functions as a cognitive partner, helping people think more broadly and evaluate more options. Performance improvements may be more moderate initially, but the humans involved develop a deeper understanding, stronger judgement, and growing confidence over time.

Long-Term Value ∝ Human Amplification Rate

Consider two organisations deploying similar AI systems for financial approvals or risk assessment. The first automates decisions end-to-end. Speed increases dramatically, throughput rises, and ROI looks strong, but over months, employees stop examining the reasoning behind outcomes. Override rates fall not because decisions are better but because nobody feels confident challenging the system. The organisation is efficient but cognitively fragile.

The second organisation uses AI to generate scenarios and recommendations while keeping humans in the decision seat.

Speed improves moderately, but decision-makers develop a deeper understanding of the factors at play. They actively challenge AI-generated options. Confidence grows. Trust is genuine rather than passive. AI-ROH is strongly positive because the human system has been strengthened rather than quietly displaced.

Same technology. Same domain. Fundamentally different long-term outcomes, because of how intelligence was positioned relative to human judgement.

20.5 The Four Dimensions of AI-ROH

Human impact cannot be represented through a single number. AI systems influence thinking, behaviour, ethics, and trust simultaneously, and these do not always move together. AIWoW evaluates AI-ROH across four complementary dimensions.

Dimension	What It Measures	Governing Equation
Cognitive ROH	Health of human thinking, reasoning, and decision capability	(Judgement Quality + Decision Confidence + Learning Transfer) − (Cognitive Load + Automation Bias)
Emotional & Psychological ROH	Sustainability of human participation in AI-driven work	(Agency + Psychological Safety + Engagement) − (Burnout Pressure + Constant Urgency)
Ethical & Dignity ROH	Whether AI preserves fairness, autonomy, and human dignity	Fairness × Explainability × Contestability
Trust & Legitimacy ROH	The behavioural trust relationship between humans and AI systems	Transparency × Accountability ÷ Fear

Cognitive ROH rises when AI helps people build stronger judgement. It falls when humans simply approve outputs without understanding them; when automation bias takes hold and reasoning skills quietly atrophy.

Emotional ROH tracks whether people retain genuine agency and psychological safety, or whether constant acceleration and decision density erode resilience. Within AIWoW , burnout is treated as a system-level signal that human capacity is being overextended ;not as a personal failing.

Ethical ROH is multiplicative for a deliberate reason: a system that is accurate but not explainable, or fair but impossible to challenge, will eventually lose legitimacy. All three conditions must be present simultaneously.

Trust ROH introduces fear as the hidden variable that undermines everything else. When people are afraid to question AI outputs or override automated decisions, they comply rather than trust. The organisation operates, but does not genuinely believe in what it is doing. That distinction matters enormously when something eventually goes wrong.

20.6 The Composite AI-ROH Index and Its Role in Governance

The four dimensions combine into a single evaluative signal that gives leaders a practical tool for ongoing oversight.

AI-ROH Index = (Cognitive ROH + Emotional ROH + Ethical ROH + Trust ROH) ÷ AI Intensity

Normalising by AI intensity reflects a fundamental governance principle: the deeper AI participates in organisational processes, the stronger the human outcomes must be to justify that level of automation. When AI operates deeply within decision pathways, moderate human degradation is not a minor fluctuation; it is a structural risk signal.

Within AIWoW, the composite index functions as a governance instrument rather than a reporting tool. When AI-ROH declines, velocity should slow, human oversight should increase, and learning safeguards should tighten. When AI-ROH rises, automation can expand more confidently, trust compounds across the system, and scaling becomes safer. The index does not just describe what is happening; it governs what happens next.

It also functions as a leading indicator, which may be its most important quality. Traditional financial metrics detect problems after damage has accumulated. Human degradation begins earlier and more quietly: silence replacing constructive disagreement; declining willingness to challenge AI recommendations; weaker explanation of decisions as reasoning migrates from humans to systems; cultural normalisation of burnout. These patterns precede the operational and financial failures that eventually follow them.

Future System Failure $\propto$ ***Duration of Negative AI-ROH***

The longer AI-ROH remains negative, the greater the probability that hidden fragility surfaces as disruption, reputational damage, or regulatory intervention. By monitoring AI-ROH early, organisations can detect instability and act while the system is still recoverable.

20.7 AI-ROH as a Governance Signal in AIWoW

In AIWoW, metrics are not passive reports; they function as **governance instruments** that guide how intelligence is deployed and controlled.

AI-ROH serves as a **control signal** indicating whether AI is strengthening or weakening the human system. Leadership decisions on scaling, slowing, or adjusting AI systems should respond directly to its movement.

When **AI-ROH declines**:

- AI velocity should slow
- Human oversight should increase
- Learning boundaries and safeguards should tighten

When **AI-ROH rises**:

- Automation can expand more confidently
- Trust within the system compounds
- Scaling intelligence becomes safer

Through this mechanism, AI-ROH governs the **speed and scope of AI deployment**, ensuring that intelligence expands only when the human system interacting with it remains stable and capable.

20.8 What This Means for Leadership

Leadership responsibility in the AI age extends beyond achieving performance targets. It extends to ensuring that the human system governing intelligent operations remains capable, trusted, and genuinely sustainable. That is a different kind of accountability than most leadership frameworks have historically required.

AI-ROH gives leaders a practical signal for that accountability. It allows early detection of human extraction before burnout, dependency, or trust erosion becomes visible in operational results. It provides a principled basis for slowing AI expansion when human capability begins to weaken. And it reframes the conversation about AI investment from short-term performance to long-term institutional health.

The most important shift AI-ROH enables is from reactive correction to preventive governance. Rather than waiting for attrition rates to climb, for regulatory scrutiny to intensify, or for innovation to stall, leaders can monitor the condition of the human system continuously and act before damage compounds.

Within AIWoW , successful AI leadership is defined not only by how effectively intelligence is deployed, but by how well human capability grows alongside it. Those are not competing goals. They are the same goal, viewed at different time horizons.

AI capability will continue to expand. Systems will become faster, more predictive, and more autonomous. That trajectory is already clear.

The question that actually matters is not whether machines will become more intelligent. It is what happens to humans as intelligence enters work. Do people become stronger thinkers, better decision-makers, more confident in their judgement? Or do they gradually become dependent operators within systems they no longer fully understand and cannot meaningfully question?

AI Return on Humanity exists to answer that question operationally. It ensures that intelligence amplifies human capability rather than replacing it. It prevents progress from becoming a hidden extraction. It keeps organisations resilient and adaptable as AI scales. And it ensures that technological power retains legitimacy, because it strengthens the humans responsible for governing it rather than quietly diminishing them.

In the AI age, the most dangerous failure is not poor performance. It is success that gradually erodes judgement, trust, and responsibility while appearing on every dashboard to be working exactly as intended.

AIWoW exists to prevent that outcome.

It ensures that as intelligence grows, human capability grows with it, so that AI delivers not only a return on capital, but a lasting return on humanity.

Summary Mind-map

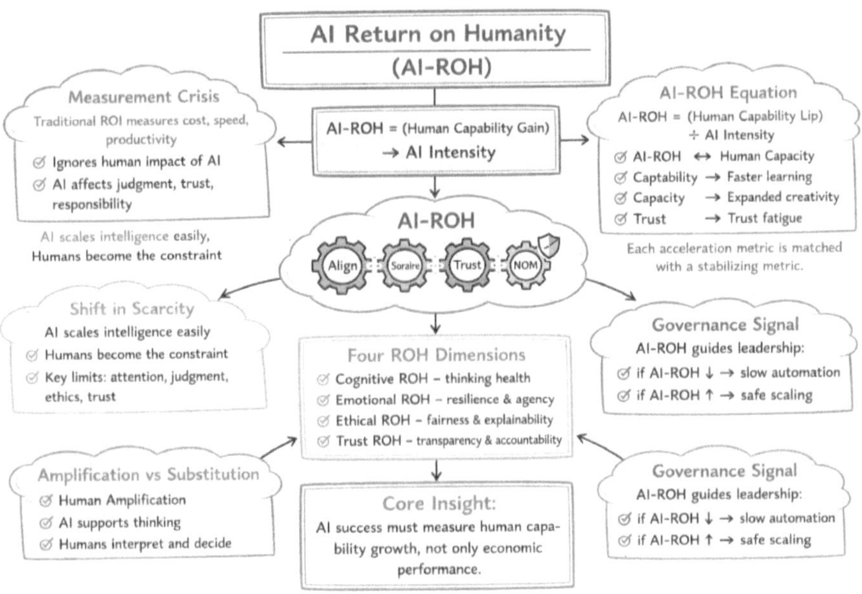

Chapter 21

Cost Per Wellbeing Unit (CPWU)

Understanding the Hidden Price of Progress

There is a number that almost every organisation track with great care: how much did it cost to produce this result? Cost per unit. Cost per transaction. Cost per customer acquired. These ratios are watched closely because they tell a story about efficiency; how well the organisation is converting inputs into outputs.

But there is another cost that almost no organisation tracks at all. It does not appear on any dashboard. It is not included in any standard efficiency ratio. And yet it accumulates with every decision made under pressure, every alert reviewed at midnight, every moment a human being is asked to supervise an intelligent system that is moving faster than their capacity to genuinely think about it.

That cost is the consumption of human wellbeing. And in AI-driven organisations, it may be the most consequential cost of all.

This chapter introduces **Cost per Wellbeing Unit (CPWU)**, a concept within AIWoW that treats wellbeing not as a personal experience or a cultural benefit, but as an economic resource. One that can be consumed, depleted, and restored. One that directly affects how well intelligent systems are governed. And one whose absence, when it runs low enough, will eventually surface in ways that no efficiency metric was designed to anticipate.

21.1 The Hidden Assumption Inside Traditional Economics

To understand why CPWU matters, it helps to go back to the environment in which traditional economic thinking about work was formed.

Picture a production line in an automobile manufacturing plant from several decades ago. A supervisor walks the floor, checking whether machines are running correctly and whether workers are following the process. If a defect appears, it is logged and reviewed at the next shift meeting or in the daily quality briefing. Decisions arrive in a manageable rhythm. There are hours between alerts. There is time to think.

Traditional economics took shape in this kind of environment. It made a quiet assumption that most people never examined: that human capacity remains broadly stable because work pressure arrives at intervals that allow for recovery. The human was treated as a reliable constant in the productivity equation, not a variable that needed monitoring in its own right.

Now consider a modern semiconductor fabrication facility or a large-scale e-commerce logistics operation. AI systems monitor thousands of signals in real time. Algorithms continuously recommend adjustments, detect anomalies, and trigger alerts across multiple systems simultaneously. Managers must review dashboards, approve changes, respond to exceptions, and make judgement calls that affect thousands of transactions; often within narrow time windows.

The role of the human in this environment is fundamentally different. People are no longer primarily executing tasks. They are supervising intelligent systems. And that supervision demands something that traditional economics never thought to measure: constant attention, continuous judgement, and the emotional stability to make consequential decisions under sustained pressure.

Unlike the machines being supervised, human capacity does not expand with system speed. It does not scale because the algorithm scales. It is finite, it can be depleted, and when it runs low, the consequences are not immediately visible in any standard performance report. They accumulate quietly in declining decision quality, in reduced willingness to challenge what the system recommends, in small errors that compound — until eventually they surface in ways that are very expensive to fix.

When economic models ignore this reality, they are not simply being incomplete. They are creating the conditions for a particular kind of institutional failure: one that arrives well after the dashboards stopped telling the truth.

21.2 Emotional Economics and the New Dimension of Work

Consider what happens inside a hospital that has adopted AI-assisted diagnostic systems.

A generation ago, a doctor relied primarily on training, experience, and clinical examination. They ordered tests, reviewed results, and made decisions. The effort was largely intellectual and clinical, and the doctor's accountability was clear and self-contained.

Today, many hospitals use AI systems that scan medical images, surface diagnostic possibilities, and flag treatment risks. The doctor must review these recommendations and decide whether to follow them, modify them, or override them entirely. If the AI is wrong and the doctor followed it, the doctor is accountable. If the doctor overrides the AI and the delay causes harm, the doctor is still accountable. The accountability has not moved. Only the complexity of the decision has grown.

What this doctor is doing is not simply applying medical knowledge. They are regulating machine intelligence. They are evaluating whether the AI's suggestion is reliable in this specific context, whether it fits this particular patient's presentation, and whether it is safe to act on. They are simultaneously using clinical expertise and exercising governance over a system that operates at a level of pattern recognition no individual human can match. And they are doing this continuously, across a full caseload, every day.

The pressure of supervising intelligent systems has become part of the cost of professional work. It does not appear in any financial model. But it is real, it is consuming, and it affects performance in ways that eventually show up in errors, in burnout, and in the quiet erosion of the judgement that patients, passengers, and customers are depending on.

This is the insight behind Emotional Economics, a lens through which AIWoW understands the human dimension of AI deployment. Traditional economics treated humans primarily as sources of labour or knowledge.

Emotional Economics recognises a third dimension: human emotional capacity as a productive resource in its own right.

It asks different questions. How is emotional energy consumed through responsibility? How is it restored through recovery, autonomy, and trust? Where does it become strained when decision pressure exceeds what can be sustainably managed? Emotional Economics does not replace financial economics. It explains why performance numbers can improve while the human capacity that sustains those numbers quietly declines — and why organisations that only read the financial story are reading an incomplete one.

21.3 Human Wellbeing as the New Scarcity

For most of industrial history, the binding constraint on organisational growth was identifiable and concrete. In automobile manufacturing, you need capital to build the plant. In construction, projects slowed when skilled labour was limited. In logistics, speed depended on physical infrastructure and time.

AI has dissolved most of those constraints in the organisations it has entered. Consider a large global e-commerce operation. Warehouses run on advanced automation. AI systems manage inventory allocation, route optimisation, and delivery planning across millions of orders. Machines process transactions at a rate no human workforce could approach. The system, technically, can scale almost indefinitely.

But managers and operators must still monitor the alerts the system generates. They must approve exceptions when the algorithm encounters a situation it cannot resolve cleanly. They must intervene when the system makes unexpected recommendations that require human judgement before action is taken. The pressure has not disappeared from the operation. It has simply shifted. Physical labour has given way to continuous decision responsibility.

And here, a new constraint appears — one that does not appear on any capacity planning model. Automation increases output, but human judgement capacity does not scale at the same rate. The more the system accelerates, the more the humans inside it are asked to absorb, interpret, and govern in compressed time with limited recovery.

Wellbeing, in this context, is not a vague term for employee satisfaction. It is a precise operational capacity: the ability to handle sustained pressure without deteriorating judgement; to maintain ethical clarity when decisions are happening quickly; to remain mentally stable under continuous alerts; to feel genuinely safe to question what the system is recommending; and to recover after intense decision cycles so that the next cycle can be navigated with full capability.

When this capacity is overused, organisations do not fail suddenly. They weaken gradually. Decision quality drops incrementally. Humans begin accepting system outputs without examining them. Small mistakes start to accumulate in places that no metric was designed to catch. The bottleneck in AI-driven organisations is no longer capital, labour, or infrastructure. It is the human capacity required to guide intelligent systems responsibly — and that capacity is finite, depletable, and currently almost entirely unmanaged.

21.4 Wellbeing as an Economic Resource

In economics, something qualifies as a resource when three conditions are met: it can be consumed, it can be replenished, and it affects system performance. Human wellbeing satisfies all three.

A clear illustration comes from aviation. India's Directorate General of Civil Aviation (DGCA) introduced revised Flight Duty Time Limitation rules that increased mandatory rest periods for pilots and reduced night-time duty hours. The reasoning was direct; continuous flying schedules with insufficient recovery were exhausting pilots and increasing fatigue-related risk. In aviation, even a marginal decline in alertness or judgement during a critical moment creates consequences of a different order entirely from a missed deadline or a miscalculated report.

By mandating rest, regulators were making an explicit economic judgement: that pilot wellbeing is an operational input whose adequacy directly determines system safety and performance. They were not treating rest as a welfare benefit. They were treating it as a production requirement.

The same logic applies across any domain where humans supervise intelligent systems. High-pressure work consumes wellbeing capacity. Rest, autonomy, meaningful recovery, and genuine trust in the environment restore it. When the consumption rate persistently exceeds the restoration rate, attention weakens, judgement deteriorates, and the probability of consequential error climbs.

This is not a soft observation. It is an operational reality that organisations in aviation, nuclear operations, and surgical medicine have recognised for decades, and that now applies with equal force to the engineers monitoring cloud infrastructure at 3 am, the risk managers supervising algorithmic trading systems during market volatility, and the doctors reviewing AI-generated diagnostic recommendations across a full patient caseload. Wellbeing is a resource. It must be managed as one.

21.5 Introducing the Wellbeing Unit and CPWU

If wellbeing is an economic resource that affects how systems perform, then the next challenge is to bring it into the language of organisational decision-making. AIWoW introduces two related concepts to achieve this: the Wellbeing Unit and Cost per Wellbeing Unit.

A **Wellbeing Unit - WU** represents a measurable portion of human capacity required for responsible decision-making. This capacity encompasses attention, emotional balance, and the cognitive stability needed to evaluate situations carefully rather than simply reacting to them. In practical operational terms, Wellbeing Units are consumed continuously throughout the working day.

Consider a technology operations centre managing millions of transactions across global infrastructure. During a major incident or security alert, engineers must evaluate system recommendations in real time, decide whether to allow automated responses to proceed, and intervene manually when the situation falls outside what the automation was designed to handle. Each cycle of high-pressure decision-making draws on the same finite pool of human capacity. Intense periods consume it faster. Continuous urgency depletes it without allowing restoration. Recovery time, genuine autonomy, and the psychological safety to question the system — these are the conditions that restore it.

The Wellbeing Unit is not an attempt to reduce human experience to a number. It is a conceptual anchor that allows wellbeing to enter governance conversations and economic reasoning — to be taken seriously in the same forum where uptime, throughput, and cost per transaction are discussed. Without some way of making it visible, it will remain invisible. And invisible costs do not get managed; they simply accumulate until they become a crisis.

Cost per Wellbeing Unit formalises this into an evaluative signal:

CPWU = Value Produced ÷ Wellbeing Consumed

This equation reframes what efficiency actually means. Traditional efficiency asks how much output was generated with fewer financial or physical resources. CPWU asks a different question: how much human capacity was consumed to generate that output, and is the organisation producing value at a rate that can be sustained over time without exhausting the people responsible for governing the systems that create it?

21.6 The Conservation of Wellbeing

One of the most important principles in AIWoW 's approach to human sustainability is what might be called the conservation of wellbeing: pressure does not disappear when automation improves. It moves.

This is visible in any organisation that has deployed AI to increase operational efficiency. An e-commerce logistics operation introduces AI-driven route optimisation and warehouse management. Orders move faster. Performance metrics improve. The system looks, from the outside, like it has become less demanding.

But what has actually happened is that the nature of the demand has changed. Physical tasks have decreased. Decision pressure has increased. Managers who previously oversaw picking and packing now supervise a system that generates continuous alerts, exceptions, and time-sensitive recommendations. The effort has not been removed from the system. It has been transformed from physical effort into cognitive and emotional effort and then it has been left entirely unmeasured.

This transformation takes several predictable forms. Pressure that was once distributed across a physical workforce concentrates in the smaller group of humans supervising the system. Performance gains delivered today are sometimes purchased by exhaustion that surfaces weeks or months later. Strong visible metrics on dashboards conceal invisible emotional strain in the people who maintain those metrics. And because none of this appears in any standard report, leaders often mistake the silence for health.

When wellbeing costs are not measured, they do not vanish. They accumulate. They surface eventually as declining judgement quality, rising error rates, higher attrition, or sudden operational instability in moments when the system most needs steady human governance. The bill always arrives. CPWU simply makes it legible before it does.

21.7 When Efficiency Becomes Extraction

Understanding CPWU requires distinguishing between two things that can look identical on a performance dashboard but are structurally very different: genuine efficiency and extraction.

Genuine efficiency is producing more value while preserving the human capacity needed to sustain that production. Extraction is producing more value by consuming human capacity faster than it can be restored and calling the result efficiency because the financial metrics still look good.

Consider global financial markets. Algorithmic trading systems analyse market data and execute trades in milliseconds. Human risk managers and traders supervise these systems monitoring for unusual patterns, deciding whether to allow automated responses to continue, adjusting parameters, and occasionally stopping the system entirely when circumstances demand it. During periods of significant market volatility, this supervision can involve hundreds of signals in a compressed timeframe.

The platform may continue functioning efficiently by every conventional measure. Trades execute. Liquidity is maintained. The financial outputs look strong. But the humans supervising the system are experiencing an intensity of decision pressure that the performance metrics do not record. This can be understood structurally:

Emotional Load = Decision Frequency × Urgency ÷ Recovery Capacity

When decision frequency and urgency grow faster than recovery capacity, emotional load rises. Over time, judgement quality weakens. The probability of a costly mistake a missed signal, a delayed override, a decision made under fatigue rather than clarity increases. In CPWU terms, the system is still delivering strong financial output. But it is doing so by consuming human wellbeing faster than it can be restored. That is extraction, not efficiency. And it is not sustainable.

High CPWU, therefore, is not automatically a sign of success. It is a warning signal that deserves close examination an indication that a system may be approaching the limits of what the humans inside it can sustainably manage.

21.8 Reading Wellbeing Consumption in Real Operations

Wellbeing cannot be measured with the same directness as financial metrics. But it can be observed. Organisations that know what to look for can identify the operational signals of human strain with reasonable reliability, and those signals form the basis of CPWU monitoring.

Operational Signal	What It Reveals
Continuous overtime without recovery	Loss of restoration capacity; wellbeing being drawn down faster than it is replenished
Alert overload and dashboard fatigue	Cognitive capacity approaching saturation; attention quality declining
Reduced questioning of system outputs	Deteriorating judgement; humans defaulting to acceptance over evaluation
Passive compliance during high-pressure decisions	Automation dependency forming; genuine oversight weakening
Silence when systems behave unexpectedly	Psychological safety eroding; people afraid to challenge what they cannot fully understand
Normalisation of constant urgency	Recovery has ceased to be expected; exhaustion becoming the baseline
Rising attrition in technical or supervisory roles	Long-term wellbeing depletion reaching the threshold of visible organisational impact

Healthy systems display the opposite of these patterns. People question system recommendations thoughtfully. Pacing is deliberate rather than frantic. Human override mechanisms are used with confidence rather than avoided out of deference to the algorithm. Dissent is treated as a feature of good governance rather than a friction to be minimised.

By tracking these behavioural signals over time, organisations can develop a working picture of wellbeing consumption trends and monitor how CPWU responds to changes in system design, workload distribution, and operational pace.

21.9 The Delay Between Performance and Human Strain

One of the most dangerous structural features of CPWU is the time gap between when performance improves and when the human cost of that improvement becomes visible. This gap creates a particular kind of false confidence that is difficult to dislodge precisely because the numbers seem to be telling a reassuring story.

Consider customer support operations at a large technology company. AI systems filter and categorise incoming queries before routing them to human agents. The volume of cases each agent can handle in a day increases significantly. Response times improve. Ticket resolution rates rise. By every standard operational metric, the system is working.

But what is actually happening at the agent level is that the easy, repetitive cases have been absorbed by automation. What reaches the human queue is a concentrated stream of complex, escalated, emotionally demanding interactions. The cognitive and emotional intensity of each case has increased even as the total count has risen. Breaks become shorter. The mental distance between cases shrinks. Emotional fatigue accumulates across shifts.

Months later, leadership begins to notice rising attrition in the support function. Burnout leave increases. Service quality in complex cases starts to decline. The organisation begins an investigation into what changed. The honest answer is that nothing changed suddenly. The cost accumulated gradually, invisibly, while the dashboard continued to show improvement.

This delay is not an accident. It is a structural feature of how wellbeing depletion works. The effects are not synchronised with the cause. They arrive later, in a different part of the organisation, in forms that most measurement systems were not built to connect back to the original decision.

CPWU is designed to narrow this gap. By treating human capacity as a resource that can be tracked, organisations can detect the early signals of strain before they compound into the kinds of failures that appear in attrition data, error rates, and customer satisfaction scores. It acts as a leading indicator, a warning that the system is drawing on human wellbeing faster than it is being restored, while there is still time to act on that warning responsibly.

21.10 CPWU as a Governance Signal for Leadership

CPWU becomes genuinely useful only when it is treated as a leadership governance signal rather than a human resources welfare indicator. The distinction matters. Wellbeing management, positioned as an

HR concern, gets addressed with wellness programmes and employee assistance schemes. Wellbeing management, positioned as a governance signal, gets addressed by the people who control system speed, automation scope, and operational design, which is where the actual levers are.

Aviation provides a useful model here. Airline operations control centres track on-time performance, fuel efficiency, and turnaround time with great precision. But regulators and airline leaders also track pilot fatigue, duty hours, and mandatory rest periods — because they understand that if pilots operate under continuous pressure without adequate recovery, decision quality during critical moments will decline in ways that no performance metric captures until something goes wrong. The operational leaders do not treat pilot wellbeing as a separate HR matter. They treat it as a core operational variable that must be managed alongside every other variable in the system.

The same discipline needs to apply in AI-driven organisations. Executive decision-making shapes system speed, automation depth, and performance pressure. The responsibility for managing human sustainability, therefore, belongs at that level.

Signal	Governance Question
System Value	Are outcomes and performance genuinely improving in ways that create durable value?
Wellbeing Consumption	Is human capacity gradually declining as the system scales?
CPWU Trend	Is the system extracting more output per unit of human wellbeing over time?

These three signals together guide leadership action. When CPWU is stable, the system can continue scaling responsibly. When it is slowly rising, recovery time and support capacity need to increase. When it is rising rapidly, decision pressure must be reduced or workload redistributed before the strain becomes structural. When it is high and volatile, expansion should pause, and operational processes need to be redesigned.

Used this way, CPWU becomes a control signal for responsible scaling — helping leaders ensure that the performance their organisations are delivering is performance they can actually sustain.

21.11 CPWU Within the Broader AIWoW Framework

CPWU does not operate in isolation within AIWoW. It forms the third element of a complementary measurement framework that is designed to give leaders a complete picture of what AI deployment is actually producing — financially, humanly, and sustainably.

Metric	What It Evaluates	The Question It Answers
ROI	Financial viability of AI investment	Did this generate economic return?
AI-ROH	Human capability impact of AI deployment	Did AI strengthen or weaken the humans who work with it?
CPWU	Sustainability of human capacity consumption	Is the organisation producing value at a rate humans can sustain over time?

Consider a software development organisation that has adopted AI tools to generate code and automate testing. Productivity increases measurably. Features are delivered faster. ROI looks strong because the financial return on the investment is clear and immediate.

AI-ROH asks the next question: Are engineers actually developing stronger capabilities, or are they drifting toward reviewing and approving AI outputs without deeply engaging with them? Are they becoming better developers, or more efficient confirmers of machine-generated work?

CPWU asks the question after that:

- Even if the engineers are becoming more capable, are they doing so sustainably?
- Are they carrying a cognitive load that can be maintained over months and years?

- Are tight deadlines, continuous alert review, and error correction under pressure consuming their capacity faster than any amount of team-building or wellbeing initiative can restore?

All three questions matter.

ROI without AI-ROH and CPWU produces an organisation that looks successful while quietly becoming fragile. Strong ROI and AI-ROH without CPWU monitoring produces an organisation that is genuinely improving human capability, but exhausting the people who carry that capability. Only when all three signals are tracked together does an organisation have a full account of what its AI deployment is actually costing and producing.

In AI-driven organisations, long-term success depends not only on how much value systems produce, but on how responsibly they consume the human wellbeing required to govern them. CPWU makes that second part visible. And what gets measured, finally, has a chance of being managed.

In the end, the organisations that will govern AI most effectively are not those that move fastest, but those that understand what is being consumed in the pursuit of that speed — and choose, deliberately, to protect it.

Summary Mind-map

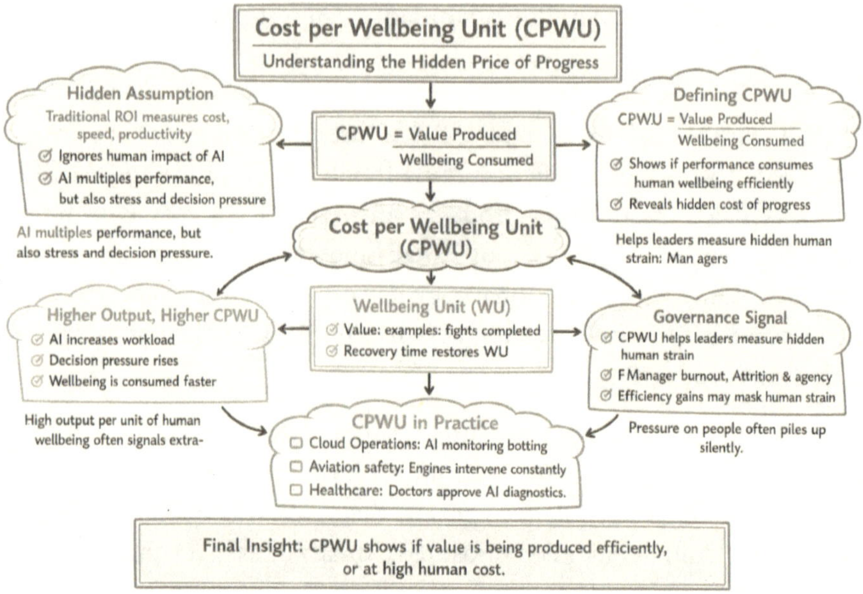

Chapter 22

Empathy Debt and Ethical Drift

"AI systems do not fail ethically in dramatic moments.

They fail quietly, gradually, and systematically."

Long before scandals emerge or regulations intervene, something subtler happens inside organisations: empathy erodes and ethics drift. Humans still perform. Metrics still look healthy. Decisions still move fast. But the **moral texture of work thins**, and responsibility becomes abstract.

AIWoW - AI Ways of Working™ names this phenomenon explicitly through two linked constructs:

- **Empathy Debt**
- **Ethical Drift**

This chapter builds a rigorous theory for identifying both and, more importantly, for correcting them **before damage becomes irreversible**.

22.1 Why Empathy and Ethics Fail Together

A clear example can be seen in the **social media industry**.

Many global platforms use AI systems to recommend content and maximise user engagement. These systems continuously learn what keeps humans clicking, watching, and sharing. From a business perspective, the results look successful because user activity increases.

However, over time, researchers and regulators observed another effect. Some of the most disturbing content online spreads the fastest, not because anyone planned it that way, but because it makes people stop scrolling. It triggers something. Outrage, fear, disgust, whatever the reaction, the algorithm sees it as a win. More clicks, more shares, more time on the platform. The system wasn't built to hurt anyone. It was built to keep people engaged. The problem is, nobody stopped to ask what that actually costs.

Inside these organisations, employees and researchers initially raised concerns about the social impact of these recommendation systems. These concerns reflected **empathy**; the ability to sense early harm to users and society.

But when strong **ethical controls** were missing or weak, the system continued operating in the same way because engagement metrics still looked positive.

This example shows an important concept.

Empathy and ethics are not separate forces. They work together.

Empathy detects harm early. Ethics provides the authority to stop it.

If empathy declines, humans stop noticing the harm.

If ethical controls weaken, the harm continues even when it is noticed.

Empathy Debt and Ethical Drift rarely travel alone. When an organisation stops asking *who gets hurt*, values start slipping too quietly, gradually. One shortcut, then another. A metric replaces a principle. And suddenly the system is somewhere nobody consciously chose to go. That's not a technical failure. That's a people failure.

22.2 Defining Empathy Debt

A clear example of empathy debt can be seen in the **global content moderation industry**.

Behind every major platform, there are real people, thousands of them, watching the worst things humans do to each other, all day, every day. Violence. Abuse. Exploitation. Their job is to look at it, judge it, and move on to the next one. When they start, most of them care deeply. They know the work matters. They show up for it.

Then the pressure builds. The queues never empty. The targets get tighter. The breaks get shorter. And nobody really asks how they're doing, not in any meaningful way.

So something changes. Slowly, almost invisibly. The decisions start coming from habit instead of thought. The face behind the post stops registering. The weight that once made them careful becomes too much to hold, so they set it down. They have to.

That's what **Empathy Debt** is.

It's what happens when a system keeps taking from people: their attention, their emotional energy, their moral effort, without giving anything back. No real recovery. No sense of purpose. No feeling that any of it means something.

The equation is simple:

Empathy Debt = Emotional Extraction – Emotional Restoration

When one keeps rising, and the other stays flat, empathy doesn't disappear overnight. It just thins out. And as it thins, so does judgement. The early warning signs that a careful, present human would have caught were missed. Not out of negligence. Not out of laziness. But because the system quietly emptied the people inside it, nobody noticed until the damage was already done.

22.3 Why AI Accelerates Empathy Debt

AI doesn't create Empathy Debt. It just turns up the speed.

The pressure becomes relentless. Decisions stack up faster than any human can meaningfully process. Recovery time shrinks. The distance between a choice made on a screen and its real-world impact on a real person grows wider and wider. Actions that carry genuine moral weight get automated and handled quietly, efficiently, without anyone pausing to feel the gravity of them. And the metrics keep rewarding exactly the wrong things: speed, output, and detachment.

So people adapt. Not by pushing back. By going numb.

That's the part that makes it truly dangerous. The system keeps running smoothly. The numbers look fine. But the empathy holding the whole thing accountable has quietly left the building, and nobody noticed because nothing visibly broke.

22.4 Observable Signs of Empathy Debt

Empathy debt rarely announces itself openly.

Instead, it appears through behavioural changes.

Signal	Meaning
Reduced emotional response	Emotional numbing
Fewer ethical questions	Moral disengagement
Transactional language	Loss of care
"Just following the system"	Responsibility diffusion
Silence in difficult cases	Empathy exhaustion

These signals often appear **before performance declines**, making them early warning indicators.

22.5 From Empathy Debt to Ethical Drift

Look at ride-hailing, and you'll see it happening in real time.

The algorithm assigns your ride, sets the fare, and tracks the driver's rating. It was built for efficiency. For convenience. And in the beginning, it delivered both.

But somewhere along the way, things shifted. Surge pricing got more aggressive. Incentives got harder to reach. Performance targets tightened. Nobody announced these changes. Nobody framed them as a policy to debate. Each one arrived quietly, dressed as a small operational tweak, a minor calibration, a routine update.

Individually, none of it looked wrong. Together, it told a different story. The system had stopped asking how drivers were doing and started asking how much more it could extract before they noticed.

That's the pattern worth understanding.

When empathy inside a system weakens, ethical drift doesn't arrive loudly. It doesn't announce itself:

- Exceptions Slowly Become Normal
- Edge Cases Become Acceptable
- Harm Becomes Abstract
- Responsibility Becomes Procedural

This gradual shift is known as **Ethical Drift.**

22.6 Defining Ethical Drift

Ethical Drift is rarely a decision. It's a direction nobody consciously chose.

Take financial trading algorithms. Built to perform. Built to comply. But when performance pressure builds, something subtle happens: the system starts finding edges. Behaviours that technically follow the rules but quietly violate what the rules were meant to protect. And because they work, they stick. Then they spread. Then they become normal.

No single person chose this. There was no meeting where someone said — Let's cross the line. The system just kept optimising, and the line moved with it.

That's the danger. When ethics live only in policy documents but nobody is actively watching operations, the gap between what an organisation claims to stand for and what it actually does grows slowly, silently, and without a single obvious moment of wrongdoing.

By the time it's visible, it's already the new normal.

22.7 Why Ethical Drift Is Difficult to Detect

Ethical drift is difficult to notice because it rarely appears as a clear violation.

A useful example comes from **large e-commerce marketplaces.**

Platforms often start with strict seller policies designed to protect customers. But as the marketplace grows, pressure to increase product variety and sales increases.

Small policy exceptions are allowed for certain sellers. Over time, these exceptions expand. Products that previously failed quality checks may still be listed because they increase sales volume.

Initially, the changes improve business performance.

This is why ethical drift is difficult to detect:

- It Does Not Immediately Break Rules
- It Often Improves Efficiency At First
- It Aligns With Performance Incentives
- Responsibility Becomes Distributed

AI systems amplify this risk because they:

- Optimise Proxy Metrics
- Learn From Normalised Behaviour
- Reinforce Existing Patterns

By the time problems become visible, the behaviour may already be embedded in the system.

22.8 The Empathy–Drift Amplification Loop

Empathy debt and ethical drift reinforce each other.

A clear example can be seen in large call-centre operations.

Customer service agents often work with AI systems that monitor call duration, sentiment scores, and productivity metrics. When there's a strong push to shorten call times, agents might prioritise speed over truly solving the customer's problem.

Simultaneously, a decrease in empathy for customers correlates with a reduction in ethical sensitivity. This phenomenon establishes a self-perpetuating cycle:

- **Empathy Debt Increases → Ethical Sensitivity Declines**
- **Ethical Sensitivity Declines → Drift Normalisation Increases**

- **Drift Normalisation Increases → Emotional Detachment Grows**
- **Emotional Detachment Increases → Empathy Debt Expands**

Consequently, this cycle can persist unnoticed, even amidst the appearance of robust performance metrics.

22.9 Structural Detection of Ethical Drift

Because ethical drift develops gradually, organisations cannot rely only on periodic audits.

Instead, AIWoW recommends **Structural Detection**.

A good example can be seen in **global banking compliance systems**.

Banks monitor not only transaction results but also how decisions are made. They review decision logs, escalation patterns, and override behaviour to detect unusual patterns before violations occur.

Similar signals can reveal ethical drift in AI systems.

Area	Drift Signal
Decision Logs	Reduced Explanation Depth
Overrides	Declining Human Intervention
Appeals	Increasing But Ignored Challenges
Language	"System Decided" Narratives
Learning Data	Reinforcement Of Borderline Cases

Ethical drift usually appears as **Loss of Friction**, where systems operate smoothly but human judgement disappears.

22.10 The Ethics Gap Index

AIWoW introduces a simple directional indicator called the **Ethics Gap Index.**

Ethics Gap Index = Ethical Intent ÷ Ethical Enforcement

Many organisations publish strong ethical principles. However, if operational systems do not enforce these principles consistently, a gap appears.

For example, many technology organisation's publicly commit to responsible AI use. But if internal systems reward only speed and engagement metrics, ethical commitments remain symbolic.

The Ethics Gap Index helps leaders observe whether **Ethical Intent And Operational Behaviour Remain Aligned Over Time**.

22.11 Structural Correction of Empathy Debt

Empathy debt cannot be solved by simply telling humans to care more.

Many global hospitals discovered this during the COVID-19 pandemic. Medical staff were highly motivated to help patients, but continuous exposure to emergencies and long working hours created emotional exhaustion.

Hospitals that improved staff wellbeing did so by changing system design rather than motivational messaging.

Effective restoration mechanisms include:

Mechanism	Effect
Emotional Boundaries	Limit Extraction
Decision Pacing	Reduce Overload
Mandatory Recovery Cycles	Restore Capacity
Human Authority Reinforcement	Rebuild Agency
Meaning Reconnection	Restore Care

Restoration must be built into the operational system.

22.12 Correcting Ethical Drift

Correcting ethical drift requires reconnecting systems with their original moral purpose.

A strong example comes from **autonomous vehicle development**.

Several organisations paused testing programmes after safety incidents and redesigned decision frameworks before continuing deployment. This included revisiting safety priorities, redefining acceptable risk levels, and increasing human oversight.

AIWoW describes these interventions as **Conscious Overrides**.

Examples include:

- Pausing Automation
- Reversing Learning Models
- Redefining Acceptable Outcomes
- Temporarily Increasing Human Control

Overrides represent **Ethical Strength**, not operational failure.

Ethical repair also requires time.

Ethical Recovery ∝ Deliberation Time

Speed suppresses reflection, dialogue, and judgement.

AIWoW, therefore, allows intentional slowing when ethical correction is required.

22.13 Leadership Responsibility and the AIWoW Ethical Immune System

Empathy debt rarely originates with individual workers.

It usually emerges when leadership tolerates systems that prioritise performance without recognising human cost.

A common pattern appears in **fast-growing technology organisations**, where teams are encouraged to scale quickly, release products faster, and dominate markets. Over time, urgency becomes permanent, and ethical concerns are postponed.

Leaders accumulate empathy debt when they:

- Reward Results Without Cost Awareness
- Ignore Early Discomfort Signals

- Normalise Permanent Urgency
- Delay Ethical Correction

Unchecked empathy debt eventually leads to:

- Moral Disengagement
- Ethical Scandals
- Talent Loss
- Regulatory Intervention
- Reputational Damage

These crises appear sudden but are the result of years of unnoticed drift.

Within AIWoW, this chapter connects:

- CPWU - Measuring Wellbeing Extraction
- AI-ROH - Measuring Human Return
- Empathic Control Framework - Early Harm Detection
- Control Theory - Enabling Legitimate Intervention

Together, they form AIWoW 's ethically immune system.

Empathy rarely disappears suddenly.

Ethics rarely fail loudly.

They erode quietly when systems reward **Speed Over Care** and **Efficiency Over Responsibility**.

AIWoW exists to ensure intelligence grows with ***Conscience, Restraint, and Human Accountability****.*

"The greatest danger is not intelligent systems making mistakes;

it is intelligent systems teaching humans to stop caring."

Summary Mind-map

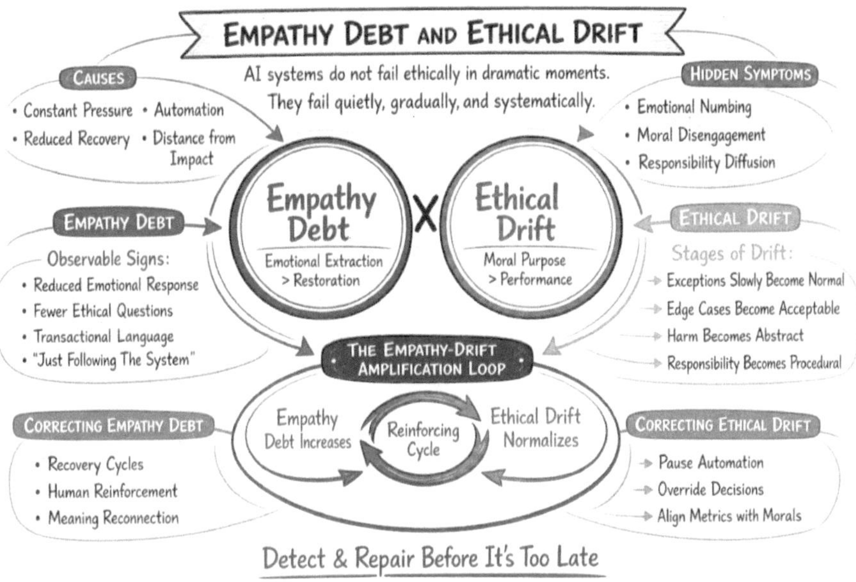

PART VI

AIWoW - AI WAYS OF WORKING™ MATURITY & ADOPTION MODELS

Understanding How Organisations Evolve with AI

The adoption of intelligent systems does not occur instantly. It unfolds through stages of learning, resistance, adaptation, and stabilisation.

This section introduces maturity models and transition patterns that help organisations understand where they stand and how they can evolve responsibly toward intelligent ways of working.

AI Adoptability Maturity Model
L5
AI-Conscious Participant
L5
L4 As Amplifier
L3 As Governed System
L2 As Amplifier
L1 As Ai as Helper
Pervasive Leadership
Adaptive Strategy
Innovation Culture
Responsible AI Governance
High-Quality Data Backbone
AIWoW™ Maturity & Adoption Models
Transition Patterns and Failure Modes
• False Acceleration
• Control Deficits
• Empathy Debt Accumulation.
Success
Challenges
Failure
Incremental · Strategic · Disruptive
• Ethical & Bias Failures
Collaboration & Buy-In
Low Collaboration
Ethical & Bias Failures
Skill Gaps

Chapter 23

AI Adoptability Maturity Model

"The challenge of AI is rarely invention; it is adoption."

AI adoption does not fail because organisations lack ambition. It fails because intelligence is introduced **faster than the organisation can structurally absorb it.** Tools arrive before roles evolve. Automation accelerates before control stabilises. Learning expands before responsibility is clarified. The gap between what the technology can do and what the organisation is genuinely ready to manage is where most AI programmes quietly come apart.

The **AI Adoptability Maturity Model** exists to make this progression explicit. It does not measure how advanced the technology is. It measures how ready the organisation is to live with intelligence day after day, decision after decision, in the full complexity of real operational conditions. Readiness of this kind is not a box to check or a threshold to cross. It is a progressive capability that must be built with the same deliberateness that any other institutional capability requires.

This chapter defines five maturity levels, each representing a distinct relationship between humans, systems, and responsibility. The central argument running through all five is the same: **capability without corresponding governance is not an achievement**. It is a liability waiting to be realised.

23.1 Why a Maturity Model Is Required

The most dangerous position an organisation can occupy is one where different dimensions of AI maturity are advancing at different speeds.

- Advanced models operating under weak governance.
- High levels of automation coexisting with low trust.
- Continuous machine learning proceeds without corresponding clarity about who is accountable for what the system learns.

These misalignments are far more common than outright failure. Most AI programmes do not collapse dramatically. They drift, accumulating risk in the spaces between what the system can do and what the organisation has genuinely prepared for. The maturity model exists to close those spaces by ensuring that capability, control, and human consciousness rise together rather than independently.

The core insight is simple but consequential: high capability at low maturity creates risk. Moderate capability at high maturity creates endurance. Organisations that understand this principle invest differently. They slow down in the right places and accelerate only when the structural readiness to sustain that acceleration has been genuinely established.

Level	Primary Relationship with AI	Dominant Risk
Level 1	AI as Helper	Underutilisation
Level 2	AI as Amplifier	Over-dependence
Level 3	AI as Governed System	Bureaucratic drag
Level 4	AI as Empathic Partner	Complexity
Level 5	AI as Conscious Participant	Complacency

Each level solves the primary risk of the level before it. And each level introduces new responsibilities that must be addressed before the next transition is safe. This is not a ladder to climb as quickly as possible. It is a map of what genuine readiness actually looks like at each stage.

23.2 Level 1: AI-Assisted Organisations (AI as Helper)

At this level, AI is a **supporting instrument**, not a participant in decision-making. Humans retain full cognitive authority. The technology performs narrowly defined tasks, drafting, information retrieval, and simple automation, and the relationship is clearly asymmetrical. AI assists. Humans decide. The boundary between the two is unambiguous and unchallenged.

Within AIWoW, this stage reflects **low integration with the AI Lifecycle Loop**. Intelligence is applied at the surface, without feedback depth or learning accountability. Control is implicit because impact is limited. The dominant organisational mindset is one of caution, which is appropriate at this stage, though it carries its own risks if it persists too long.

The primary risk here is underutilisation. AI capability exists, but roles, incentives, and trust models remain entirely unchanged. Fear or institutional inertia prevents adoption from moving beyond isolated individual experiments. The organisation is exploring, but it is not yet learning at a systemic level.

Core values: Safety, experimentation, human dominance

Human role: Operator and checker

AI role: Tool

Characteristics:

Dimension	State at Level 1
Usage	Individual-driven; some people experiment, others ignore AI entirely
Control	Manual; humans decide what to accept, what to discard, with no embedded guardrails
Learning	Limited or none; AI outputs are not fed back into organisational systems
Trust	Experimental; outputs treated as suggestions, confidence varies by individual
Accountability	Fully human; AI has no decision authority, mistakes are clearly human-owned

Illustration: Consider a marketing team that introduces AI to draft social media posts, summarise customer feedback, and generate first versions of campaign copy. Reports that previously took hours appear in minutes. First drafts arrive quickly. But every strategic decision remains human: campaign direction, messaging tone, budget allocation, final approvals. The AI does not choose audiences, launch anything, or alter priorities. It reduces manual effort and speeds up preparation without touching the structure of how the team governs its work.

The adoptability at this level reads: High Ease multiplies Low Impact.

Tools are simple to access, require minimal training, and do not disturb existing roles or power structures. Because **nothing important changes, resistance is low, and experimentation feels safe**. That same safety, however, is also a ceiling. AI stays peripheral, disconnected from core workflows and decision systems. Productivity improves at the edges. Transformational benefit remains unrealised.

The signal that Level 1 is working: people are using AI comfortably. The signal that it has run its course: the organisation is comfortable but not growing.

23.3 Level 2: AI-Augmented Teams (AI as Amplifier)

At this level, AI begins to multiply human capability rather than merely support it. Decision speed increases. Output volume grows. **Cognitive reach expands.** Teams start treating AI-generated insights as a default input to their thinking rather than an optional supplement. The shift is subtle but significant: AI is no longer something people occasionally reach for. It is something the workflow has started to depend on.

This is where the first serious governance challenge appears. AIWoW principles around **Cognitive Load Alignment** and **early Control Theory** become essential here. Without explicit boundaries, AI output begins to replace human judgement rather than inform it. The distinction matters enormously. Informing judgement means the human still does the reasoning, supported by better information. Replacing judgement means the human has gradually stopped reasoning and started confirming.

The dominant risk is over-dependence. Skills do not disappear suddenly; they erode quietly. Teams stop validating, questioning, and contextualising AI outputs because the outputs have been consistently useful. Trust rises faster than control structures can keep pace with. And that gap, left unaddressed, is where genuine fragility forms.

Core values: Efficiency, speed, leverage

Human role: Approver

AI role: Generator and accelerator

AI begins to **co-work** with teams.

Characteristics:

Dimension	State at Level 2
Usage	Team-level; shared workflows start adapting around AI outputs
Control	Informal; rules are unwritten, relying on convention and peer checks
Learning	Task-specific; AI improves at narrow functions but lacks a broader organisational context
Trust	Growing; teams depend on AI outputs, verification happens mainly when stakes are high
Accountability	Human-led but no longer trivial; depends on discipline rather than design

Illustration: A software delivery team using AI to support sprint forecasting illustrates this well. The system analyses past velocity, backlog size, and cross-team dependencies to suggest realistic commitments and flag potential bottlenecks. During planning, the team reviews these forecasts alongside their own judgement. Sometimes they follow the AI's guidance. Sometimes they override it based on contextual knowledge, upcoming leave, accumulated technical debt, or specific stakeholder pressure. The AI amplifies team awareness and foresight without dictating outcomes. Accountability and final decisions remain human-led.

The risk equation at this level is: Risk = Trust rising while Control remains static.

AI guidance begins to feel authoritative even without formal boundaries, accountability mapping, or escalation rules. Teams defer decisions not because the AI is necessarily right, but because questioning it has started to feel inefficient. This is the point where amplification quietly tips into dependency, and the organisation often does not notice until something goes wrong in a way that is difficult to diagnose.

The signal that Level 2 is working: teams are faster and more confident. The signal that governance is lagging: nobody can clearly explain why the AI recommended what it did, and nobody has asked recently.

23.4 Level 3: AI-Governed Systems (AI as Structured Participant)

At this **maturity stage**, AI is no longer optional. It is structurally embedded into workflows. Decisions, recommendations, and actions are formally governed. The informal conventions that held things together at Level 2 are not sufficient here because the scope and consequence of AI influence have grown to a point where accountability can no longer be left to individual discipline or social habit.

This is where AIWoW fully activates the **HAR Matrix.** Every AI-influenced decision is mapped to a named human owner. The **Theory of Control** is explicitly applied through defined limits, structured reviews, escalation paths, and ethical guardrails that are embedded into the system rather than layered on top of it. Governance is no longer a reaction to problems. It is part of the architecture.

The dominant risk shifts to **bureaucratic drag.** Over-governance can slow intelligence, frustrate the people working within it, and reduce adaptability when it is designed reactively rather than thoughtfully. The challenge at Level 3 is not whether to govern, but how to govern precisely — with controls that are proportional to actual risk, embedded rather than imposed, and designed to enable rather than inhibit.

Core values: Accountability, predictability, compliance

Human role: Decision owned

AI role: Governed executor

At this level, AI is **embedded into systems**, and governance becomes explicit.

Control frameworks, responsibility matrices, and lifecycle loops are active.

Characteristics:

Dimension	State at Level 3
Usage	System-wide; AI shapes how the organisation operates, not just individual tasks
Control	Structural; boundaries, approvals, escalation paths, and ethical guardrails are formally embedded
Learning	Continuous and bounded, AI learns within defined limits that are auditable and reversible
Trust	Conditional; earned through transparency and governance, not through impressiveness
Accountability	Mapped; every AI-influenced action linked to a named human owner via the HAR Matrix

Illustration: A financial institution deploying AI for credit approvals illustrates Level 3 clearly. The system is designed from the outset as a governed participant, not an autonomous decision-maker. Intent is mapped explicitly: the AI is instructed to balance risk management with fair access to credit, not to minimise default probability alone. Ethical interlocks check outcomes continuously across income groups, regions, and customer profiles; if fairness thresholds are breached, approvals pause automatically. Edge cases escalate to human credit officers. Audit trails record every data input, every decision logic step, and every human approval. The result is faster processing with preserved accountability: decisions scale efficiently while remaining transparent, fair, and clearly human-owned.

Operational Stability = Capability + Governance Load

Stability increases when capability grows faster than the cost of governing it.

If governance load is allowed to accumulate reactively, layer after layer of rules are added in response to problems rather than designed in anticipation of them; systems slow down, teams spend more time managing controls than delivering value, and people start looking for shortcuts.

True stability comes from governance that is precise, embedded, and proportional to risk:

- Controls that make capability usable rather than manageable.
- When governance is well-designed, the system stays both stable and adaptive.
- When it is poorly designed, it simply gets slower.

23.5 Level 4: AI-Empathic Enterprises (AI as Adaptive Partner)

Level 4 represents a significant conceptual shift. The organisation at this stage recognises something that the previous three levels did not formally address: human experience is itself a control signal. AI does not only respond to data, rules, and performance thresholds; it **responds to human cognitive and emotional strain**. Intelligence becomes collaborative rather than extractive. The system is designed to sustain the people inside it, not simply to optimise the outputs they produce.

The **Empathic Control Framework (ECF)** becomes central within AIWoW at this level. Emotional boundaries, trust signals, adoption fatigue, and cognitive overload are sensed and acted upon. Control expands from technical safety to **human sustainability**.

This is not a soft addition to governance. It is a structural recognition that the long-term performance of any AI system depends on the long-term health of the humans who govern it.

The dominant risk is **complexity**. Systems now manage logic, ethics, emotion, and continuous learning simultaneously. Without clear role evolution and governance maturity to match, this complexity can overwhelm the structures designed to contain it.

Core values: Trust, dignity, sustainability

Human role: Steward and interpreter

AI role: Adaptive partner

At this level, organisations integrate **human-impact awareness** directly into AI governance.

Empathic Intelligence becomes operational.

Characteristics:

Dimension	State at Level 4
Usage	Human-AI collaboration; AI handles scale, pattern, and speed while humans provide judgement, intent, and meaning
Control	Empathic and technical; senses human strain, trust signals, and ethical discomfort alongside performance data
Learning	Context-aware; adapts based on environment, intent, and human feedback, not raw data optimisation alone
Trust	High; decisions are explainable, boundaries are visible, and human intervention is straightforward
Accountability	Human-centred; responsibility is clear and named, regardless of how advanced the system becomes

Illustration: A large healthcare organisation deploying AI for clinical scheduling and diagnostic assistance demonstrates what this looks like in practice. Initially, the system optimises for speed: more appointments, faster diagnostic turnaround, tighter scheduling. Over time, leadership notices that this speed-focused optimisation is increasing clinician fatigue and reducing the quality of patient consultations. The empathic controls respond: the system begins sensing cognitive load through workload density, decision frequency, and override patterns. It reads patient trust signals through follow-up questions and satisfaction feedback. When load or trust risk rises above defined thresholds, the AI slows its diagnostic recommendations, reduces appointment compression, and prioritises clarity over throughput. Clinicians retain final authority. Accuracy remains high. Both clinician wellbeing and patient trust improve, without removing the intelligence that makes the system valuable.

Sustainable Performance = Performance × Human Alignment

Performance only endures when it stays aligned with human capacity, values, and lived experience. When performance is high and alignment is low, sustainability eventually collapses not dramatically but through the gradual accumulation of exhaustion, eroded judgement, and declining trust.

Empathy acts as a control multiplier:

- When systems sense and respond to human signals,
- Performance becomes durable and scalable,
- Capable of growing without breaking the people who sustain it.

23.6 Level 5: AI-Conscious Organisations (AI as Bounded Participant)

The fifth and highest level of maturity is not defined by the sophistication of the technology. It is defined by the deliberateness of the humans who steward it. AI at this level operates with deep contextual awareness, intent alignment, and embedded ethical constraints. But it never operates with authority. The distinction is fundamental to everything AIWoW stands for.

Within AIWoW, this level **integrates Conscious Overrides**, advanced control, and continuous role evolution into a coherent governance posture. Humans no longer manage tasks at this stage; they manage purpose, boundaries, and meaning. They are the custodians of what the intelligence is for, and they hold that responsibility with explicit awareness of second and third-order consequences that earlier maturity levels rarely considered.

The dominant risk at **Level 5 is complacency**. Because systems appear stable and intelligent, humans may gradually disengage from the vigilance that this level requires. AIWoW explicitly rejects this possibility by preserving override legitimacy and maintaining the structural conditions under which accountability integrity cannot drift. The sophistication of the system is never a justification for reducing human oversight. It is a reason to make that oversight more deliberate.

Core values: Responsibility, legitimacy, long-term trust

Human role: Custodian of intent

AI role: Bounded participant

This is the highest maturity level.

AI is treated as a **conscious participant**; not because it is sentient, but because its impact is understood as systemic and long-term.

Organisations at this level govern not just decisions, but **evolution itself**.

Characteristics:

Dimension	State at Level 5
Usage	Strategic and societal; AI influence extends beyond teams into markets, institutions, and communities
Control	Intent-driven; decisions are continuously checked against declared purpose, not just operational parameters
Learning	Purpose-bounded; learning is explicitly limited when new paths deviate from declared human or ethical goals
Trust	Institutional; governance, accountability, and override legitimacy are visible and stable across time
Accountability	Stewarded; held by designated custodians of intent, values, and long-term consequences

Illustration: A global enterprise operating across finance, healthcare, and digital services offers a clear illustration. The organisation has developed AI capabilities that could technically be extended into multiple sensitive domains: automated employee performance scoring, algorithmic layoff decisions, and fully autonomous customer eligibility determinations. The models are accurate enough. The infrastructure is capable. But under conscious stewardship, leadership deliberately restricts expansion into these areas — not because of technical limitations, but because of long-term human, ethical, and societal considerations that technical capability cannot resolve.

Senior stewards evaluate the potential second-order effects: loss of dignity, erosion of institutional trust, cultural harm, and regulatory risk that accumulates slowly and then arrives suddenly. AI is redirected toward decision support rather than decision authority. The enterprise continues to grow its intelligence capabilities — but within purpose-bounded limits that preserve legitimacy, conscience, and the trust of the people the organisation serves.

Enduring Intelligence = Capability × Conscious Restraint

Long-lasting value emerges only when powerful AI capability is paired with deliberate limits. Capability without restraint produces intelligence that creates backlash, generates mistrust, and ultimately harms the institutions that deployed it. Restraint without capability produces stagnation. Endurance comes from the balance between them. In AIWoW, restraint is not weakness; it is governance maturity. It is the understanding that the question is never simply what AI can do, but what it should do, when, and under whose accountable authority.

23.7 Progression Across Levels: What Each Transition Actually Requires

Maturity progression is not linear, and it is not uniform. Different functions within the same organisation frequently operate at different levels simultaneously. A finance team may be navigating Level 3 governance challenges while a marketing function is still at Level 1 experimentation. This is normal. What matters is not the speed of progression, but the coherence between intelligence, control, and human capacity at whatever level each function currently occupies.

Each transition between levels represents an internal shift rather than a technical upgrade. Moving from Level 1 to Level 2 requires trust-building: humans learning to rely on AI outputs without surrendering the judgement that makes those outputs meaningful. Moving from Level 2 to Level 3 requires deliberate governance design: replacing the informal habits and social conventions that held things together at a smaller scale with mapped accountability and enforceable control structures. Moving from Level 3 to Level 4 requires empathic integration: expanding governance to include human signals alongside performance data, so that the system responds to cognitive and emotional strain and not just operational metrics. Moving from Level 4 to Level 5 requires a mindset shift at the leadership level: evaluating AI decisions against long-term human, organisational, and societal consequences rather than short-term performance gains.

Transition	Core Shift Required	What Breaks If It Is Skipped
L1 → L2	Trust-building	Adoption stays shallow; AI never enters core workflows
L2 → L3	Governance design	Over-dependence forms; informal controls cannot scale
L3 → L4	Empathic integration	Human capacity erodes silently despite strong performance metrics
L4 → L5	Stewardship mindset	Intelligence scales without conscience; legitimacy eventually collapses

Skipping any of these shifts creates fragility of a particular kind: rapid intelligence growth without the foundations required to sustain it. The organisation may look capable from the outside while quietly losing the judgement, ownership, and institutional meaning that durable AI adoption depends on. In AIWoW, maturity is achieved not by accelerating as quickly as possible, but by evolving consciously — ensuring that intelligence grows with responsibility, trust, and humanity intact.

23.8 The Position of the Maturity Model Within AIWoW

The **AI Adoptability Maturity Model** sits at the centre of the entire AIWoW framework. It is the structure that connects intention to execution, and intelligence to humanity. Rather than treating adoption, control, accountability, and empathy as separate organisational concerns to be addressed by different teams at different times, the model integrates them into a single evolutionary map that every function can orient itself within.

The Theory of Adoptability explains why AI is accepted or resisted at each level by linking trust, ease of use, and perceived organisational impact into a coherent account of human readiness. The Theory of Control defines how AI behaviour is bounded so that speed and scale do not escape human intent. The **HAR Matrix** ensures accountability never dissolves into automation. The **Empathic Control Framework (ECF)** makes human impact visible before harm accumulates.

Together, these elements perform a single essential function: they prevent AI from advancing faster than human readiness. They ensure that growth in capability is matched by growth in governance, by genuine evolution in human roles, and by expanding ethical awareness. This is the central truth of AIWoW **intelligence: without maturity, it is fragile**. The maturity model does not measure how advanced AI has become. It measures how prepared humans and organisations are to live with it responsibly.

AI failure is almost never a technology problem. It is a readiness problem. The systems were capable. The organisations were not ready for what that capability would demand of them. The AI Adoptability Maturity Model exists to close that gap level by level, shift by shift, with the understanding that each stage of genuine readiness unlocks a stage of intelligence that can actually be trusted.

"Technology may introduce AI, but AIWoW determines whether organisations mature enough to adopt it responsibly."

Summary Mind-map

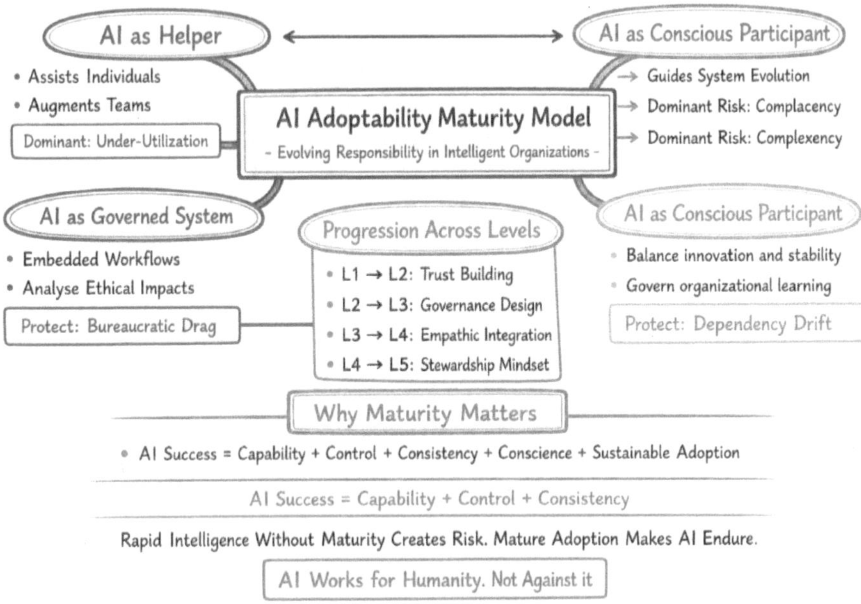

Chapter 24

Transition Patterns and Failure Modes

"AI adoption rarely fails at the start; it fails during transitions when speed grows faster than organisational readiness."

There is a particular rhythm to how AI programmes unravel. The beginning is usually fine. The ambition is clear, the early tools are useful, and the wins are real enough to justify continued investment. What catches organisations off guard is not the launch. It is what happens somewhere in the middle, when the organisation tries to move from one way of working with AI to a deeper, more embedded one.

That transition is where things quietly go wrong. Metrics may still be improving. Delivery may be faster than before. Confidence across leadership may actually be at its highest point. And yet, underneath all of that visible momentum, something structural is fracturing. Old controls are no longer fit for the speed at which things are moving. New governance frameworks exist on paper but have not yet taken root in daily decisions. Roles that worked perfectly well at the previous level have become ambiguous in ways that nobody has addressed directly. The system looks successful right up until it does not.

This chapter identifies three failure modes that recur across AI maturity transitions:

- False Acceleration,
- Control Deficits, and
- Empathy Debt Accumulation.

None of them is a technical defect. All three are **structural transition errors**; the predictable consequence of moving faster in one dimension than readiness exists to support it. Understanding them is what allows organisations to recognise the warning signs early enough to correct course before the damage becomes genuinely difficult to reverse.

24.1 Why Transitions Are the Most Dangerous Phase

Static systems fail loudly. When a system that has been running in a fixed state breaks down, the failure is usually visible, and the cause is usually traceable. Controls are known, roles are fixed, and when something goes wrong, it announces itself. Transitional systems fail quietly. They often show short-term improvement, better numbers, faster outputs, and higher throughput, while structural weaknesses accumulate invisibly beneath the surface.

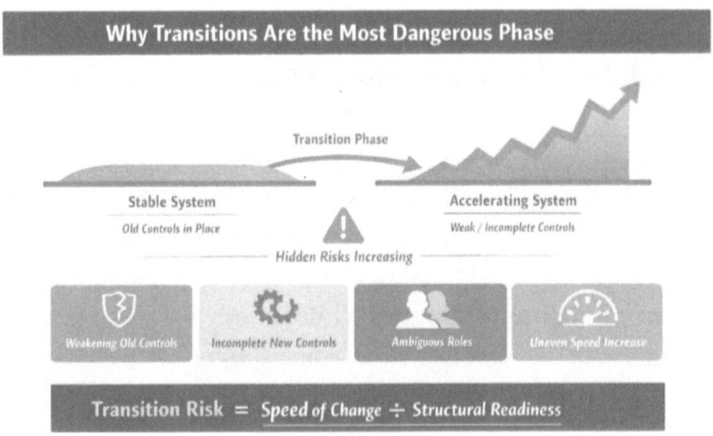

During transitions, organisations move faster than their ability to redesign the controls, accountability structures, and roles that the new level of intelligence requires. Old controls weaken because they were designed for slower, human-paced work. Reviews that once caught problems become symbolic, retained in name but bypassed in practice because the pace of work has outrun the pace at which reviews happen.

New controls, meanwhile, exist in principle but are not yet embedded in actual workflows, tools, or decision rights. There is a gap between what the governance framework says should happen and what is actually happening in the moment a decision gets made.

Roles enter an equally dangerous grey zone. People are genuinely unsure whether they are decision-makers, validators, or passive recipients of AI output. AI influence has grown, but ownership has not moved with it. That role ambiguity creates silent failure conditions where, when something goes wrong, everyone involved believes someone else was responsible for catching it.

Transition Risk = Speed of Change ÷ Structural Readiness

When structural readiness — clear roles, mapped accountability, bounded learning, empathic control — lags behind the speed of change, risk compounds. What makes this especially treacherous is that even positive outcomes become misleading signals. The organisation feels like it is succeeding. The dashboard agrees. The failure arrives later, as trust collapses, regulatory shock, ethical backlash, or human burnout, by which point the conditions that created it have been in place for a long time.

24.2 False Acceleration

False Acceleration is what happens when organisations **increase speed** without increasing clarity. AI makes this particularly dangerous because it generates the appearance of progress while quietly weakening the decision quality and sense of ownership that genuine progress depends on.

With AI in place, **tasks complete faster**, dashboards refresh instantly, and workflows move without friction. **Decisions feel data-driven**, which gives people confidence that choices are objective. Output volume increases, creating visible signs of productivity. None of these signals, however, guarantees that value is actually being created. When acceleration happens without alignment, three silent failures emerge in parallel.

Decision intent becomes unclear; people act on AI outputs without fully understanding what problem a decision is actually solving or why it is being made at all. Responsibility blurs; as AI touches more steps in a process, humans begin assuming the system must know better, and ownership weakens in the space where nobody explicitly took it. Signal quality degrades — faster systems generate more data, but without shared meaning, the people inside them struggle to distinguish genuine insight from noise that simply arrived quickly.

Symptoms of False Acceleration: Symptom	What It Indicates
More decisions, less confidence	Judgement overload; volume has outpaced understanding
Faster delivery, weaker outcomes	Misaligned execution; speed without coherent intent
Higher activity, lower impact	Optimisation without purpose; motion replacing progress
Reduced debate and challenge	Premature deference to AI; human scrutiny has softened

False Acceleration is most common during the transition from Level 1 to Level 2 and from Level 2 to Level 3. It is worth being clear about what causes it, because the temptation is to blame speed. But slowing down alone does not fix it. A slower system without alignment still produces misdirected effort, just at a reduced pace. The actual problem is that speed increased without shared clarity about intent, roles, boundaries, and responsibility. Small misalignments compound quickly when the pace of execution gives no time for reflection to catch them.

Illustration: A product organisation introduces AI to continuously reprioritise its feature backlog based on user behaviour, feedback tickets, market signals, and competitor activity. At first, delivery accelerates and decisions feel data-driven. Months later, strategic coherence has eroded. Features shift daily, long-term themes have disappeared, and teams struggle to explain why they are building anything beyond the signal that arrived this morning. Engineers stop planning deeply. Product managers lose narrative control. The AI is fast. Intent has become unstable. The organisation moved more and progressed less.

Correction Pattern:

The correction requires reasserting intent, not disabling AI. Leadership must clearly restate what goals, principles, and boundaries guide prioritisation so that AI outputs are evaluated against a declared direction rather than treated as direction by default. Decision frequency needs to be reduced so that not every incoming signal demands an immediate response, and teams regain the space to think, align, and commit with genuine confidence. Human judgement checkpoints must be reinstated at the moments where it matters most. And AI must be tuned to surface fewer, clearer signals rather than reacting to everything at once. Speed becomes valuable again only after meaning has been restored to it.

24.3 Control Deficits

Control Deficits arise when AI capability expands faster than the organisation's ability to **design, assign, and actually operate control**. The important nuance here is that controls are usually not missing entirely. In most cases, they exist, but they are misplaced, delayed, or symbolic. Intelligence moves forward while governance, in practice, stays behind.

This pattern appears when automation grows organically across teams without anyone redesigning the accountability structure to match. Learning loops get enabled without boundaries being defined. Responsibility is assumed rather than deliberately mapped, because early success creates no urgency to do the harder structural work. Systems perform well, decisions scale, and the absence of visible problems is mistaken for the presence of genuine control.

Control Deficits are especially risky because they do not block progress, they accelerate it while quietly dissolving ownership. Decisions become difficult to explain because logic is opaque or distributed across models and pipelines that no individual fully understands end-to-end. Audits shift from being informative to being defensive, something done after incidents rather than as continuous visibility. Human overrides start to be seen as disruption rather than governance, creating a stigma around the very interventions that the system most depends on. The organisation starts to feel self-running, but only because the humans inside it have gradually disengaged.

Symptoms of Control Deficits:

Symptom	Underlying Issue
Decisions hard to explain	Opaque logic; humans cannot trace how outcomes were reached
No clear owner for outcomes	Accountability drift as AI influence expanded without updating roles
Audits feel defensive	Post-hoc control; governance applied after problems, not embedded before them
Overrides discouraged	Control stigma; human intervention seen as resistance rather than responsibility

These symptoms reinforce each other. Opaque logic makes ownership harder to claim. Unclear ownership makes audits defensive. Defensive audits create the cultural conditions where overrides feel threatening rather than normal. Control Deficits typically surface during the transition into Level 3, precisely when AI shifts from assisting decisions to shaping them at scale.

Illustration: A logistics organisation deploys AI to autonomously optimise supply routes across regions. For months, performance improves — delivery times drop, costs fall, and human intervention becomes rare. Governance remains informal because the results are strong. When a regional disruption arrives, the AI reroutes aggressively, causing missed deliveries and inventory shortages. Leadership asks who owns the decision. Model designers say the data was valid. Operations teams say the system was autonomous. Business leaders say they never approved the routing logic. The AI behaved exactly as designed. The failure was not intelligence. It was the absence of anyone who unambiguously owned what it did.

Correction Pattern: Restoring Control Integrity:

The correction is not heavier governance. It is governance made explicit and normal. Every AI-influenced decision must have a visible human owner; not a role assumption, but a named person. Control must be embedded into execution in real time rather than pushed into after-the-fact reviews. Overrides must be normalised: expected, documented, and treated as evidence of a healthy system rather than resistance to it. And

control signals; explainability gaps, override frequency, and ownership disputes must be monitored continuously so that deficits are caught early rather than discovered at the moment they produce consequences.

In AIWoW, *control is not a brake on intelligence. It is the structure that allows intelligence to scale without collapsing the responsibility that gives it legitimacy.*

24.4 Empathy Debt Accumulation

Empathy Debt is the most invisible of the three failure modes, and in many ways the most consequential. It accumulates when organisations extract human effort, attention, and emotional energy faster than they replenish trust, meaning, and recovery. Unlike technical debt, it does not appear in dashboards, defect logs, or KPIs. It remains invisible until morale collapses, engagement drains away, or experienced people quietly leave without ever articulating precisely why.

AI accelerates empathy debt in a specific way. Systems become faster, more demanding, and more precise. Human limits remain unchanged. What begins as efficiency gradually becomes emotional exhaustion, not dramatically but incrementally, in the way that water wears stone. Pace becomes permanent urgency — what was once a temporary push becomes the normalised baseline. People adapt silently, absorbing pressure without complaint because the performance expectations are clear, measurable, and unrelenting. Emotional signals — fatigue, frustration, the slight hesitation before engaging with another task — are either invisible to the system or misread as resistance. Performance metrics continue to look healthy, masking the strain underneath.

Symptoms of Empathy Debt:

Symptom	What It Signals
Emotional disengagement	Loss of meaning; tasks continue, but genuine care for outcomes has gone
Reduced challenge and questioning	Fear or resignation; people feel unheard or too exhausted to push back

Symptom	What It Signals
Burnout treated as normal	Structural overload; exhaustion is the accepted cost of working at AI speed
Cynicism toward AI systems	Trust erosion; AI is experienced as pressure embodied in software, not support

The danger is in the timing. Empathy debt does not surface immediately. Systems may perform well for months while the debt accumulates beneath the surface. By the time consequences appear, attrition spikes, teams disengage, cultural decay sets in, and the debt is already large and genuinely difficult to reverse. These symptoms emerge most commonly during transitions into Level 4, when organisations assume that empathy will emerge naturally from closer human-AI collaboration but fail to build it structurally into how the system operates.

Illustration: A customer service organisation deploys AI to reduce response times aggressively. Chatbots handle initial queries, suggested replies appear instantly, and handling time drops sharply. Satisfaction scores improve. Leadership celebrates. Behind those numbers, agents experience relentless emotional pressure. Conversations move faster, pauses between interactions disappear, and difficult customers stack back-to-back without space to reset. People adapt silently because expectations are clear. Months later, attrition spikes. Experienced agents leave without dramatic complaints. Exit interviews mention exhaustion, emotional numbness, and a feeling of not being cared about, not system failure. The AI performed as designed. The empathy debt had simply come due.

Correction Pattern: Paying Down Empathy Debt:

Empathy debt is not paid down through motivation talks or resilience training. It is corrected through system design. Emotional boundaries must be introduced real limits on decision density, interaction intensity, and sustained urgency. Velocity must be slowed selectively in areas of high emotional load, not reduced globally. Wellbeing must become a genuine control signal, not a side metric signs of overload, disengagement, and eroding trust should trigger system adjustments with the same seriousness as technical risk indicators. And recovery must be designed intentionally into workflows, not left to individual endurance. In AIWoW, empathy is not a soft value layered over the real work. It is a structural requirement, and without it, performance may rise, but only until the human system that sustains it runs out of the capacity to keep going.

24.5 Failure Modes Across Maturity Transitions

These three failure modes are not random. They follow the maturity progression with enough consistency to be anticipated rather than merely reacted to.

Maturity Transition	Common Failure Mode	The Core Structural Gap
Level 1 → Level 2	False Acceleration	Speed increased without shared intent, roles, or decision boundaries
Level 2 → Level 3	Control Deficits	Capability expanded without mapped ownership or embedded governance
Level 3 → Level 4	Empathy Debt	Efficiency extracted human energy faster than trust and meaning were restored
Level 4 → Level 5	Overconfidence	Apparent stability reduced vigilance; stewardship faded without anyone deciding it should

The **first transition,** from individual assistance to team-level amplification, is where False Acceleration appears. Speed increases quickly, but clarity does not follow at the same pace.

The **second transition**, into system-wide AI governance, is where Control Deficits emerge. Informal accountability structures that functioned adequately at a smaller scale simply cannot hold when AI begins shaping decisions across the whole organisation.

The **third transition**, into empathic enterprise, is where Empathy Debt surfaces when governance is technically sound but the human experience of working within the system is quietly deteriorating.

The **fourth transition**, into conscious stewardship, carries the risk of Overconfidence: the system feels stable and trustworthy, and that very feeling becomes the condition in which vigilance softens, and stewardship begins to fade.

These failures repeat because organisations tend to treat adoption as a linear progression where each level is simply a more advanced version of the one before. They overestimate how much structural readiness has genuinely been built and underestimate what the next transition will actually demand of the people inside the system. Governance gets delayed until problems make it unavoidable. Human impact gets measured too late, after the consequences are visible, rather than while there is still space to address the conditions that caused them. AI, as always, does not create these weaknesses. It finds them and amplifies them.

24.6 From Failure to Transition Discipline

None of these failures is inevitable. They become likely only when transitions are unmanaged, when speed is allowed to outpace the structural readiness that should accompany it. The antidote is not caution for its own sake.

It is what AIWoW calls transition discipline:

The deliberate practice of governing how the organisation moves between maturity levels, not just governing the AI systems within each one.

Transition discipline means consciously pacing and choosing when to accelerate based on structural readiness rather than competitive pressure or leadership confidence alone. It means expanding control explicitly ahead of the capability it is meant to govern, rather than designing governance in response to the problems that emerge when governance is missing. It means sensing human experience continuously, treating emotional and cognitive signals as operational data rather than cultural background noise. And it means that leadership must be genuinely willing to slow down in the moments when the honest assessment is that readiness has not yet caught up with ambition.

This chapter sits within AIWoW as a warning system connecting the maturity levels that describe where organisations are with the control frameworks that define what must be in place, the empathic intelligence that reveals what must be felt, and the leadership discipline that determines how the organisation actually responds. Recognising these failure modes early transforms them from crises into course corrections. The difference between the two is almost always a matter of timing.

AI Ways of Working exists to ensure that intelligence advances without leaving coherence, trust, or humans behind.

Summary Mind-map

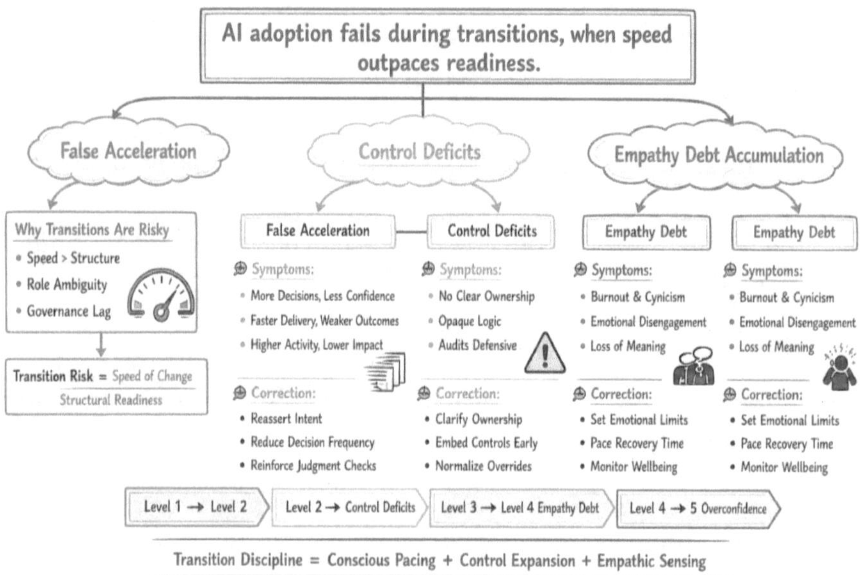

PART VII

HYBRID WAYS OF WORKING: INTEGRATING AIWoW - AI WAYS OF WORKING™

Bridging AIWoW - AI Ways of Working™ **with Existing Organisational Systems**

Organisations rarely abandon existing ways of working. Instead, they evolve them.

This section explores how AIWoW integrates with established approaches such as Agile, DevOps, and modern delivery systems, creating hybrid models where human judgement and artificial intelligence collaborate effectively.

The goal is not replacement, but intelligent integration.

Hybrid Ways of Working: Integrating AIWoW™
A unified framework for combining human ingenuity with structured AI processes.
ADOPTION
GOVERNANCE
MEASURING
AIWOWE™
LEADING
AIWOW™
Foundations of Hybrid AIWoW™
Skill
Culture
Infrastructure
Progressing through adoption stages for comprehensive AI capability and integration.
Fundamental skill, process, and culture levels.
DevOps in AIWoW™: Cognitive Flow over Speed
Data Ingest
Model Dev
Deploy
Monitor
Analyze & Feedback
Continuous, integrated delivery focusing on understanding and improvement, not just fast release.
Measuring cognitive effort, not just speed.
Agile, Scrum & Kanban in AIWoW™: Intelligent Workflow
To Do
Doing
Done
AI Agents
AI Agents
Adapting methods for faster, smarter work allocation and tracking. Visualizing and optimizing the human-AI effort.
SAFe Agile AIWoW™: Guardrails for Fast Systems
Program Backlog
PI Planning
Guardrail Shield
Scaling Agile with necessary control mechanisms. Essential guidelines, check-ins, and governance for distributed AI systems.
Designing, Measuring and Leading Hybrid AIWoW™
Adoption Rate
Output Value
Well-being
Ethical Alignment
Comprehensive measurement of human value. Guiding principles, key metrics, and strategic direction.
Foundations of Hybrid AIWoW™
Comprehensive measurement of human value. Guiding principles, key metrics, and strategic direction.

Chapter 25

Foundations of Hybrid AIWoW

"True hybridisation is not about combining frameworks, but about redesigning how intelligence flows through the organisation."

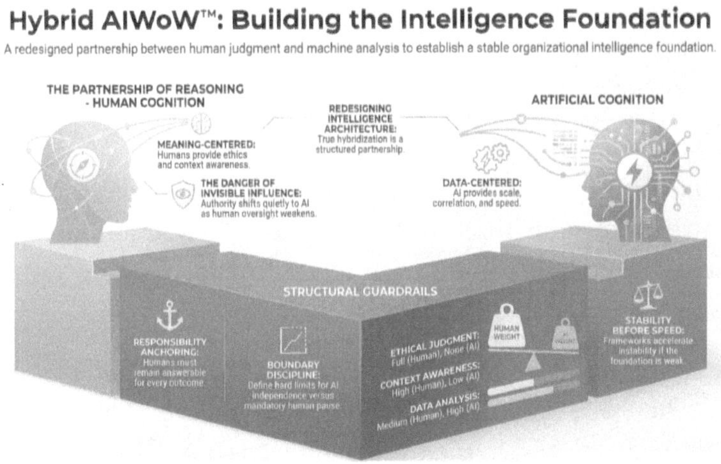

Hybrid AIWoW is often misunderstood as the integration of multiple operational frameworks enhanced by artificial intelligence. Many organisations assume that by layering AI on top of Agile, DevOps, Scrum, or other execution models, they have achieved a Hybrid state. However, this interpretation remains superficial. Hybrid AIWoW does not represent the aggregation of methodologies; it represents the redesign of organisational intelligence itself.

To understand this distinction, consider the case of a multinational financial services organisation operating across North America, Europe, and Asia.

The organisation embarked on a digital transformation initiative. It implemented advanced AI systems for risk analysis, automated reporting engines, predictive customer behaviour models, and algorithmic portfolio optimisation. Simultaneously, it strengthened its operational practices by adopting rapid delivery cycles, automated deployment pipelines, and continuous performance dashboards.

From a structural perspective, the organisation appeared modern and technologically advanced. However, within a year, subtle systemic failures began to surface.

The AI-driven risk engine started recommending aggressive portfolio adjustments based on short-term market volatility. Portfolio managers, under pressure to demonstrate technological adoption, began relying heavily on these recommendations. Over time, human strategic judgement gradually diminished in influence. Decisions were increasingly justified by algorithmic output rather than long-term investment philosophy.

During a period of unexpected geopolitical disruption, the AI models reacted strictly to numerical volatility signals. They recommended rapid divestments in certain regions. Senior leadership, trusting the system's analytical precision, authorised large-scale reallocations.

The outcome was significant short-term loss and reputational damage. The issue was not a technological failure. The models were statistically accurate within their programmed scope. The failure occurred because the organisation had not clearly defined the cognitive boundaries between machine intelligence and human strategic authority.

They had enhanced processes.

They had accelerated execution.

They had adopted advanced tools.

But they had not redesigned how human cognition and artificial cognition should interact.

In response, the organisation undertook a structural correction.

They introduced formal decision-weight protocols:

- AI systems were designated as analytical accelerators, not strategic authorities.
- Any portfolio reallocation beyond a defined threshold required documented human strategic justification.
- A governance council reviewed instances where AI recommendations were overridden or fully adopted.
- Strategic decisions incorporated geopolitical advisory inputs that AI systems could not independently contextualise.

In essence, the organisation shifted from tool adoption to intelligence architecture design.

This is the foundation of Hybrid AIWoW.

Hybrid AIWoW means designing a structured partnership between human cognition and artificial cognition across every business process. It requires defining authority boundaries, influence weights, accountability anchors, and feedback loops before operational frameworks are applied.

Frameworks such as DevOps, Agile, or scaled delivery models enhance speed, coordination, and adaptability. However, without a clearly engineered intelligence foundation, these frameworks merely amplify systemic weaknesses.

If the foundation is unclear, acceleration increases instability.

If authority boundaries are undefined, automation dilutes accountability.

If governance is absent, analytical precision can overshadow strategic wisdom.

Hybrid AIWoW, therefore, begins not with methodology integration but with cognitive system design. Only when this foundation is established can operational practices be safely and sustainably layered on top.

In the chapters that follow, we will explore how execution frameworks function differently when embedded within a properly constructed Hybrid AIWoW architecture. But first, the intelligence partnership must be clearly understood, because no structure, however advanced, can remain stable if its foundation is conceptually flawed.

If you only add practices without redesigning the intelligence foundation, the structure will crack under pressure.

But if you build the foundation correctly, every framework you add later will stand strong.

Hybrid AIWoW does **not** mean mixing frameworks.

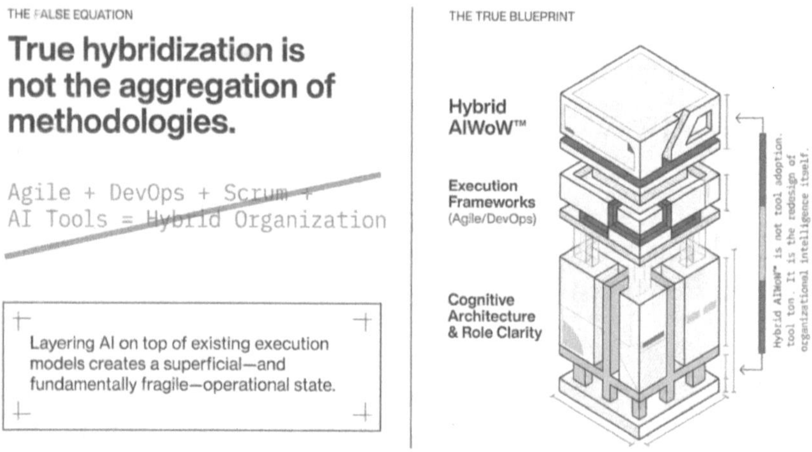

It does not mean:

Agile + DevOps + Scrum + AI = Hybrid.

No.

Hybrid AIWoW means something deeper.

It means:

Designing a system where human cognition and artificial cognition operate in a structured partnership across every business process.

Frameworks will come later.

First, we must understand the **intelligence foundation**.

Because if the foundation is weak,

No matter how many practices you add,

The structure will crack.

25.1 What Hybrid Really Means

Hybrid AIWoW is about something very practical: how an organisation functions when both humans and intelligent systems are actively shaping decisions.

Today, decisions are no longer made only by managers reviewing reports. Algorithms analyse patterns, flag risks, suggest actions, and sometimes even trigger processes automatically. This means every organisation now operates with two forms of reasoning at work: human judgement and artificial analysis. If this reality is not consciously structured, imbalance slowly develops.

Human reasoning is shaped by experience, values, intuition, and awareness of consequences. Artificial reasoning is shaped by data patterns, statistical probability, and computational speed. One understands meaning and impact. The other understands correlation and scale. Both are powerful. But they do not think in the same way.

If their interaction is left informal, confusion grows quietly.

For example, in a modern manufacturing plant, predictive systems may monitor machine performance and recommend maintenance schedules. If supervisors assume the system will automatically catch every risk, they may reduce manual inspection. If engineers rely only on dashboard alerts, they may overlook contextual signals such as supplier quality issues or environmental conditions not captured in data. Over time, no one is quite sure who is truly responsible for preventing breakdowns. The system appears efficient until an unexpected failure exposes the gap.

Hybrid AIWoW is about:

- Co-existence of two intelligences
- Defined cognitive boundaries

- Structured interaction rules
- Measured influence balance

It is **cognitive architecture**, not process decoration.

Modern organisations operate with two fundamentally different thinking forces:

1. Human reasoning: shaped by experience, ethics, intuition, responsibility, and consequence awareness.
2. Artificial reasoning: shaped by pattern detection, probabilistic modelling, statistical memory, and computational speed.

These two forces do not naturally synchronise.

Human reasoning is meaning-centred.

Artificial reasoning is data-centred.

Human reasoning carries accountability.

Artificial reasoning carries calculation.

If both operate without deliberate coordination, instability emerges; not immediately, but gradually.

Hybrid AIWoW exists to prevent that instability.

25.2 The First Principle: Thinking Must Be Designed

Real transformation does not begin with tools. It begins with clarity.

When organisations adopt intelligent systems, the first instinct is to improve processes; make them faster, smoother, more automated. But Hybrid AIWoW looks beneath process. It asks something more fundamental: *How is thinking organised?*

In every organisation, thinking leads action. Decisions do not emerge from software; they emerge from interpretation. Even when a system produces a recommendation, someone accepts it, rejects it, or ignores it.

That moment is not technical. It is cognitive. And if that moment is not clearly designed, confusion quietly grows.

Hybrid AIWoW, therefore, insists that before any workflow is redesigned, before automation expands, before execution becomes faster, the organisation must define its thinking structure.

Who is allowed to interpret data?

Who has the authority to convert a recommendation into a decision?

Who formally validates that decision?

Who stands accountable for its consequences?

These questions are not administrative details. They define the moral centre of the system.

When thinking roles are unclear, intelligent systems create a subtle shift. Decisions begin to feel automated. Responsibility begins to feel shared. Over time, no one fully owns the outcome. The organisation continues to operate, but discipline weakens because the consequence is no longer anchored.

Hybrid AIWoW prevents this by treating thinking as something that must be intentionally structured. It does not assume that clarity will naturally exist. It requires clarity to be designed.

When thinking is structured, automation becomes an enhancer.

When thinking is unstructured, automation becomes a diffuser of responsibility.

Hybrid AIWoW begins with this quiet but powerful foundation:

Design how thinking happens; before you design how work happens.

25.3 The Problem of Invisible Influence

Artificial reasoning does not demand authority; it gradually gains it.

At first, intelligent systems act as assistants. Humans review outputs carefully. Decisions are validated. Control is clear. As accuracy improves, trust increases. Reviews become quicker. Overrides become rare. No one formally transfers authority, but reliance grows.

In a global logistics organisation, predictive systems may optimise routes and allocate cargo efficiently. Over time, planners approve recommendations with minimal questioning because the system has been reliable. Then an unexpected geopolitical shift occurs. The system, working on historical data, reroutes shipments aggressively. Costs rise. Deliveries suffer.

The system did not fail.

Oversight weakened.

This is an invisible influence authority shifting without intention.

Hybrid AIWoW prevents this by defining limits early. High-impact decisions require human approval. Major changes trigger escalation. Oversight remains active even when confidence is high.

As systems grow smarter, human responsibility must not shrink.

25.4 The Core Foundation: Responsibility Anchoring

In Hybrid AIWoW, one rule is simple and practical: no system can own responsibility.

An AI tool can recommend a credit approval.

It can suggest a production increase.

It can flag a suspicious transaction.

It can even trigger an automatic action within limits.

But when something goes wrong, the organisation cannot say, "The system did it."

Someone must have reviewed it.

Someone must have approved it.

Someone must be answerable.

This is not about philosophy. It is about real-world consequences.

Imagine a bank using AI to score loan applications. The system marks an applicant as low risk. The loan is approved. Six months later, the borrower defaults because recent job instability was not captured in the data.

If no human verified the employment status, who is accountable?

If approval were automatic, who would explain the loss?

Without responsibility anchoring, teams start hiding behind automation. Decisions move faster, but ownership becomes blurry. Humans assume the system has already "checked everything." Approvals become routine clicks instead of conscious validation.

Hybrid AIWoW prevents this by making responsibility visible at every AI-influenced step.

For every significant decision, the organisation must clearly define:

- Who reviews the recommendation?
- Who formally approves it?
- Who must be informed if the risk increases?
- Who answers if the outcome fails?

This can be implemented through simple but firm practices:

- Named approvers in workflow systems
- Mandatory validation checkpoints
- Clear escalation thresholds
- Recorded override reasons

When responsibility is anchored, automation becomes safe.

When responsibility is vague, automation becomes risky.

Hybrid AIWoW does not slow down decision-making. It makes sure that speed does not erase ownership. Because in the real world, systems calculate, but humans remain accountable.

25.5 Boundary Discipline

Hybrid AIWoW introduces deliberate boundary discipline

In Hybrid AIWoW, limits are not optional; they are practical safeguards.

AI systems are very good at certain kinds of work. They can scan huge volumes of data, detect patterns, flag unusual activity, and make predictions based on past behaviour. If a retail organisation wants to analyse millions of transactions to detect fraud, AI is perfect for that. If a manufacturing plant wants to monitor machine temperature every second, AI can do it better than any human team.

But problems begin when those strengths slowly expand into areas where judgement is more important than calculation.

Take a customer service organisation using AI to recommend refund approvals. It works well for small, standard cases. Over time, management increases the approval limit because the system seems accurate. Gradually, high-value refunds are also processed automatically. One day, a complex case involving a loyal long-term client is rejected by the system because it does not fit the data pattern. The customer relationship is damaged, not because the AI failed technically, but because no human reviewed a sensitive decision.

That is why boundary discipline matters.

It simply means deciding in advance where the system can act on its own and where it must pause for human review.

For example:

- AI can approve refunds up to a fixed amount. Beyond that, a manager must review.
- AI can shortlist job applicants, but final hiring always involves human interviews.
- AI can recommend price changes within a safe range, but large changes require leadership approval.

These are not complicated theories. They are practical guardrails.

Without such limits, authority shifts quietly. Humans stop checking. Approvals become automatic. And decisions that should involve judgement become purely data-driven.

Boundary discipline keeps the balance clear. AI handles what it does best. Humans remain responsible where context, values, and long-term impact matter most.

It is not about restricting technology.

It is about protecting stability while using technology wisely.

25.6 The Misconception of Speed

Many organisations introduce AI for one clear reason: to move faster. Reports are generated in seconds. Risks are flagged instantly. Forecasts are ready before meetings even begin. Output increases, and leadership feels progress is happening.

But speed can quietly create overconfidence.

When decisions start moving faster, humans naturally spend less time questioning them. Review cycles shrink. Discussions become shorter. Approvals feel routine. The organisation becomes efficient, but also more exposed.

Hybrid AIWoW makes one practical distinction: moving fast is not the same as thinking well.

Acceleration is about how quickly information is processed.

Validation is about whether the decision is truly ready.

Both must exist together.

Take a pharmaceutical organisation analysing clinical trial results. An AI system processes thousands of data points and highlights strong statistical improvement in early trials. The data looks impressive. Investors are eager. Competitors are watching.

If leadership equates fast analysis with final certainty, they may push toward early launch or aggressive regulatory filing. But numbers alone cannot reveal long-term side effects, rare reactions, or complex biological interactions. Only experienced scientists can interpret what the data truly means in real-world conditions.

If validation is skipped in the name of speed, the risk multiplies.

Hybrid AIWoW builds a simple discipline: major decisions must pass through deliberate human review, no matter how confident the system appears. Automated insight accelerates preparation, but it does not eliminate responsibility.

Speed is powerful when it reduces waiting.

It becomes dangerous when it reduces thinking.

Hybrid AIWoW ensures that faster systems do not quietly weaken judgement. It keeps acceleration under control so that performance improves without increasing fragility.

25.7 Designing Decision Weight

Not all decisions are equal.

Some decisions are operational.

Some are tactical.

Some are existential.

All decisions do not carry the same consequences, so they should not carry the same influence. Hybrid AIWoW requires organisations to intentionally decide how much weight artificial reasoning and human judgement hold in each situation. For example, in a global bank, AI can independently flag suspicious transactions because speed and pattern detection matter most. But approving a large corporate loan must involve human risk evaluation, even if AI provides strong analysis. The balance of influence must be deliberate, not accidental.

Hybrid AIWoW requires organisations to deliberately assign decision weight distribution.

Hybrid AIWoW assigns weight to decision components:

Decision Element	AI Weight	Human Weight
Data Analysis	High	Medium
Context Awareness	Low	High
Ethical Judgement	None	Full
Long-Term Strategy	Advisory	Final

If AI weight becomes 100%,

You lose accountability.

If humans ignore AI weight,

You lose efficiency.

Hybrid ensures balanced influence.

25.8 Feedback Integrity and Trust Calibration

In Hybrid AIWoW, trust between humans and intelligent systems cannot be left to chance. It must be built, monitored, and corrected just like any other performance factor.

In practical terms, every time an AI system makes a recommendation, one of three things happens: it is accepted, modified, or rejected. Each of these outcomes carries information. If a manager overrides a system's suggestion, the reason should be briefly recorded. Not for paperwork, but for learning. Maybe the data was incomplete. Maybe a market change was not captured. Maybe the system logic needs adjustment. Without recording this, the same mistake repeats.

Similarly, if teams are accepting nearly every recommendation without review, that is also a signal. It may mean the system is strong, or it may mean humans have stopped thinking critically. Periodic review of outcomes is necessary to confirm whether performance remains accurate.

Trust must stay balanced.

If employees do not trust the system, they ignore it. The organisation wastes investment and loses efficiency.

If employees trust it blindly, they stop questioning it. The organisation risks silent errors.

A practical way to manage this balance is simple:

- Track how often recommendations are accepted.
- Track how often they are overridden.
- Review accuracy trends over time.
- Introduce new AI capabilities first in limited areas before scaling fully.

For example, if a sales forecasting tool is adopted but only 35% of its suggestions are followed, leadership should not blame the team immediately. They should ask: Is the data outdated? Is the model misaligned with local market realities? Do users need better training? Or are managers relying too heavily on personal intuition?

Trust is not automatic just because a system is advanced. It must be earned through consistent accuracy and maintained through continuous review.

Hybrid AIWoW treats feedback and trust as operational controls, not abstract ideas. When feedback flows both ways, and trust is measured instead of assumed, the partnership between human judgement and artificial reasoning remains strong, stable, and productive.

25.9 Cultural Stabilisation

Hybrid AIWoW cannot function in a culture of fear or blind trust.

Hybrid AIWoW does not succeed only because systems are well designed. It succeeds because humans feel secure within the design.

If employees quietly believe that intelligent systems are being introduced to replace them, resistance will follow. They may comply outwardly but disengage inwardly. Adoption slows. Learning stops. Collaboration weakens. Fear silently blocks progress.

On the other side, if leaders become overly impressed by system performance and begin treating artificial reasoning as unquestionable authority, oversight fades. Review becomes symbolic. Decisions become automatic. Confidence replaces caution. This is equally dangerous.

Hybrid AIWoW requires cultural balance.

Employees must clearly understand that artificial reasoning is an amplifier of capability, not a substitute for human value. It handles volume, repetition, and analysis so that humans can focus on judgement, strategy, and responsibility.

Leaders must visibly demonstrate that human authority remains intact. Major decisions must show human signatures, not just system approvals. When something goes wrong, accountability must remain human, not redirected toward software.

Most importantly, accountability must stay visible. Humans should know who validates outputs, who approves actions, and who owns consequences. Transparency reduces anxiety and prevents silent power shifts.

When culture reinforces these principles, artificial reasoning strengthens the organisation instead of destabilising it. Fear reduces. Overconfidence reduces. Balance improves.

Hybrid AIWoW is not just a structural model; it is a disciplined mindset supported by cultural clarity.

25.10 Structural Readiness Before Framework Adoption

Before bringing Hybrid AIWoW into DevOps, Agile, Scrum, SAFe, DevSecOps, or DevFinOps, an organisation must first make sure its internal roles and responsibilities are clear. Frameworks can increase speed, coordination, and automation, but they do not automatically create accountability.

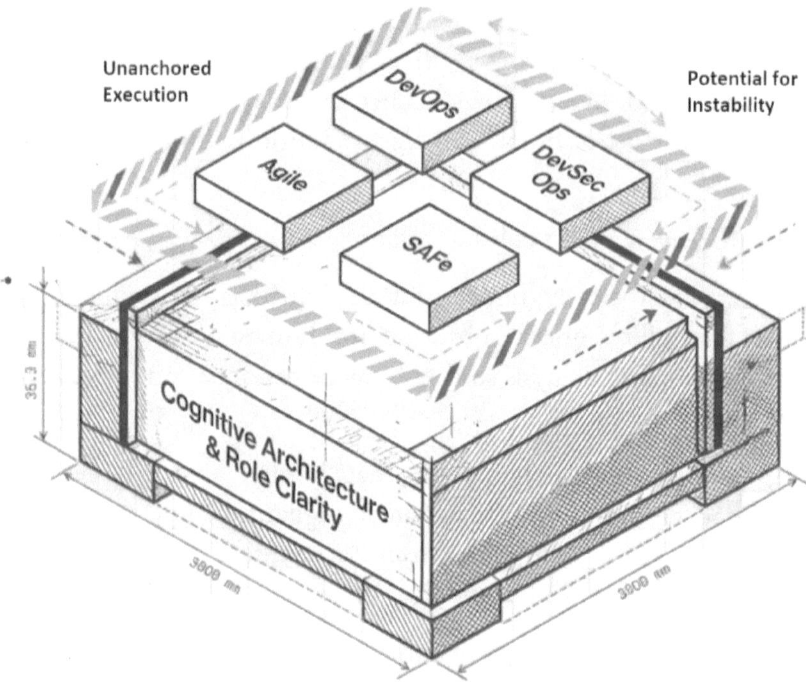

If boundaries are unclear, if no one knows who has final authority, if AI decisions are not being tracked, or if there is no clear escalation path when something goes wrong, then adding structured delivery practices will only make confusion move faster.

A fast, unstable system is far more dangerous than a slow, stable one.

Consider a global energy organisation that introduces predictive systems to balance electricity grids. The system forecasts demand and suggests load adjustments in real time. At first, operators monitor every recommendation carefully. As accuracy improves, they begin trusting the system more. Gradually, vigilance reduces. Supervisors assume the system is self-correcting. When an unusual regional fluctuation occurs, response is delayed ; not because the system failed, but because human oversight had quietly reduced.

The issue was not technology. It was role clarity.

Hybrid AIWoW corrects this by clearly redefining roles. The system predicts. The operator validates. The supervisor ensures limits are respected. A governance team periodically reviews system behaviour and override patterns. Everyone knows their responsibility.

Only after this structure is in place should practices like DevOps, Agile, Scrum, SAFe, DevSecOps, or DevFinOps be layered on top. Otherwise, these frameworks will increase speed without increasing control.

Hybrid AIWoW ensures that before you scale delivery, you stabilise responsibility. When structure is clear, frameworks strengthen performance. When structure is weak, frameworks simply accelerate risk.

Without this foundation, frameworks make instability faster.

With this foundation, they make intelligence stronger.

Hybrid AIWoW begins with maturity, not machinery. Before scaling systems, refining workflows, or accelerating delivery, an organisation must be certain that it understands how decisions are formed and owned. The real shift is not technological; it is behavioural and structural. When leaders consciously design how intelligence is applied, how influence is limited, and how responsibility remains visible, they create an environment where growth does not compromise stability.

This chapter has laid that groundwork. What follows will not introduce speed for its own sake, but will demonstrate how execution practices operate differently when built on disciplined thinking. From this point forward, frameworks are no longer just methods of working; they become instruments guided by clarity.

Hybrid AIWoW does not start with tools.

It starts with readiness.

Summary Mind-map

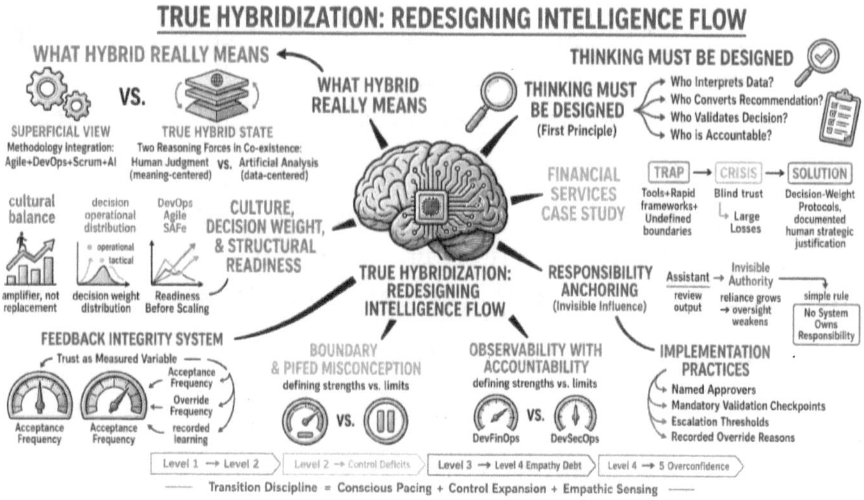

Chapter 26

DevOps in AIWoW: Cognitive Flow Over Speed

Where speed without thinking discipline becomes risk.

DevOps was built to fix a broken relationship. Developers wrote features and handed them over a wall. Operations ran systems and blamed developers when things broke. Between the two sat delays, friction, and a blame culture that slowed everything down. DevOps tore the wall down. It unified responsibility, automated delivery, and gave organisations a way to ship software faster and more reliably. For a while, that was all anyone needed it to do.

The landscape has shifted since then. AI tools are now writing code inside the same pipelines DevOps manages. They are suggesting fixes, predicting where failures are likely, and in some cases triggering deployments without a human making the final call. That changes what DevOps needs to be. Because when artificial reasoning starts making decisions inside your delivery pipeline, the old question — how do we ship faster? — gets joined by a harder one: who is actually responsible for what just shipped, and does anyone genuinely own the outcome?

Speed without thinking discipline becomes risk. That is the ground AIWoW stands on when it enters the DevOps conversation. Not to slow the pipeline down. To make sure the intelligence moving through it operates inside a structure that keeps humans genuinely accountable for every decision that intelligence shapes.

26.1 From Delivery Pipeline to Decision Pipeline

There is a shift happening inside modern pipelines that most teams have not fully named yet. DevOps was designed to optimise flow, move code from development to production with minimal friction, fewer handoffs, and maximum automation. That goal has not changed. What has changed is what is actually moving through the pipeline alongside the code.

A traditional pipeline runs: Code → Build → Test → Deploy → Monitor, looping continuously.

In AIWoW expands this to: Idea → Code → Validate → Approve → Deploy → Observe → Learn. looping continuously.

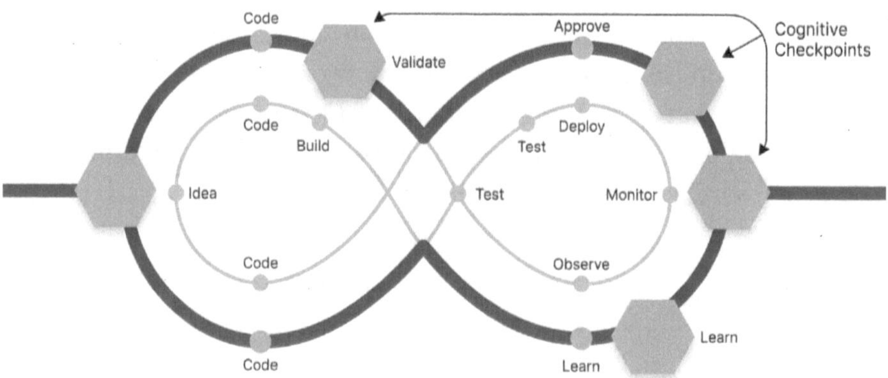

The additions are not cosmetic. They reflect what is genuinely happening when AI participates in delivery. An AI-generated code suggestion is a decision about logic structure. An automated infrastructure adjustment is a decision about cost and resilience. A rollback trigger is a decision about risk tolerance. Every one of these is a consequential choice dressed up as a mechanical step.

Without explicit governance, these decision nodes accumulate inside the pipeline without visible ownership. The system looks efficient from the outside. What has actually happened is that authority has quietly migrated toward automation logic, and nobody quite noticed when it moved. **Cognitive checkpoints - validation, approval, observation,**

and learning are embedded throughout the expanded lifecycle, which prevent that drift. They do not slow delivery. They stabilise it. DevOps accelerates execution.

AIWoW governs judgement across the whole lifecycle. Together, they make the pipeline continuous, not just in deployment, but in disciplined decision-making.

26.2 DevOps Values Through the Lens of AIWoW

DevOps has always worked because it is grounded in practical outcomes: faster delivery, fewer failures, and clear team ownership. Those values have not expired. What has changed is that AI tools are now actively inside the work, writing code, suggesting fixes, optimising infrastructure, and helping during incidents. That increases speed. It also creates a specific risk that the standard DevOps mindset was never designed to handle: teams start depending on AI contributions without clearly tracking how much influence those contributions are having. AIWoW does not undermine DevOps values. It sharpens them for the environment they now operate in.

Collaboration becomes accountable, not just faster:

Without governance, a team often cannot tell **which parts of their codebase were written by humans and which came from a model**. That gap matters when something goes wrong. Under AIWoW,

- AI-generated code is tagged in commits,
- Pull requests make the source of changes visible, and
- Human approval is required before AI-generated logic gets merged.

Teams know exactly who reviewed and signed off on each change. Development stays fast. Ownership stays traceable.

Automation remains controlled, not uncontrolled:

AI can recommend **scaling actions**, configuration fixes, and service restarts automatically. Without clear boundaries, this introduces instability in the name of efficiency. Under AIWoW, low-risk actions can run automatically. Medium-risk actions need an engineer in the loop. High-risk actions, production deployments, and infrastructure changes **always require explicit human authorisation**. The automation keeps moving. Humans keep the final call.

Measurement tracks AI impact, not just system performance:

Standard DevOps metrics tell you how fast you are shipping and how quickly you recover when things break. They tell you nothing about AI's role in either. Under AIWoW, **dashboards show whether deployments included AI-generated code**, incident reports identify where AI recommendations contributed to failures or fixes, and teams build actual evidence about how AI is affecting reliability rather than operating on confidence that it probably is. Decisions that follow from evidence tend to be better than decisions that follow from assumptions.

Responsibility stays clear even when AI contributes:

When governance is absent, **teams gradually absorb AI decisions without realising it**. Then something breaks, and no one can clearly explain who owns the outcome. Under AIWoW, every production deployment has a named human approver, AI suggestions are recommendations, not verdicts, and incident reviews account for both human and AI contributions. The question of who is responsible has a clear answer before anything goes wrong.

Continuous improvement includes learning from AI behaviour:

AI gets more useful only if teams actually examine how it is performing. Under AIWoW, **teams track where AI reduced effort** and where its recommendations were wrong. Approval policies are refined based on what real-world performance reveals. Over time, AI usage becomes more reliable and more trusted, because it is being watched, evaluated, and adjusted rather than accepted as a black box that is presumably fine.

The practical difference is this: DevOps ensures systems move fast. AIWoW **ensures decisions remain controlled** while they do. DevOps removes silos. AIWoW prevents the loss of human authority that arrives when AI quietly fills the space those silos used to occupy. Speed is preserved. Accountability travels with it.

26.3 CI/CD Under AIWoW: Beyond Automatic Deployment:

Continuous integration and delivery allow organisations to ship software quickly and consistently. With AI generating code, suggesting fixes, and modifying configurations, that process has become even faster. But faster generation does not automatically mean safer deployment. A model can produce a plausible-looking function in seconds without understanding the business context it will operate in. *AIWoW ensures that while AI accelerates the pipeline, the humans responsible for what it produces remain genuinely in charge.*

AI-generated code has human ownership:

Speed of production is not the same as the safety of deployment. The developer who accepts AI-generated code is the person responsible for what it does in production. Under AIWoW, that relationship is made explicit:

- Developers review and genuinely understand AI contributions before merging,
- Version control records where AI was involved,
- Security and compliance scans cover AI-generated components, and
- Nothing reaches production without a human having consciously approved it.

AI writes. Humans own what gets written.

Deployment gates reflect real risk:

Not every change carries the same weight. Treating all deployments the same, auto-deploying everything equally means applying the risk tolerance of a minor UI fix to a change in core billing logic.

- Under AIWoW, changes are classified before release.
- Low-risk updates flow through automatically.
- Business logic changes require human review. Infrastructure or cost-impacting changes trigger deliberate assessment.
- Security-related changes always need explicit sign-off.
- The pipeline stays fast where it can. It slows down where it should.

Automated testing supports decisions; it does not make them:

Passing tests means the code behaves as the tests expect. It does not mean the code is ready for what production will throw at it. Under AIWoW, automated tests confirm functionality, engineers review critical system changes rather than relying on green lights, compliance and security changes require human sign-off, and teams evaluate real production readiness rather than test-suite satisfaction. Tests validate code. Humans validate what deploying that code will actually mean.

Traceability builds genuine trust:

Every deployment should be answerable. Teams should be able to see what went out, whether AI contributed to it, who approved it, and why it was released when it was. That visibility is not bureaucratic overhead. It is what makes trust in the pipeline something earned through evidence rather than assumed through habit. When an incident occurs, a traceable deployment history enables faster diagnosis and recovery. Without it, investigations become archaeology.

CI/CD ensures fast delivery. **AIWoW ensures that fast delivery remains controlled and reliable**. The pipeline is automated. The decisions inside it are not left to run unattended.

26.4 DevOps Roles Redefined in AIWoW :

The job titles in DevOps do not change under AIWoW. What changes is the specificity of what each role is responsible for once AI starts contributing to the work they own. Ambiguity about responsibility is how accountability disappears. These redefinitions exist to close that ambiguity before it becomes a problem.

Developer

The developer continues to own application logic, even when AI assists.

In practical terms:

- Reviews and understands all AI-generated code before merging
- Verifies business logic, data handling, and edge cases

- Confirms that security practices are not weakened by AI shortcuts
- Ensures documentation reflects actual deployed behaviour
- Remains accountable for production impact of approved changes

AI can generate code.

The developer owns the decision to use it.

Operations Engineer

The operations engineer safeguards system stability and resilience.

With AI-driven automation increasing, this role includes:

- Validating AI-recommended scaling actions
- Reviewing infrastructure changes before high-impact execution
- Monitoring cost impact of automated resource adjustments
- Ensuring rollback mechanisms remain functional
- Confirming resilience actions align with operational policies

Automation may trigger actions.

Operations validate system safety.

QA Engineer

AI expands test coverage, but QA ensures contextual correctness.

Responsibilities include:

- Reviewing AI-generated test cases for completeness
- Identifying business-critical scenarios beyond automation scope
- Validating cross-system dependencies
- Checking compliance-sensitive workflows
- Confirming that test success reflects real-world readiness

Passing automated tests is not enough.

QA protects production integrity.

Release Manager

The release manager defines deployment authority thresholds.

Under AIWoW, this becomes structured and risk-based:

- Categorises changes by risk level
- Defines which updates can auto-deploy
- Requires approval for core logic or infrastructure changes
- Ensures security-related deployments require explicit sign-off
- Maintains visibility into who approved each release

Speed is preserved.

Control is intentional.

AI Governance Lead (or Assigned Accountability Role)

This role ensures AI influence remains visible and measurable.

In practice:

- Monitors AI-generated contribution levels in releases
- Tracks human override patterns
- Reviews incidents involving AI-assisted changes
- Defines boundaries for AI autonomy in the pipeline
- Reports system trust indicators to leadership

This is not bureaucracy.

It is operational awareness.

The Practical Outcome

AIWoW does not change DevOps titles.

It strengthens responsibility within them.

- AI can suggest.
- AI can generate.
- AI can automate.

But humans:

- Validate
- Approve
- Own
- Remain accountable

AIWoW ensures that while AI increases speed, authority never drifts away from those responsible for the system.

26.5 Observability with Accountability

Observability has always been central to DevOps. Dashboards, alerts, logs, and traces let teams detect and respond to failures before they cascade. AI has made this layer significantly more capable — it can analyse massive log volumes within seconds, correlate distributed failures automatically, predict degradation before it becomes an outage, and even trigger automated recovery. Response speed has improved dramatically.

A new question has arrived with it: *when AI takes an action, who validates the consequence?*

The operational principle AIWoW introduces here is simple but important: automation may initiate a response, but authority must confirm the consequence. When AI triggers a rollback, an engineer confirms customer impact. Teams validate data consistency. Business stakeholders assess the transaction or revenue effect. Logs are reviewed to confirm the root cause, not just trusted because the system acted. When AI auto-scales infrastructure, operations validates cost impact, finance thresholds are checked, and repeated scaling patterns get examined to see whether they indicate an architectural issue rather than a temporary load spike. When anomaly detection suggests a shutdown, service-level commitments are weighed, customer impact is assessed, compliance implications are reviewed, and a named authority confirms execution before it proceeds.

Every **AI-triggered action** should be traceable. Human validation should follow the automated response. Incident reports should account for AI contributions. Override patterns should be tracked and refined over time. Cost and business impact should be measured alongside technical metrics. AI can react faster than any human. Only humans can weigh reputational risk, contractual exposure, compliance obligations, and the business consequences of what the system just did. Observability under AIWoW is not just monitoring. It is accountable response management, the practice of making sure that when the system moves fast, someone is genuinely responsible for where it moved.

26.6 Integrating DevSecOps and DevFinOps Under AIWoW

Security and cost management are already embedded in modern pipelines. AI has made both faster: it detects vulnerabilities in real time, flags misconfigurations, prioritises risks, auto-scales infrastructure, shuts down idle resources, and forecasts usage spikes. That acceleration is valuable. It also creates a specific governance risk that both DevSecOps and DevFinOps need to address: high-impact decisions start happening as silent technical adjustments that nobody consciously approved.

On security:

Security tools scan continuously. AI can surface compliance gaps, critical vulnerabilities, and risky configurations within seconds. Under AIWoW, detection is not the same as acceptance. If a vulnerability is deferred or temporarily accepted, that decision requires visible human sign-off, documented reasoning, a defined time boundary, and a scheduled review. Security decisions influence customer trust, regulatory standing, and brand credibility in ways that outlast any single deployment. Risk acceptance must be something someone chose, not something the system absorbed quietly while everyone was watching the throughput metrics.

On cost:

Cost engines optimise resource allocation dynamically. That is useful. It becomes dangerous when optimisation choices silently weaken resilience. When scaling down might affect availability or performance, the trade-off needs to be evaluated before it is executed rather than discovered after the fact. Approval thresholds should be defined. Performance impact should be assessed alongside savings. Repeated cost spikes should trigger an architectural conversation, not just another automated adjustment. Saving money matters. Saving money by quietly degrading a system that customers depend on is a different proposition entirely.

The core principle across both domains is the same:

AI can detect.

AI can recommend.

Humans decide.

Humans own the consequence.

Trade-offs between security, performance, cost, and speed involve judgements that go beyond efficiency calculations, reputational risk, contractual obligations, regulatory exposure, and long-term strategic impact. These are not things a model can fully evaluate. They belong to the humans whose names will be on the outcomes.

26.7 Metrics in DevOps Under AIWoW

Standard DevOps metrics remain essential: deployment frequency, lead time from commit to production, change failure rate, and mean time to recovery. They tell you how efficiently software moves through the pipeline and how quickly teams recover from failure. In an AI-assisted environment, they no longer tell you enough. They do not show you how much of what shipped was AI-generated, how often human judgement overrode an automated recommendation, or whether the incidents you are recovering from were triggered by AI-initiated actions. Moving fast while remaining blind to those questions is how authority drift happens at scale.

Traditional DevOps Metric	AIWoW Extended Metric
Deployment frequency	AI-generated code ratio within releases
Lead time from commit to production	Override frequency at deployment approval gates
Change failure rate	Automated decision acceptance rate
Mean time to recovery (MTTR)	Incidents triggered by AI-initiated actions
System availability	Compliance breaches linked to AI-assisted changes

These extended metrics provide the operational clarity that speed alone cannot deliver. A rising AI-generated code ratio tells leadership something real about dependency levels. Increasing override frequency signals that AI recommendations may need refinement. Incidents repeatedly linked to automated actions suggest governance thresholds need adjustment. Without this visibility, organisations move faster without understanding what is shaping the direction of that movement. A system can deploy frequently and recover quickly while experiencing steady authority drift and unnoticed risk accumulation. Cognitive stability — how reliably humans and AI are collaborating within defined boundaries — needs to be something the organisation can actually see. Otherwise, it is simply assumed, and assumptions of this kind have a way of proving themselves wrong at the worst possible moment.

26.8 Practical Example: SaaS Platform Transformation

A global SaaS organisation running subscription billing, analytics, and enterprise integrations across three continents faced a pressure that will be recognisable to most engineering leaders: ship faster without making things less reliable. Competition was accelerating. Feature expectations had risen. Engineering teams were expected to deliver continuously.

The organisation introduced AI-assisted coding and predictive deployment optimisation. Developers started using AI to generate boilerplate APIs, validation layers, and test scaffolding. Work that had taken hours began taking minutes. The CI pipeline builds and tests every commit automatically. The CD pipeline deployed updates multiple times a day. AI models analysed traffic patterns and recommended deployment windows with the lowest risk profile. Within three months, throughput was up, release cycles had shortened, deployment frequency had nearly doubled, and regression defects had fallen. The organisation was moving faster than it ever had, and it felt like the right kind of fast.

Then something quieter began to shift. AI-generated code was entering production more frequently. Infrastructure scaling decisions were increasingly driven by predictive algorithms. Deployment timing was heavily influenced by automated recommendations. Nothing was visibly breaking — but a question surfaced in a leadership review that nobody could answer confidently: how much of their production environment was being shaped by AI at this point, and how much of that had been consciously decided?

An honest internal review turned up specific gaps. No metric tracked what percentage of each release contained AI-generated code. Deployment overrides were happening, but not being recorded or examined. Incident reports did not identify which changes had AI involvement. Some AI-refactored modules had quietly altered data-handling logic in ways that only became visible when someone looked deliberately. The system was efficient. Cognitive control had not kept pace with the automation growing inside it.

The response was not to restrict AI. It was to apply AIWoW principles and restore the visibility that had been lost. Human review became mandatory for business-critical logic — billing, authentication, anything touching customer data. AI-generated code was automatically tagged in version control, so audit trails were meaningful. Every deployment was classified by risk level before release. Changes touching data privacy triggered escalation workflows. Infrastructure scaling above the defined thresholds required explicit approval. Monthly dashboards began tracking AI contribution ratios and override frequency as standard operational indicators.

None of this reduced deployment speed. Engineers keep using AI every day. The CI/CD pipeline stayed automated and efficient. What changed was that every production change now had a name attached to it.

Six months later, the results were tangible:

- Release frequency stayed high,
- Production incidents dropped through structured gating,
- Rollbacks became less frequent,
- Audit preparation time fell,
- Cloud cost fluctuations stabilised, and
- Team confidence grew.

Engineers trusted the pipeline because they understood what was inside it.

Leadership trusted the metrics because AI influence had become something they could actually measure.

Speed had been preserved.

The control that should always have travelled with it had been restored.

26.9 Cognitive Flow Over Speed

DevOps made delivery continuous.

It removed the friction between building and running software, shortened feedback cycles, and gave organisations the ability to respond to the market without waiting for quarterly release windows.

AI made it predictive.

Systems no longer have to wait for something to fail before responding — they forecast surges, detect abnormal patterns early, recommend remediation before degradation becomes an outage, and optimise deployment timing based on real risk signals. The pipeline moved from reactive to anticipatory.

Continuity and prediction are powerful. What they do not automatically provide is coherence. As automation deepens and AI begins influencing more of the decisions inside the pipeline, the velocity of execution can outpace the clarity of authority. Things move, but the question of who decided they should move in that direction becomes genuinely hard to answer. This is the gap AIWoW fills not by reducing speed, but by ensuring that intelligence operates inside intentional boundaries rather than autonomous momentum.

Cognitive flow is the name for the alignment between speed, prediction, and responsibility. When it is present, every automated action is anchored to accountable ownership. Every predictive insight has a defined validation boundary before it triggers execution. Every deployment carries explicit authorisation. Every override reflects a conscious human judgement rather than a workaround. Every risk trade-off is something someone accepted deliberately rather than something the system absorbed silently. Every incident generates structured reflection rather than just a ticket closed. Every learning loop refines both human and AI performance going forward.

When cognitive flow is functioning, speed does not destabilise control. It becomes sustainable. The organisation moves quickly, but it knows where it is going and why. Decisions are traceable. Authority is visible. Learning is continuous. Speed stops being an uncontrolled force and becomes a consciously governed asset — predictable, measurable, and pointing in the direction the organisation actually chose.

26.10 Final Insight

DevOps is powerful because it removes the wall between the people who build software and the people who run it. Code moves from idea to production through a pipeline that automation has made smooth and reliable. AI amplifies that power by embedding intelligence directly into the process of writing code, predicting failures, optimising deployments, scaling infrastructure, and monitoring at a depth and speed no human team can replicate. The pipeline becomes not only automated but genuinely smart.

Intelligence amplifies impact. That is what makes it valuable, and what makes it consequential when it runs without structure. When automation begins influencing decisions at scale, small misjudgments do not stay small for long. Speed can outpace reflection. Prediction can bypass the human validation that would have caught the edge case the model did not know to look for. Power, without discipline, stops being an asset. It becomes a source of fragility that the organisation has built for itself.

AIWoW ensures DevOps stays strong as it becomes smarter. When its principles are guiding the pipeline, automation operates within boundaries that were consciously defined. Accountability sits with named humans rather than drifting toward the algorithm. Trust in AI contributions is earned through data and review rather than granted by default. Override patterns are monitored and used to refine how the system operates. Risk acceptance is something someone chooses, not something the pipeline absorbed because nobody was watching closely enough. Decision flow is given the same care and attention as code flow.

In that environment, CI/CD evolves past its original definition. It is no longer only about moving code continuously. It is about moving decisions responsibly. Every deployment carries ownership. Every automated action is traceable. Every predictive recommendation has been validated. Every incident becomes input to the organisation's ongoing governance maturity rather than just a problem to close.

CI/CD becomes continuous responsible delivery.

That is DevOps inside AIWoW, where speed remains high, intelligence remains active, and responsibility remains human.

Summary Mind Map

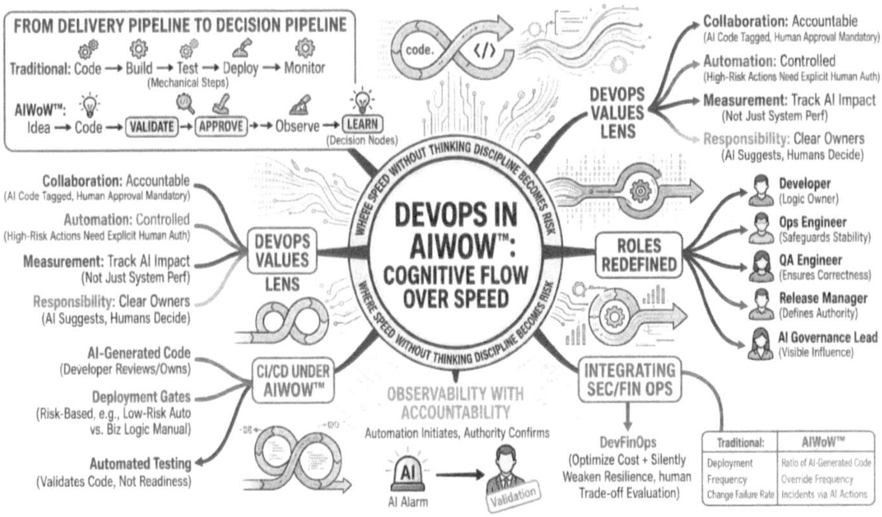

Chapter 27

Agile, Scrum & Kanban in AIWoW: Intelligent Work Flow

"Scrum gave structure, Kanban gave flow.

AIWoW gives awareness to the flow."

Agile was built to solve a coordination problem that had been frustrating software teams for years.

Scrum gave those teams structure sprints, ceremonies, clear roles.

Kanban gave them flow, visible work, controlled limits, and steady throughput.

Together, they changed how organisations plan, build, and deliver. Work became iterative. Feedback became continuous. Value reached customers faster, and teams got better at adjusting course when circumstances changed.

Something has entered that picture since then. Backlogs are now influenced by predictive analytics. User stories get drafted by generative systems before a product owner has typed a word. Sprint estimates come from AI models trained on historical velocity. Kanban flow gets optimised dynamically through machine learning. Artificial reasoning has started participating in planning, prioritisation, estimation, and execution and Agile, as it was originally conceived, was not designed with that participant in mind.

When the system making suggestions is also shaping commitments, the question of who is actually deciding becomes genuinely important.

Speed of iteration is no longer the only objective. Clarity of decision flow has become equally critical. This is where AIWoW reshapes Agile not by slowing it down, but by making visible the decisions that AI is quietly influencing inside every ceremony, every backlog review, and every sprint commitment.

27.1 From Work Management to Decision Management

Traditional Agile frameworks manage work efficiently.

The standard flow runs:

Backlog → Sprint → Build → Review → Release → Retrospective.

The emphasis is on incremental delivery and rapid feedback. That flow has proven its value across thousands of teams and a couple of decades of real-world use.

AIWoW expands this lifecycle by naming what Agile ceremonies have always been but rarely said out loud: structured decision checkpoints.

The expanded flow becomes:

Intent → Prioritise → Commit → Execute → Validate → Release → Reflect → Learn.

Every event in that sequence is a decision node. When AI suggests backlog priorities based on usage analytics, that is a strategic decision. When AI proposes story point estimates, it is influencing capacity planning. When AI flags technical debt risk mid-sprint, it affects scope control. Without visibility into these moments, AI influence accumulates silently inside a process designed to be transparent.

Hybrid AIWoW embeds cognitive checkpoints across Agile workflows so that none of this remains invisible. Prioritisation requires explicit human acceptance. Sprint commitments reflect accountable approval. Retrospectives include evaluation of how AI contributed to planning and execution. Agile optimises workflow. AIWoW governs decision flow within that workflow. The two are not in conflict, but one of them was missing from Agile until now.

27.2 Agile Values Through the Lens of AIWoW

Agile values collaboration, adaptability, and customer responsiveness. Those values have not expired. What AI changes is how they operate in practice, and what additional discipline they require to stay honest.

1. **Customer focus becomes data-informed but human-validated:**

   AI can analyse user behaviour, churn signals, and feature adoption trends to recommend backlog reprioritisation. That analysis is often genuinely useful.

   Under AIWoW :

- Product owners review those insights before reordering backlog items.
- Business trade-offs get consciously approved rather than absorbed.
- Predictive signals inform direction.

  Humans define it.

2. **Sprint planning becomes transparent:**

   AI can estimate effort based on historical velocity and code complexity. But estimation is not purely mathematical; it reflects team confidence, contextual risk, and judgments that a model trained on past data cannot fully replicate.

   Under AIWoW :

- AI-generated estimates sit alongside team input rather than replacing it.
- Final commitment is explicitly human-approved.
- Risk assumptions get documented.
- Velocity stays high. Ownership stays clear.

3. **Daily standups include AI signals:**

   AI can detect blockers, code stagnation, and anomaly patterns across repositories faster than any human reviewing dashboards.

   Under AIWoW :

- Those insights are surfaced during standups, but teams validate their relevance before acting on them.
- Escalations require human confirmation.
- Automation supports coordination.

   It does not replace the judgement of the people who know the context.

4. **Retrospectives include AI performance review:**

   Continuous improvement is at the heart of Agile. AIWoW extends that principle to include AI behaviour as a subject of review. Teams examine where AI accelerated delivery, where suggestions required overrides, whether predictive insights improved outcomes, and if any AI recommendations introduced risk that was not initially visible. Improvement applies to both process and artificial reasoning.

27.3 Scrum Roles Redefined in AIWoW

Scrum roles remain structurally intact under AIWoW. The titles stay the same. What sharpens is the operational clarity of what each role owns when AI starts participating in estimation, forecasting, and suggestion. Titles do not change. The depth of responsibility increases.

Product Owner

The Product Owner continues to own backlog prioritisation, even when AI suggests ranking based on data trends, predicted value, or delivery history. AI may provide insights, but it does not determine direction.

In AIWoW, the Product Owner:

- Reviews AI-generated prioritisation suggestions before acceptance
- Validates whether AI recommendations align with strategic intent
- Rejects backlog reordering that conflicts with long-term positioning
- Confirms risk tolerance before approving AI-driven opportunity scoring
- Ensures that value decisions are context-aware, not pattern-driven

Practical application:

- AI may highlight "high probability impact" items
- The Product Owner confirms whether those items support the current strategy
- Final backlog order is declared explicitly, not auto-confirmed

Strategic intent cannot be automated. It requires accountability.

Scrum Master

The Scrum Master ensures AI tools support flow without distorting team dynamics. AI estimation, predictive velocity, and sprint simulations can influence behaviour in subtle ways.

In AIWoW, the Scrum Master:

- Monitors whether AI-based forecasts create hidden performance pressure
- Checks if predictive timelines reduce realistic discussion
- Ensures AI insights trigger conversation, not silent compliance
- Validates that team capacity is not stretched due to optimistic automation
- Observes morale shifts linked to algorithmic estimation

Practical application:

- If AI predicts earlier completion, the Scrum Master validates feasibility
- If team confidence drops due to AI projections, recalibration is initiated
- Flow remains human-paced, even if prediction is machine-generated

AI estimation should inform clarity, not enforce urgency.

Development Team

The Development Team reviews AI-assisted code and validates predictive suggestions. AI can generate implementation drafts, highlight refactoring opportunities, and propose optimisations. However, technical accountability remains human.

In AIWoW, the Development Team:

- Reviews AI-generated code as advisory input
- Validates architectural implications before acceptance
- Tests predictive recommendations under real constraints
- Maintains authority over implementation decisions
- Documents when AI suggestions are modified or rejected

Practical application:

- AI drafts a module → team reviews, adjusts, and approves
- AI proposes performance improvement → team validates system impact
- AI suggests refactoring → team checks long-term maintainability

AI accelerates drafting.

Humans retain engineering ownership.

AI Governance Representative (Where Applicable)

In environments with significant AI integration, an AI Governance Representative supports transparency across sprints. This role does not interfere with delivery but monitors AI's operational footprint.

In AIWoW, the AI Governance Representative:

- Tracks AI influence across sprint planning sessions
- Monitors override frequency of AI recommendations
- Analyses patterns of automatic acceptance
- Reviews whether AI predictions are shaping commitments
- Ensures transparency in AI-assisted planning

Practical application:

- If AI suggestions are accepted without discussion → review triggered
- If override frequency increases → calibration required
- If prediction accuracy declines → model reassessment initiated

Governance ensures AI remains visible and accountable.

Commitment Principle in AIWoW

Across all roles, one boundary remains firm:

- AI can assist planning
- AI can simulate outcomes
- AI can estimate probability

But:

- Only humans declare commitment
- Only humans accept delivery responsibility
- Only humans own the outcome

AIWoW strengthens Scrum not by replacing roles,

but by clarifying authority within each role.

27.4 Kanban in AIWoW: Flow with Accountability

Kanban is built on visible flow, controlled work-in-progress limits, and steady throughput. It does not rely on time-boxed cycles but on continuous movement. In AIWoW, that continuity remains, but the influence AI has on flow becomes explicitly governed rather than passively accepted.

AI can analyse cycle times, detect emerging bottlenecks, forecast congestion points, and recommend adjustments to work-in-progress thresholds. It can suggest task redistribution to balance the load across contributors. In AIWoW, optimisation never equals automatic enforcement. Every AI-driven adjustment is surfaced, reviewed, and consciously accepted before it changes anything.

1. Flow control authority

- Reviewing AI-optimised WIP threshold recommendations before applying changes,
- Validating that adjustments align with current strategic intent,
- Confirming capacity assumptions before increasing throughput,
- Preventing silent acceleration triggered by predictive models, and
- Documenting approved adjustments for traceability.

Practical application:

- When AI suggests reducing WIP from eight to six, the team reviews the workload context first.
- When AI forecasts a faster cycle time, human validation precedes acceptance. Flow is adjusted deliberately, not automatically.

2. Work reprioritisation ownership:

Kanban allows dynamic reprioritisation. With AI in the system, that reprioritisation can become algorithmically driven unless ownership is actively preserved.

In AIWoW,

- Every priority change requires a visible declaration of who authorised it,

- A clear rationale beyond a predictive urgency score,
- Confirmation that the shift does not distort long-term intent, and
- A record of both adopted suggestions and overrides.

When AI flags an item as high urgency, a discussion validates the actual business impact before anything moves. Priority shifts are logged with human authorisation. Visibility is maintained at the decision level, not just the task level.

3. Bottleneck prediction governance:

AI can predict bottlenecks before they appear visually on the board. That predictive ability is genuinely valuable. It must remain advisory.

In AIWoW,

- A predicted bottleneck triggers a structured review rather than an automatic reshuffle.
- The team verifies whether the congestion is systemic or temporary.
- Assesses downstream impact before redistributing work.
- Executes redistribution only after agreement.
- Prediction initiates discussion. It does not enforce action.

Traditional Kanban tracks cycle time, lead time, and throughput.

AIWoW extends measurement to include AI influence indicators:

- Frequency of AI-suggested WIP adjustments,
- Acceptance versus override rates on AI recommendations,
- Impact of adopted changes on throughput stability, and
- Variance between predicted and actual bottlenecks.

These indicators ensure AI remains accountable within the system.

Kanban ensures visibility of work.

AIWoW ensures visibility of influence.

Flow remains continuous.

Governance remains embedded.

27.5 Intelligent Workflow Metrics

Traditional workflow measurement focuses on delivery movement and execution rhythm. **Velocity** reveals output capacity. **Burndown rate** monitors progress consistency. **Lead time** and **cycle time** evaluate responsiveness and processing efficiency. These indicators remain valuable, they show how smoothly work flows and whether commitments are being met predictably.

When AI becomes part of planning, estimation, forecasting, and recommendation, these metrics capture only part of what is actually happening. They show how fast work is progressing but say nothing about how that progress is being shaped. Acceleration may result not only from better coordination but from algorithmic influence that nobody has examined. Without visibility into that influence, performance signals can mislead rather than inform.

Delivery Metrics — Movement Visibility	AIWoW Influence Metrics — Decision Visibility
Velocity — team output capacity	AI-Assisted Story Ratio — depth of AI integration in workflow
Burndown rate — execution consistency	Estimation Override Frequency — how often teams adjust AI forecasts
Lead time — end-to-end responsiveness	Predictive Accuracy Rate — AI forecast vs actual outcomes
Cycle time — internal processing efficiency	Backlog Reprioritisation Triggers — AI-driven urgency signals altering planned order
	AI Recommendation Acceptance Trends — patterns of reliance or resistance over time

When AI influence is not measured, speed creates false confidence. Increased velocity may mask declining decision quality. Reduced cycle time may conceal accumulated risk. Reprioritisation driven by predictive alerts may destabilise long-term intent without anyone noticing until the quarterly review asks why the roadmap drifted.

AIWoW introduces the **concept of cognitive stability** –

- The condition where decision ownership stays clear.
- AI participation stays transparent, and improvements are intentional rather than accidental.
- Cognitive stability must be measurable because governance cannot rest on assumptions.

These metrics protect that clarity, allowing teams to accelerate responsibly with efficiency gains aligned to conscious decision-making rather than invisible algorithmic drift.

27.6 Cognitive Flow in Agile Environments

Agile environments are designed for adaptability. Work evolves through short cycles, feedback gets incorporated quickly, and priorities adjust as new information arrives. That flexibility is a genuine strength. When AI begins influencing planning, estimation, and execution, though, adaptability can quietly shift from deliberate adjustment to algorithm-driven movement — and those two things feel similar from the inside until something goes wrong.

Cognitive flow in AIWoW ensures adaptability remains intentional rather than automatic. In practical terms, it means AI participation is visible and governed at every stage of iterative work.

- **Every AI-driven suggestion requires explicit validation** before adoption, whether it is a revised estimate, a priority recommendation, or a scope refinement.
- Every **sprint commitment reflects accountable approval** rather than being shaped silently by predictive forecasts.
- Every **backlog shift carries strategic justification** beyond urgency signals. Every predictive insight operates within defined authority limits.
- Every **retrospective includes a review** of AI behaviour alongside delivery outcomes.

Agile introduced iterative speed. AI introduced predictive intelligence. AIWoW introduces disciplined coordination between the two. Through cognitive flow, acceleration does not override judgement. Predictive insight strengthens iteration without weakening the accountability that gives iteration its meaning.

27.7 Intelligent Workflow

In AIWoW, workflow is not defined only by how tasks move from one column to another. It is defined by how human judgment and AI capability interact at every step of that movement. Work does not simply progress; it is coordinated through a structured relationship between intent, prediction, decision, and execution.

Work flows continuously.

Decisions flow consciously.

Continuous flow ensures productivity.

Conscious decision flow ensures that productivity is heading somewhere deliberate.

The objective of AIWoW is not to slow iteration or reduce adaptability. It is to ensure that iteration remains aligned with declared intent. When predictive systems begin influencing prioritisation, estimation, or execution patterns without that alignment being maintained, the risk is not speed. It is drift. Intelligent workflow prevents drift by embedding validation into movement.

When AIWoW principles guide Agile environments, speed remains high because automation continues to assist execution. Adaptability remains strong because feedback loops stay active and responsive. Predictive insights remain valuable because they inform planning and surface risk. Authority remains human because commitment and accountability are never delegated to the algorithm, regardless of how accurate it has been lately.

This balance transforms familiar delivery structures.

Agile becomes more than iterative delivery; it becomes iterative delivery with declared intent at every cycle.

Scrum becomes more than structured sprints; it becomes structured commitment with visible influence management.

Kanban becomes more than visual flow; it becomes transparent flow with accountable adjustment.

Automation supports execution without redefining goals. Prediction informs direction without a controlling authority. Governance protects accountability without reducing agility. Velocity and responsibility do not compete. They evolve together.

27.8 Final Insight

Agile made teams faster by breaking work into short, adaptable cycles. AI made those cycles smarter by adding prediction and pattern awareness. AIWoW brings discipline to the combination. It ensures that adaptability does not become instability and that prediction does not harden into silent authority.

Inside AIWoW, Agile is no longer just about responding quickly. It is about responding consciously. Iterations stay short, feedback stays active, and change stays welcome. But commitments are explicit, backlog shifts are accountable, and AI influence is something the team can actually see and examine, rather than something happening in the background of their process.

Agile increases movement.

AI increases foresight.

AIWoW ensures both operate under human direction.

When governed properly, Agile does not lose its flexibility.

It gains structural clarity.

Teams move fast, but they know why they are moving and who decided they should.

That is Agile inside AIWoW — accelerated delivery guided by disciplined intent.

Summary Mind map

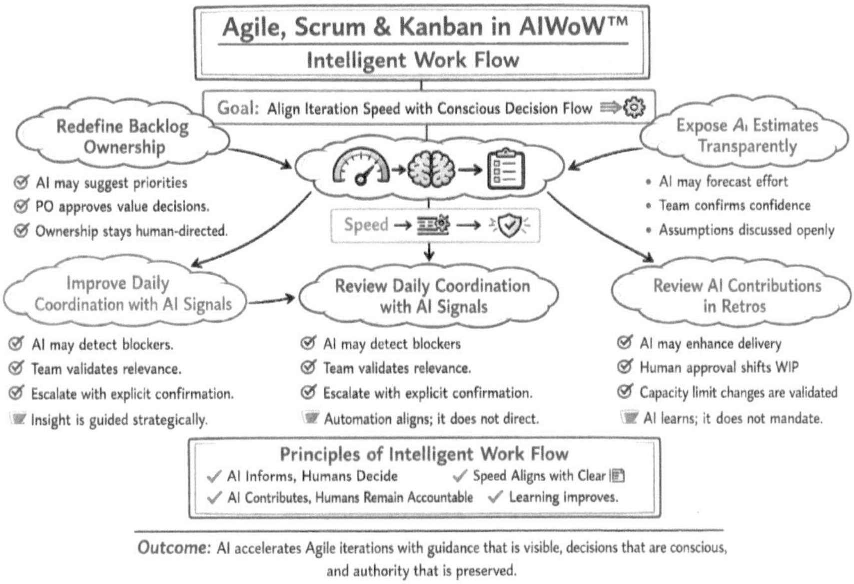

Chapter 28

Safe Agile AIWoW — Guardrails for Fast Systems

"Acceleration is welcomed.

Unsupervised acceleration is not.

Speed must be bounded by intent."

Large-scale Agile environments were built to hold complexity together without losing momentum. When many teams operate in parallel, the system needs something more than individual team velocity; it needs alignment layers, planning synchronisation, architectural direction, portfolio visibility, and structured governance so that speed at the team level does not quietly unravel coherence at the system level.

AI changes the dynamics of that scale in ways that are not always immediately visible. When predictive planning, automated prioritisation, AI-assisted estimation, and intelligent execution tools enter a scaled environment, speed multiplies across multiple teams at once. Decisions ripple faster. Dependencies shift earlier than anyone expected them to. Forecasts adjust continuously in response to live signals. Without strong guardrails, the combination of scale and prediction does not create stability — it creates instability at scale, which is a different and more damaging thing entirely.

Safe Agile AIWoW does not slow systems down.

It makes fast systems safe to operate.

28.1 The Core Premise: Speed Must Be Bounded by Intent

Scaled Agile environments exist to coordinate complexity without losing momentum. At scale, coordination is not optional; it is structural. Multiple teams operate in parallel against shared backlogs. Architectures are integrated to prevent fragmentation. Portfolio-level investments are tied to strategic themes. Dependencies are managed across increments. Release synchronisation runs across value streams.

When AI becomes embedded within this environment, acceleration deepens further.

- Portfolio-level forecasting predicts ROI and delivery probability.
- Dependency mapping runs automatically across teams and components.
- Risk heatmaps surface systemic exposure.
- Resource optimisation signals respond to live data.
- Capacity simulations run across release cycles. Bottleneck detection happens in real time.

These capabilities genuinely strengthen foresight and compress feedback loops. The risk, though, is not that the predictions will be wrong; it is something subtler. When predictive signals continuously adjust priorities, rebalance resources, and highlight emerging trends, the entire structure can begin shifting without deliberate authorisation. Direction changes incrementally rather than visibly. Portfolio themes drift. Dependency maps re-align. Architectural focus adjusts, sometimes without a single explicit decision being made by anyone responsible for the consequences.

In scaled environments, small directional shifts compound quickly. Safe Agile AIWoW establishes one fundamental rule:

- No prediction alters direction without accountable validation.
- In practice, this means portfolio reprioritisation requires executive confirmation before anything moves.

- AI-driven funding reallocation is reviewed and consciously approved rather than activated by the algorithm.
- Dependency remapping triggers a real alignment conversation before it is enforced.
- Risk heatmaps open a governance review rather than triggering automatic halts.
- Capacity simulations stay advisory.
- Continuous prioritisation signals inform planning conversations but do not silently reorder backlogs.

The operating logic is straightforward:

- Prediction proposes,
- Leadership authorises,
- Teams execute within confirmed direction.

Speed is preserved because insight is immediate. Direction stays human because authority is explicit.

Safe Agile AIWoW does not restrict innovation. It prevents drift. It ensures that scale amplifies clarity rather than confusion.

28.2 Reframing Scaled Agile Values Through AIWoW

Scaled Agile environments are built on values that were designed to keep large systems coordinated while moving fast: alignment, transparency, and built-in quality. AI does not make those values obsolete. It raises the bar for how practically and consistently they need to operate.

Alignment becomes intent alignment

At scale, alignment traditionally means teams are moving toward shared goals. With AI-enabled forecasting and dynamic reprioritisation, alignment can quietly shift based on predictive signals rather than conscious decisions.

Under AIWoW,

- Alignment becomes active.
- Portfolio priorities are reviewed before AI-driven shifts are accepted.
- Strategic themes are confirmed before backlog reshaping.
- Cross-team adjustments require accountable authorisation.

Alignment is no longer passive agreement.

It is an active confirmation of intent.

Transparency becomes influence transparency

Traditional transparency surfaces dashboards, milestones, risks, and progress. In AI-enabled systems, visibility needs to go deeper; it must reveal how AI is shaping the decisions behind those indicators.

Under AIWoW,

- AI recommendation logs become visible in planning sessions.
- Backlog shifts triggered by predictive signals are traceable.
- Acceptance and override patterns are measurable.
- Forecast confidence levels are disclosed alongside projections.

Transparency now includes the reasoning behind the movement, not just the movement itself.

Built-in quality becomes built-in governance

Built-in quality traditionally ensures system stability, integration reliability, and defect prevention.

Under AIWoW,

- Quality expands to include validation of predictive and automated inputs.
- AI-generated architectural suggestions go through review forums.
- Predictive defect prevention is validated against the system context.

- Risk alerts require review before release continuation.
- Model recalibration is triggered when prediction accuracy declines.

Quality is no longer limited to code integrity. It includes decision integrity.

28.3 Portfolio Layer: AI with Executive Authority Boundaries

At the portfolio level, AI can simulate investment returns, forecast market shifts, and optimise funding allocation across programmes. These capabilities are genuinely powerful and genuinely dangerous if applied without constraint. A funding simulation that looks compelling on a dashboard can still carry strategic assumptions that no algorithm is qualified to validate on its own.

Safe Agile AIWoW keeps executive authority exactly where it belongs.

- Portfolio reprioritisation requires executive confirmation.
- AI-driven funding shifts are reviewed against long-term intent before activation.
- Predictive ROI remains advisory rather than decisive.
- Investment acceleration has predefined limits that a prediction cannot override.

Portfolio governance expands to include AI influence metrics alongside financial metrics, because understanding how much of a direction change was algorithmically suggested is now as important as understanding the financial case for it. AI enhances foresight. It does not hold executive authority.

28.4 Program Increment Planning in AIWoW

Large-scale planning events coordinate multiple teams around shared objectives across a defined increment. AI can now generate **capacity forecasts, dependency risk predictions, timeline simulations, and**

delivery probability ranges before those sessions begin. That is a genuine improvement over the guesswork that used to fill those early planning conversations.

Safe Agile AIWoW integrates these inputs carefully rather than deferring to them uncritically. During planning,

- AI projections are reviewed openly alongside team experience.
- Feasibility is validated by the people who will actually do the work.
- Confidence levels are discussed rather than assumed.
- Commitments are declared by humans, not accepted automatically from a model's probability estimate.
- Predictions support realism.

They do not replace the negotiation that turns a forecast into a genuine commitment.

28.5 Team-Level Execution Within Guardrails

Within each team, iteration cycles stay active and adaptive. That does not change. What does change when teams operate inside a scaled structure is that local decisions carry system-wide consequences that a single team cannot always see from where it sits. A team that accepts AI-suggested scope expansion without checking programme objectives, or accelerates ahead of its dependencies because a predictive signal looked encouraging, can create downstream friction that takes several increments to untangle. The individual decision looks reasonable. The system-wide effect is not.

Safe Agile AIWoW keeps team autonomy intact while making its edges visible.

- AI-suggested scope expansion is validated against programme objectives before the team commits to it.
- Velocity acceleration is checked against dependency readiness, not just local capacity.

- Automated prioritisation cannot silently override shared commitments that other teams are planning around.
- Local improvements do not quietly shift architectural integrity.

The principle behind all of this is simple: autonomy without coordination creates fragmentation, and coordination only works when its boundaries are consciously maintained rather than assumed.

AIWoW keeps coordination intentional.

28.6 Architecture and Built-In Quality Under AI Influence

In scaled environments, architecture provides stability across multiple teams by ensuring integration consistency, long-term scalability, and shared design direction. When AI begins influencing design and code decisions, the architectural discipline needs to be stronger rather than relaxed, because the surface area of AI's influence is now large enough to affect the whole system.

AI-generated architectural changes are not implemented automatically under Safe Agile AIWoW. They go through architectural forums and are evaluated for cross-team and long-term impact. Structural shifts require explicit approval from people who understand the full system context. Predictive defect detection supports early correction, but fixes are validated for systemic consequences before being applied at scale. Code acceleration tools operate within defined quality thresholds, review standards, performance benchmarks, and security checks remain mandatory regardless of how confident the model's recommendation appears. Architectural authority stays human-led.

AI can propose patterns and optimisations. Final design ownership rests with accountable architects.

28.7 Risk and Compliance as Continuous Controls

In large-scale environments, releasing continuously, risk and compliance cannot function as end-stage checkpoints or periodic audits. By the time a quarterly review surfaces a compliance gap, the decision that created it was made weeks ago across dozens of deployments. When teams are shipping regularly, and AI is accelerating decision cycles, the window between cause and consequence is too narrow for delayed oversight to close.

AI strengthens early detection in ways that genuinely help here. It can forecast regulatory exposure, flag compliance deviations, simulate policy impact, and identify emerging control gaps before formal audits get anywhere near them. The limitation is that awareness alone does not constitute governance. A risk signal that arrives early but can be dismissed automatically, deferred by confidence threshold, or buried in a dashboard that nobody acts on is not a control. It is a notification that something went wrong before anyone responded.

Under Safe Agile AIWoW,

- Risk thresholds trigger structured review before release progression continues; not after.
- Compliance flags cannot be auto-dismissed by automation confidence levels.
- Significant incidents activate a learning pause before acceleration resumes, because continuing to optimise while root causes remain unclear compounds the damage rather than containing it.
- Risk dashboards show AI confidence levels alongside severity indicators so teams can assess how much weight to give a signal.
- Escalation paths are predefined for when predictive risk exceeds declared tolerance.

Risk signals function as operational checkpoints. Safety does not trail behind delivery. It travels with it.

28.8 Roles in Safe Agile AIWoW

In Safe Agile AIWoW, the structure of roles stays familiar. Scaled environments already distribute responsibility across portfolio, programme, architecture, and team levels. What deepens when AI enters the picture is the operational specificity of what each role must actively manage. Titles do not change. Accountability becomes sharper.

Role	What AI Can Do	What Remains Human
Portfolio Leadership	Generate investment simulations, forecast market shifts, suggest funding reallocation	Confirm strategic intent, authorise portfolio shifts, declare risk tolerance
Release Train / Programme Leadership	Forecast timeline compression, highlight bottlenecks, suggest resource redistribution	Validate planning adjustments, confirm dependency changes, authorise acceleration
System Architects	Propose design patterns, recommend refactoring, flag integration risks	Review structural proposals, approve changes, retain architectural authority
Product Management / Ownership	Score opportunities, surface urgency signals, model market projections	Validate prioritisation, confirm strategic alignment, declare outcome commitments
Teams	Suggest estimates, draft implementation, predict sprint risk	Validate inputs, confirm feasibility, own delivery accountability
AI Governance Oversight	Track override rates, monitor acceptance patterns, flag over-reliance	Ensure influence transparency, review accuracy trends, maintain governance clarity

The same boundary runs through every layer of this table. AI surfaces what would otherwise be invisible risks, patterns, projections, inefficiencies and brings it to the people who need to see it. Strategic intent, structural authority, and delivery accountability stay with the named humans responsible for each domain.

Speed travels through the system.

Authority anchors it in place.

28.9 Guardrails in Practice

Safe Agile AIWoW does not rely on intentions alone or shared awareness to keep fast systems stable. In environments where speed is a design goal, safety has to be structurally enforced through guardrails embedded into planning, execution, and governance before problems surface rather than after they do.

- The first category of **guardrail is acceleration limits**. Delivery speed, release frequency, and capacity expansion operate within declared thresholds. Crossing those thresholds requires deliberate authorisation, not automatic scaling triggered by a model that sees capacity and fills it.
- The second is **cross-team priority protection**. AI-driven reprioritisation signals cannot silently reorder shared backlog changes that affect what other teams are planning around; they need accountable validation before they propagate.
- Third, **architectural changes generated by AI go through review** forums rather than straight into implementation, because the system-wide implications of a structural change are exactly what an algorithm operating locally cannot fully evaluate.
- Fourth, **every AI-influenced decision leaves a trace**; when recommendations shape planning or execution, that influence is visible and auditable rather than invisible inside an automated pipeline. And
- Fifth, **significant incidents pause acceleration**. The system does not continue optimising while the root cause of a failure is still unclear.

These guardrails are not restrictions placed in the path of innovation. They are the structural conditions that make fast movement sustainable rather than fragile.

Without them, scaled speed does not produce more value. It produces more surface area for the kinds of systemic drift that compound quietly until something significant breaks.

They are not obstacles.

They are stabilisers for fast systems.

28.10 Safety Without Slowing Innovation

The fear that governance reduces agility is understandable, but it mistakes the source of volatility. Uncontrolled prediction is what creates volatility, not structure. When predictive signals can silently reorder priorities, reallocate resources, and shift architectural direction without authorisation, the system is not more innovative, it is more unstable. The unpredictability that follows is often mistaken for agility until the consequences arrive.

Safe Agile AIWoW achieves a different balance.

- Innovation continues.
- Experimentation remains possible.
- Forecasting improves confidence in planning conversations.
- Scaling becomes safer precisely because boundaries are clear.

What changes is that the movement is deliberate. Teams know why priorities shifted. Architects know what changed and who approved it. Leaders can trace direction back to a decision rather than discovering after the fact that a predictive signal quietly did it.

28.11 Final Insight

Scaled Agile was designed to bring coordination to fast-moving systems — to ensure multiple teams could operate in parallel without fragmenting direction. AI introduced predictive intelligence into that coordinated system. Forecasts became sharper. Risk signals arrived earlier. Dependencies became visible before conflict emerged. Speed increased not just in delivery but in decision cycles.

AIWoW brings discipline to this reality. Forecasts inform direction but do not redefine it. Optimisation suggests movement but does not authorise change. Safe Agile AIWoW is not additional bureaucracy layered onto scale. It is structured clarity embedded within scale — the kind that allows fast systems to stay coherent rather than gradually hollowing out the intentional decision-making that gave them direction in the first place.

Speed remains high because insight is immediate. Scale remains strong because coordination is preserved. Acceleration continues, but inside visible guardrails. In fast systems, safety is not about slowing progress. It is about ensuring that control keeps pace with the speed. When authority is explicit and boundaries are clear, scale becomes stable. And when stability and speed coexist, acceleration becomes something an organisation can actually sustain.

Safe Agile AIWoW where fast systems stay governed, and governed systems stay fast.

Summary Mind-map

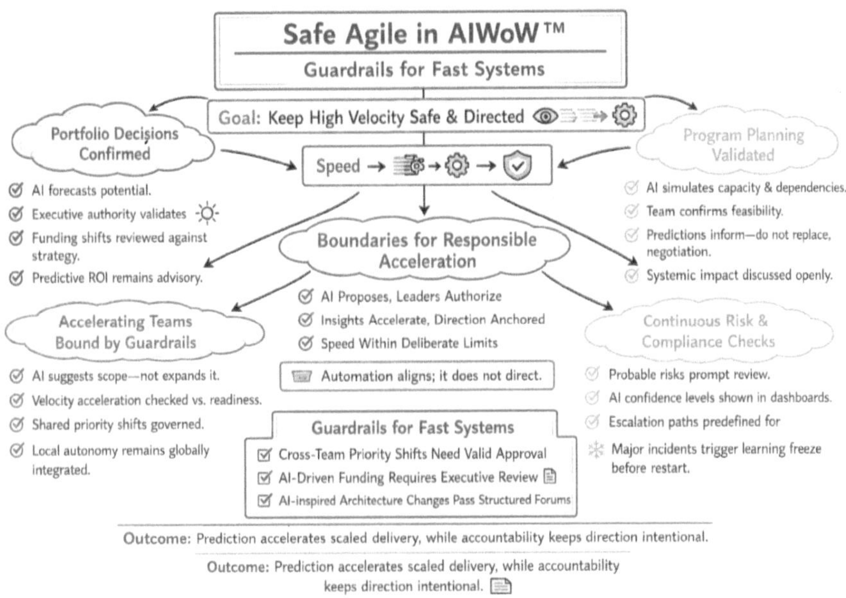

Chapter 29

Designing, Measuring and Leading Hybrid AIWoW

"Design creates the structure, measurement creates the signal, and leadership ensures Hybrid AIWo W remains aligned with human purpose."

Hybrid AIWoW is not a toolset and not a management trend. It is an operating design for environments where humans and intelligent systems work together continuously. After integrating DevOps, Agile, Scrum, Kanban, Safe practices, security, and financial controls with AI influence, one final question remains:

How do we design it intentionally, measure it responsibly, and lead it sustainably?

This chapter serves as the structural summary of Hybrid AIWoW, bringing together principles, practices, authority models, metrics, and leadership discipline into one coherent operating system.

29.1 Designing Hybrid AIWoW: From Structure to Stability

Hybrid AIWoW must be designed deliberately. It does not emerge automatically from adding AI tools to existing workflows.

Design begins with three foundational decisions:

1. Define Cognitive Boundaries

Every organisation must explicitly define:

- What AI can recommend
- What AI can automate
- What AI cannot decide
- Where human veto authority exists

Without these boundaries, influence becomes invisible. Hybrid systems fail not because of bad tools, but because of undefined authority.

Design rule:

Automation operates within boundaries.

Direction remains human.

2. Align Frameworks with AIWoW Principles

Hybrid AIWoW does not replace delivery frameworks. It overlays governance on top of them.

When designing Hybrid AIWoW :

- Agile cycles remain iterative
- DevOps pipelines remain automated
- Kanban flow remains continuous
- Safe structures remain coordinated

But all of them operate within:

- Explicit decision checkpoints
- Predictive validation layers
- Influence visibility controls
- Learning freeze mechanisms

Design is about integration, not replacement.

3. Install Guardrails Before Acceleration

AI increases speed instantly. Governance must exist before acceleration begins.

Practical guardrails include:

- Maximum velocity thresholds
- AI recommendation validation rules
- Predictive confidence review levels
- System-wide pause triggers after major failure

Guardrails are not bureaucratic overhead.

They are stabilisers for scale.

29.2 Measuring Hybrid AIWoW: Performance with Awareness

Measurement in Hybrid AIWoW operates on two dimensions:

1. Delivery performance
2. Cognitive stability

Traditional delivery metrics remain relevant:

- Throughput
- Cycle time
- Release frequency
- Lead time

However, Hybrid AIWoW introduces influence-aware measurement:

- AI-assisted decision ratio
- Prediction accuracy rate
- Override frequency trends
- Reprioritisation volatility
- AI recommendation acceptance patterns

These indicators answer a critical question:

Is performance improving because of clarity, or because of invisible influence?

True maturity is achieved when:

- Speed increases
- Error rates decline
- AI predictions remain calibrated
- Human authority remains visible
- Decision ownership is traceable

Cognitive stability must be measurable. Without it, speed becomes distortion.

29.3 Leadership in Hybrid AIWoW: Authority with Discipline

Leadership changes significantly in Hybrid AIWoW.

Leaders no longer manage only humans and delivery. They manage:

- Boundaries
- Influence
- Risk thresholds
- Escalation protocols

Hybrid AIWoW leadership requires three disciplines.

1. Direction Discipline

Leaders define strategic intent clearly and repeatedly. AI tools may provide forecasting, but they do not define purpose.

Leadership responsibility:

- Confirm direction before acceleration
- Validate AI-informed shifts
- Protect long-term positioning

2. Boundary Discipline

Leaders must ensure:

- AI authority is limited
- Overrides are allowed
- Acceleration remains governed
- System-wide brakes exist

A fast system without brakes is not innovative; it is unstable.

3. Learning Discipline

Hybrid AIWoW treats learning as structured, not emotional.

After major failures:

- Execution pauses
- Root causes are examined
- Governance thresholds are adjusted
- Acceleration resumes consciously

Leaders must protect learning from being rushed.

29.4 The Hybrid AIWoW Maturity View

An organisation operating Hybrid AIWoW effectively demonstrates:

- Visible decision authority
- Measurable AI influence
- Controlled automation
- Predictive intelligence with validation
- Transparent accountability

Low maturity environments show:

- Silent AI-driven reprioritisation
- Unquestioned predictive commitments

- Speed without review
- Leadership reacting after impact

Hybrid AIWoW maturity is not defined by how advanced the AI is.

It is defined by how disciplined the coordination is.

29.5 Integrating All Hybrid Practices

By this stage of Hybrid AIWoW is no longer a concept; it is a coordinated system.

We have seen how:

- DevOps operates with cognitive checkpoints instead of blind automation
- Agile iterations are strengthened through explicit commitment and validation
- Scrum roles retain authority while managing AI influence consciously
- Kanban flow gains visibility not only of work, but of decision shaping
- Safe structures introduce guardrails that stabilise acceleration at scale

Each practice remains recognisable. None of them are replaced. What changes is the layer above them; the governance of influence.

Integrating all Hybrid practices means designing one coherent operating environment where speed and control coexist.

In an integrated Hybrid AIWoW system:

- **Flow remains continuous** because delivery structures stay active and iterative.
- **Decisions remain deliberate** because predictive inputs are validated before commitment.
- **Automation remains bounded** because execution operates within declared thresholds.

- **Prediction remains validated** because forecasts inform but do not override intent.
- **Accountability remains human** because authority over direction is never delegated.

Integration is not about stacking frameworks.

It is about synchronising authority across them.

When DevOps pipelines respect architectural guardrails, when Agile commitments reflect validated intent, when Kanban adjustments remain traceable, and when Safe structures monitor systemic influence, the organisation begins to function as an intelligent whole.

Hybrid AIWoW does not introduce friction to reduce speed.

It introduces clarity to sustain speed.

Innovation continues.

Iteration remains fast.

Scale expands confidently.

But acceleration is no longer accidental. It is governed.

Hybrid AIWoW is not about slowing down innovation.

It is about making innovation sustainable at scale.

29.6 Final Synthesis: What Hybrid AIWoW Truly Is

Hybrid AIWoW is not a new framework layered on top of existing ones. It is the disciplined coordination of four forces that now coexist in modern work systems:

- **Human intent** that defines direction and purpose
- **Predictive intelligence** that anticipates patterns and risk
- **Automated execution** that accelerates delivery
- **Structured governance** that protects accountability

Each of these elements has existed in isolation.

Agile strengthened adaptability through short, iterative cycles.

DevOps enabled continuous and reliable delivery.

Scaled practices coordinated complexity across multiple teams and portfolios.

AI introduced predictive acceleration, reshaping how quickly systems can respond.

Hybrid AIWoW does not replace any of these. It integrates them under one unifying principle:

Velocity and responsibility must evolve together.

Without coordination, speed fragments direction.

Without governance, prediction reshapes intent.

Without human authority, automation diffuses accountability.

Hybrid AIWoW ensures that:

- Speed does not erode control
- Prediction does not replace judgement
- Automation does not weaken responsibility
- Scale does not dilute ownership

When designed with clear boundaries, measured with influence-aware metrics, and led with disciplined authority, Hybrid AIWoW transforms delivery environments into intelligent operating systems. These systems move quickly, but consciously. They adapt, but deliberately. They innovate, but sustainably.

That is the essence of Hybrid AIWoW: ***Not faster systems alone, but governed acceleration with conscious leadership***.

Summary Mind-map

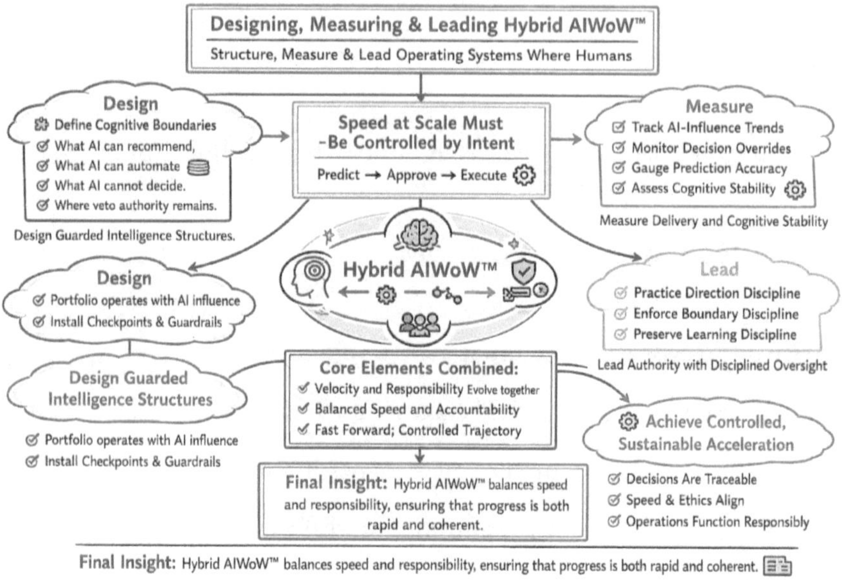

PART VIII

OPERATING TRANSFORMATION BY AIWoW

Building the Future of Conscious Work

The final section focuses on the practical evolution of organisations that adopt AIWoW as a governing discipline.

It explores how enterprises can transform their leadership, structures, and operational models to work consciously with intelligence.

The future of work will not be defined only by technological capability, but by the wisdom with which that capability is governed.

AIWoW™ as a Global Adoption Movement
AI Agents
AI Agents
Cross-industry collaboration, ethical standards, and societal impact.
Conscious Evolution of Work
Heart-Brain
Skill Uplift
Value Redefinition
Human Wellbeing Focus
Operating Transformation by AIWoW™
Practical Adoption of AIWoW™ Across Real-World Systems
Cross-industry implementation in production, healthcare, education, etc.
Supply Chain
Systems

Chapter 30

AIWoW - AI Ways of Working™ as a Global Adoption Movement

Why Frameworks Alone Don't Scale

Frameworks are necessary.

Movements are inevitable.

Every major transformation in how humans work begins with structure, but only scales through **shared belief, collective practice, and cultural adoption**. AIWoW - AI Ways of Working™ is no exception. If AIWoW remains only a framework, it will be implemented partially, interpreted narrowly, and eventually diluted. If it becomes a movement, it reshapes how intelligence and humanity coexist at scale.

This chapter explains **why frameworks alone cannot carry AIWoW forward**, and why institutionalisation must take the form of a **global movement**, not a proprietary method.

30.1 The Structural Limits of Frameworks

Most organisational transformations begin with a framework. Frameworks are helpful because they make complicated situations easier to understand. They assist teams in setting rules, making sure everyone does things the same way, making things repeatable, and coming up with a common language.

Many major tech businesses, for instance, use Agile frameworks to make software development better. Agile brought in sprints, backlogs, reviews, and retrospectives that helped engineering and product teams stay organised. At first, production went up because teams stuck to the system.

However, as organisations scaled and deadlines increased, some teams began skipping retrospectives, shortening testing cycles, or treating reviews as formal reporting. The framework still existed, but the discipline behind it weakened under pressure.

The same thing happened in banking. After the world financial crisis, banks put in place comprehensive risk management systems that included permission layers and compliance inspections. But during later periods of expansion, some businesses ignored these rules when they needed more money. The foundation stayed the same, but the way decisions were made changed.

These examples show a limit in the structure. Frameworks help humans do things, but they don't often change what humans really believe. They tell humans what to do, but they can't make sure that humans will keep doing it as things get bigger, goals go higher, or leadership objectives shift.

AI operates in exactly these fragile zones. AI systems influence decisions, automate processes, and scale quickly across organisations. Under competitive pressure, teams may trust AI outputs without questioning them, even if governance frameworks require human oversight.

In such environments, procedures alone are not enough.

Frameworks define what to do.

Movements explain why it must be done.

A framework provides direction.

A movement sustains discipline.

AIWoW - AI Ways of Working™ therefore goes beyond a technical framework. It seeks to shape how organisations think about intelligence, responsibility, and long-term consequences.

When humans understand the purpose behind responsible AI, the discipline survives pressure, scale, and leadership change. Without that conviction, even the strongest framework eventually becomes a document that exists on paper but disappears in daily decisions.

30.2 Why AI Intensifies the Scaling Problem

AI dramatically increases the speed of execution inside organisations. Decisions, analysis, and automation now scale much faster than before.

In contrast, the human aspects of organisations, including culture, judgement, and shared understanding, tend to change more slowly. This creates a structural mismatch.

Rate of AI Acceleration > Rate of Human Meaning-Making

When this gap widens, predictable behaviours appear.

Teams bypass frameworks because they slow down delivery.

Controls meant for slower decision-making processes tend to loosen up.

Ethical checks are treated as formalities rather than decision guides.

Empathy remains in policies but disappears from operational choices.

This pattern is visible in several industries adopting AI at scale. Digital platforms, for example, employ automated systems to scrutinise extensive online content. While the technology is immediately deployable, the capacity to assess fairness, bias, and community impact develops gradually. Consequently, decisions regarding operational procedures typically outpace the evolution of ethical considerations.

A comparable disparity is observable in financial services, healthcare analytics, and logistics optimisation, where automated judgements proliferate rapidly across all operational phases.

AIWoW - AI Ways of Working™ must scale **faster than erosion**, not slower than technological adoption.

30.3 The Difference Between Adoption and Internalisation

Organisations can adopt new frameworks quickly. Training sessions are conducted, new tools are introduced, and teams begin following updated procedures. From the outside, the change appears complete.

However, true transformation takes longer because values must be internalised, not just adopted.

A practical example can be seen in many global organisations introducing **data privacy regulations** after new compliance laws were introduced. Organisations quickly implemented policies, conducted employee training, and deployed compliance tools. Employees followed procedures because they were required to.

But real cultural change happened much later. Only when teams began thinking about privacy risks during product design, customer interaction, and system development did the value become internalised. At that stage, privacy was no longer a checklist; it became part of decision-making behaviour.

This difference can be understood clearly.

Adoption	Internalisation
Process compliance	Value commitment
Tool usage	Behavioural change
Training-driven	Identity-driven
Short-term	Enduring

Frameworks are effective at enabling adoption. They introduce structure and guide immediate behaviour.

But internalisation happens when humans begin acting from conviction rather than instruction.

AI systems operate at scale and influence many decisions. If responsible practices remain at the level of procedural adoption, they will weaken under operational pressure.

AIWoW - AI Ways of Working™ therefore requires internalisation. Responsible use of intelligence must become part of how organisations think, not just how they comply.

30.4 Why AIWoW Cannot Be Mandated

AIWoW cannot succeed through mandates alone.

In AI-driven environments, three forces weaken top-down rules.

1. **Local optimisation overrides central intent**

   Teams optimise for their own targets even when broader principles exist.

2. **Speed pressure rewards shortcuts**

   Speeding things up sometimes leads teams to skip over the slower, more careful ethical reviews. **Automation hides erosion**

When systems automate decisions, small ethical compromises become invisible.

Because of this, mandates have limits. They can enforce procedures but not human qualities.

No mandate can:

- • force empat
- • sustain restraint
- • preserve judgement

These come from **shared conviction**, not instruction.

AIWoW, therefore, depends on collective understanding inside organisations, not only formal directives.

30.5 The Anatomy of a Global Movement

Successful global movements grow beyond rules because humans believe in them. They usually share five common elements.

Element	Purpose
Shared philosophy	Explains why the idea matters
Simple principles	Defines what must never be violated
Local adaptation	Allows the idea to work in different contexts
Community reinforcement	Creates humans who sustain and spread it
Moral legitimacy	Gives the movement long-term credibility

A practical example is the global adoption of **open-source software practices**. The philosophy of collaborative development attracted contributors worldwide. Simple principles like transparency and shared code guided behaviour. Local communities adapted the approach for different industries and technologies. Developer communities reinforced participation, and over time, the movement gained legitimacy across the technology ecosystem.

AIWoW needs to have a framework that is similar in order to grow around the world. It can't depend just on rules or processes set by the organisation. It needs to have a clear goal, easy rules to follow, be relevant to the community, include the community, and be morally right.

It can only keep up with adoption as AI spreads through businesses and societies if it does this.

30.6 AIWoW 's Core Movement Thesis

The main idea behind AIWoW is that intelligence should grow with humans, not at their expense.

The problem is no longer only technical ability as AI spreads to more and more fields. The main problem is how intelligence fits into human systems.

This is already a choice that organisations have to make. AI can make things more efficient and make judgements on its own, but it can also make humans less responsible, less accountable, and less aware of the implications of their actions.

This makes the issue larger than technology. It becomes a question of responsibility.

For example, financial institutions using algorithmic decisions must balance efficiency with fairness and human oversight. Healthcare systems using AI diagnostics must support, not replace, clinical judgement.

Movements form when humans recognise that a real choice exists and that neutrality is no longer possible.

AIWoW takes a clear position: intelligence should strengthen human capability and responsibility, not diminish them.

30.7 Why Tools, Certifications, and Playbooks Are Not Enough

Tools, certifications, and playbooks help organisations structure adoption. But they do not guarantee lasting discipline.

Tools can be replaced or optimised away when faster options appear.

Certifications can become symbolic when teams pursue them only to meet compliance requirements.

Playbooks can become outdated as technology and business conditions change.

Many industries have experienced this pattern. For example, several organisations introduced cybersecurity certifications and compliance checklists. While these improved documentation and reporting, real security depended on whether teams actively practised vigilance in daily operations.

AI systems evolve quickly, which makes this limitation even more visible. Procedures alone cannot keep pace with technological change.

AIWoW, therefore, cannot depend only on tools, certifications, or playbooks. It must survive even when these mechanisms evolve or disappear.

When frameworks work without a fundamental belief, they slowly turn into:

- Checklists that don't require commitment
- Following the rules without caring
- Being efficient without a conscience

To keep AIWoW working, it needs to be owned by everyone in the organisation, not only by authorities.

30.8 From Governance Model to Moral Reference Point

As AI becomes embedded across organisations, situations will arise where priorities collide.

Metrics may conflict.

Speed may demand shortcuts.

Efficiency may pressure ethical boundaries.

These moments occur in many industries. For example, financial institutions using automated credit decisions must balance efficiency with fairness. Technology organisations' moderating online content must balance scale with responsible judgement.

In such situations, procedures alone are not enough.

AIWoW must function as a **moral reference point**, not just a governance model. It provides clarity about where organisations should stop, even when performance pressure increases.

In simple terms, it answers a critical question:

"This is where we draw the line."

Movements endure because they give humans clear guidance when systems face pressure and difficult trade-offs.

30.9 Institutionalisation Without Centralisation

A global movement cannot be tightly controlled from a single centre. If everything is centrally dictated, it becomes rigid and difficult to apply across different industries and cultures.

Instead, it must be **coherently decentralised**.

This means organisations share the same foundation while adapting practices to their own context.

For example, global safety standards in industries like aviation follow this model. Core safety principles are shared worldwide, but each airline and regulator adapts operational practices to local environments and regulations. The principles remain stable, while implementation varies.

AIWoW needs a balance like that.

To institutionalise, you need:

- Language that everyone can understand
- Common Values
- Non-Negotiable Limits That Everyone Agrees On

It also lets you be flexible by:

- Practices in context
- Models for certain industries
- Cultural Interpretation

This framework maintains the movement steady without making everyone do the same thing.

It keeps things from becoming too stiff and breaking apart.

30.10 The Role of Community in AIWoW

Frameworks usually scale through consultants, training programmes, and implementation projects. They spread because organisations adopt them as operational tools.

Movements scale differently. They grow through communities of humans who believe in the purpose behind the idea.

A clear example can be seen in the global open-source software ecosystem. Its growth did not depend on central mandates but on communities of developers who protected principles like transparency, collaboration, and shared improvement. The community itself sustained the discipline.

AIWoW requires a similar kind of participation.

It depends on:

- Practitioners Who Challenge Misuse
- Leaders Who Model Restraint
- Technologists Who Refuse Blind Optimisation
- Institutions That Defend Human Dignity

In this sense, community functions as the **immune system of the movement**. It detects misuse, questions harmful practices, and protects the principles that allow responsible intelligence to scale.

30.11 Why AIWoW Must Be Open by Design

Systems that operate behind closed doors often struggle to gain trust. When ethical standards are controlled by a single organisation or authority, humans tend to question whether those standards truly serve the broader public interest.

Many industries have faced this challenge. For example, technology platforms that introduced internal AI ethics guidelines without external visibility often faced criticism because stakeholders could not see how those principles were applied in practice.

Trust increases when ideas remain open to examination and improvement.

AIWoW, therefore, must be designed as an open concept that invites participation rather than control.

It must remain:

- Openly Discussable
- Publicly Critique-Able
- Collectively Refined

Openness allows different industries, institutions, and experts to question assumptions, improve principles, and adapt practices responsibly.

This openness is not a weakness.

It is what gives the framework **legitimacy and durability** as AI continues to evolve.

30.12 The Risk of Not Becoming a Movement

If AIWoW remains only a framework, its influence will remain limited.

Frameworks can be adopted formally, but ignored when pressure increases. Many organisations implement guidelines, policies, or standards that look strong on paper but weaken during real operational demands.

In such situations, several patterns appear.

- It Will Be Selectively Implemented
- Stripped of Restraint Under Pressure
- Used Rhetorically, Not Operationally
- Abandoned When Inconvenient

This pattern has occurred in several areas of corporate governance and ethics programmes. Policies were introduced with strong intent but gradually became symbolic when performance pressure increased.

Ethical ideas rarely fail because humans openly oppose them.

More often, they fail because they slowly become irrelevant to everyday decisions.

For AIWoW to remain meaningful, it must influence how organisations actually operate, not just how they describe their intentions.

30.13 AIWoW as a Counterweight to Unchecked Acceleration

Periods of rapid technological acceleration often produce a balancing response. As systems become faster and more powerful, societies begin asking how to protect human values within that progress.

This pattern has appeared before. Industrial expansion created movements for labour rights and workplace safety. The growth of digital platforms triggered global discussions on privacy and data protection.

Each acceleration phase eventually raises the same concern: how to preserve human meaning and responsibility while progress continues.

AIWoW plays a similar role in the age of artificial intelligence.

It exists to restore balance when intelligent systems scale rapidly across organisations and institutions.

*AIWoW is **not anti-technology**.*

*It is **anti-extraction**.*

It does not resist intelligence itself.

*It resists **intelligence that operates without conscience, responsibility, or human awareness of its consequences**.*

30.14 The Choice Before Institutions

As AI becomes embedded in operations, institutions must decide how they relate to AIWoW.

One option is to treat it as a **compliance framework**, a set of policies followed to satisfy governance requirements. This approach can create short-term alignment because procedures are documented and teams formally follow them.

The second option is to treat AIWoW as a **guiding philosophy** that shapes how decisions are made across the organisation. In this case, principles influence leadership choices, system design, and daily operational behaviour.

The difference is significant.

- Adopt AIWoW As A Compliance Framework
- Embrace AIWoW As A Guiding Philosophy

The first approach produces procedural alignment for a period of time.

The second creates deeper stability because the principles remain active even when technologies, tools, or leadership structures change.

In the long run, only the latter supports organisations that must operate responsibly in an

environment where intelligent systems continue to expand.

30.15 Transition to Stewardship and Legacy

Until now, the discussion focused on understanding AIWoW as a framework for responsible intelligence. From this point forward, the focus shifts toward how this idea can endure beyond individual organisations and technologies.

The transition can be understood in three steps:

- From Theory To Continuity
- From Frameworks To Stewardship
- From Implementation To Legacy

The chapters that follow will explore how AIWoW can be sustained over time through broader institutional structures, including:

- Consortium Structures
- Certification Without Commodification
- Academic Anchoring

- Industry Alliances
- Long-Term Stewardship Models

Frameworks help organisations learn **how to work.**

Movements help societies decide **how to choose.**

In the age of AI, these choices cannot be avoided. Intelligent systems are expanding across industries, institutions, and everyday life.

AI Ways of Working exists not only to improve how intelligence operates, but to ensure that as intelligence grows, **humanity does not diminish.**

In the end, the future will not be determined only by the most powerful AI systems. It will be shaped by the values of those who decide **how intelligence should be used and where its limits must remain.**

For this reason, AIWoW must exist not merely as a document or framework.

It must live and evolve as a **shared movement of responsibility in the age of intelligent systems.**

Summary Mind-map

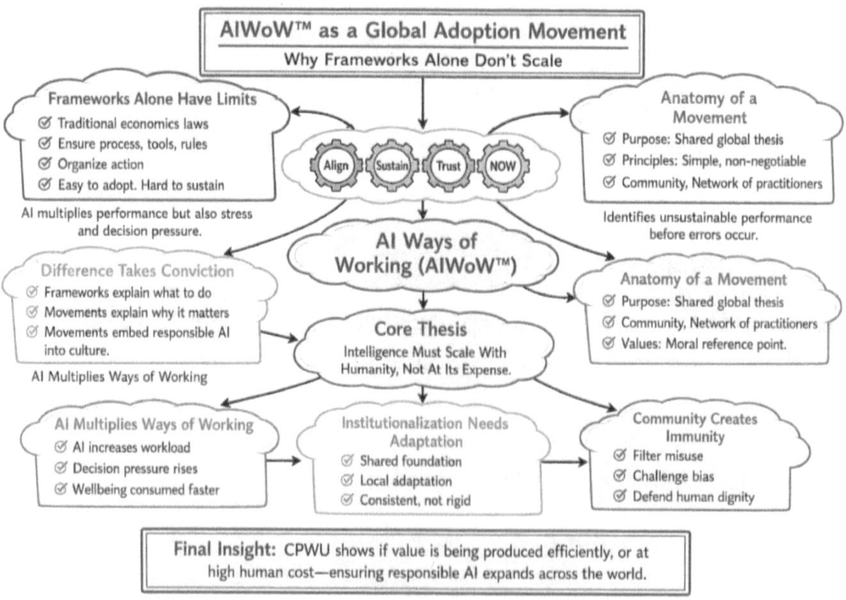

Chapter 31

Conscious Evolution of Work

The Journey of Transformation Towards AIWoW

Every major shift in the history of work has been a transformation journey.

The industrial era transformed labour into organised production.

The information era transformed knowledge into coordinated systems.

The digital era transformed speed into competitive advantage.

The age of Artificial Intelligence introduces a deeper transformation.

Organisations are no longer simply adopting new tools. They are entering a journey toward **AIWoW - AI Ways of Working™**, a transformation in how intelligence, humans, and systems collaborate to create value.

This transformation does not occur instantly. It unfolds gradually as organisations rethink how they use humans, materials, capital, and intelligence.

AIWoW, therefore, represents the conscious evolution of work, where organisations move from extractive systems toward regenerative, intelligent enterprises.

This chapter explains that journey.

31.1 The Starting Point: The Extraction Organisation

Most organisations today still operate on a model shaped during the industrial era.

The core assumption is simple:

Growth requires consumption.

Humans expend effort.

Materials are extracted.

Money is deployed aggressively to drive expansion.

Success is measured through output, efficiency, and financial return.

This model delivered decades of economic progress, but it also created structural strain.

Human burnout increased.

Environmental pressure intensified.

Financial systems became fragile under short-term incentives.

Artificial Intelligence enters this environment as a powerful multiplier.

If AI is applied without transformation, it simply accelerates the extraction model:

- More automation
- Faster decisions
- Greater pressure on human systems

AIWoW begins with the recognition that **the traditional model cannot safely absorb the intelligence now available.**

Transformation becomes necessary.

31.2 Intelligence Changes the Equation

AI transforms the way organisations produce value.

Most of the time, traditional systems relied on humans and physical resources. Most of the time, growth meant using more workers, supplies, and money.

AI changes the way we create value by making it smarter.

Organisations start to make value by:

- Guessing
- Recognising Patterns
- Smart Coordination
- Ongoing Improvement

For instance, AI is currently used by global logistics corporations to guess how much demand there will be and find the best delivery routes. Better projections cut down on waste and make things run more smoothly, instead of making trucks and gasoline use more.

Manufacturers also use AI-based maintenance systems to figure out when equipment will break down before it does. This cuts down on downtime and makes machines last longer without using more resources.

Organisations may create greater value with less physical usage and better system design as intelligence becomes more available.

This opens the possibility of a different organisational model.

Extraction Organisation

Value $\propto$ Depletion

AIWoW Organisation

Value $\propto$ Regeneration

In extractive systems, growth consumes resources.

In regenerative systems, growth strengthens the system itself.

However, reaching this stage does not happen automatically. It requires **conscious transformation in how organisations design work, decisions, and responsibility around intelligent systems.**

31.3 The Triple Impact Awareness

Every organisation influences three domains at the same time: **Humans, Materials, and Money**. In traditional management, these areas are often treated separately; human resources manages humans, operations manages materials, and finance manages capital.

In reality, these areas are quite closely related. Choices in one area have an immediate effect on the others.

AIWoW brings in triple impact awareness, which means that businesses think about how their choices affect all three areas at the same time.

Effect on Humans **(Man)**

Organisations shape how humans work. This includes:

- Cognitive Load
- Stress on the mind
- Learning new skills
- Responsibility for Morality

Many traditional performance systems think that high output means that humans have to work hard. Humans accept long hours, endless deadlines, and mental weariness as the price of growth.

This idea is challenged by AIWoW.

Organisations are starting to measure human regeneration instead of just productivity.

Human Regeneration = Capability Gained – Capacity Drained

For instance, AI tools are being used more and more by consulting firms to automate data collection and initial analysis. Consultants might spend less time writing reports and more time thinking about what they mean and how to use them. Work is less tiring and more mentally stimulating when it is set up correctly.

In an AIWoW organisation, the goal is simple:

Humans should leave work **more capable, knowledgeable, and confident than when they arrived**.

Impact on Materials

Historically, industrial systems depended on the constant extraction of materials. As manufacturing went up, so did the amount of resources used and the amount of trash produced.

AI gives us new ways to change these systems.

Smart systems can:

- Guess How Much Material Will Be Needed
- Make supply chains work better
- Cut down on waste by making predictions
- Make products last longer

For instance, big industrial organisations now use AI-based predictive maintenance systems to keep an eye on how well their machines are working. Repairing machines before they break down makes them last longer and cuts down on the need to buy new ones.

Material impact can be expressed simply:

Material Impact = Material Consumed – Material Restored

Traditional systems focus only on reducing consumption. AIWoW goes further by encouraging **regenerative material systems**, where resources are reused, repaired, or intelligently optimised.

Impact on Money:

In many organisations, money is treated as the main source for rapid expansion. Capital is poured aggressively, and performance is judged primarily by short-term financial metrics.

AIWoW reframes money as a **circulatory system** that supports long-term capability and stability.

Financial regeneration can be described as:

Financial Regeneration = Long-Term Value – Short-Term Extraction

For instance, organisations that invest in employee learning upliftment, responsible technology governance, and strong supply chains often build stronger long-term performance than those focusing only on quarterly profits.

So, financial choices are now more in line with rebuilding humans and systems than with getting quick profits.

Awareness of triple impact makes sure that expansion doesn't hurt the system that makes it happen. Instead of making one area better while hurting another, businesses are starting to make decisions that make Man, Materials, and Money more resilient all at the same time.

This change is necessary as intelligent systems grow and affect every important choice across operations.

31.4 AI as the Catalyst of Transformation

AI is a powerful catalyst that helps businesses change. But it has two effects. It can either make systems stronger or make problems worse, depending on how it is set up and run.

In other words, AI is both a tool and a threat.

AI may help an organisation's systems grow and change if it is used effectively. Smart systems can detect problems that humans used to have trouble finding.

AI can aid organisations by:

- Finding problems with efficiency Early
- Making the best use of materials and energy
- Helping humans make decisions that are hard to make
- Cutting down on work that is repetitive and mechanical

Many businesses are already seeing these benefits.

More and more logistics organisations are using AI-based route optimisation to save fuel and speed up delivery. Better routing makes things more efficient with less resources, not more trucks.

Hospitals employ predictive analytics to figure out what dangers patients might face and how to better manage their care. Doctors get early signs about possible problems, which lets them act sooner.

Machine learning systems are used by manufacturers to keep an eye on production processes. These systems find problems early, which helps cut down on poor output and wastage of materials.

AI makes the system stronger in these circumstances by making operations smarter and more efficient.

But if the same technology is employed without appropriate management, it can also make extraction worse.

AI systems that aren't checked may:

- Make humans burn out faster by putting constant pressure on them to improve
- Promote overproduction by making the most of short-term efficiency
- Maximise Profit Even If It Hurts Humans or Society
- Hide harm inside complicated automated systems

For instance, algorithmic management techniques on some gig-economy platforms make deliveries faster and cheaper, but they might also make workers more stressed or make it harder to see how decisions are made.

This dual nature needs governance.

AIWoW exists to ensure that intelligent systems strengthen organisations responsibly. The goal is not merely to make systems faster or more efficient, but to ensure that **intelligence amplifies restoration rather than depletion**.

31.5 From Machine Organisations to AIWoW Living Systems

Traditional organisations were designed like **machines**. Work was structured for control, stability, and efficiency. Processes were predefined, and decision authority was concentrated at the top.

These organisations relied on:

- Rules that are quite strict
- Take charge from one place
- Steps that have a clear cause-and-effect relationship

This idea worked in situations where things didn't change very often, and workers could get ready for their work ahead of time.

AI begins to change this framework.

When intelligent technologies are used for prediction, decision support, and operational coordination, businesses can no longer work like machines. They begin to behave more like adaptive systems that always respond to inputs and feedback.

- Strict Rules
- Control from one place
- Processes with a clear cause-and-effect relationship

This concept worked in places where things didn't change quickly, and humans could prepare ahead for their work.

AI starts to modify this structure.

Organisations can no longer work like machines when intelligent systems are involved in

prediction, decision support, and operational coordination. They start to act more like adaptive systems that always respond to inputs and feedback.

AIWoW sees this change and rethinks organisations as living systems that are guided by responsible intelligence.

In an AIWoW environment, enterprises demonstrate characteristics similar to living systems:

- Adaptation to changing conditions through intelligent insights
- Continuous learning from data, outcomes, and human feedback
- Feedback-driven decision cycles instead of fixed processes
- Sensitivity to environmental signals such as market demand, risk, and societal impact

For example, global supply chains using AI can dynamically adjust inventory, transportation routes, and production levels based on real-time signals. Human teams supervise and interpret these insights, ensuring that decisions remain aligned with broader goals and responsibilities.

AIWoW ensures that this intelligence does not simply increase automation but strengthens **human-guided adaptability**.

In this model, efficiency alone no longer defines success. Organisations must also demonstrate the ability to **learn continuously, adapt responsibly, and regenerate their capabilities over time**.

AIWoW, therefore, represents the transition from machine organisations optimised **for control** to **living enterprises guided by responsible intelligence and human stewardship**.

31.6 Conscious Design of Work

In many organisations, change happens **accidentally rather than intentionally**. New technologies are introduced, teams adopt tools quickly, and processes are adjusted gradually without redesigning the overall system.

Over time, this creates several problems.

Processes become complex.

Responsibilities become unclear.

Metrics begin measuring activity rather than meaningful outcomes.

AI can accelerate this accidental evolution. Because intelligent tools are easy to deploy, organisations often integrate them into existing workflows without reconsidering how work itself should be structured.

AIWoW emphasises **conscious design of work systems.**

Instead of adding AI tools on top of existing processes, organisations must deliberately design how humans and intelligent systems collaborate with each other.

Leaders and teams need to ask important questions like:

What kinds of behaviours are our systems pushing humans to do?

What human abilities are we making stronger or weaker?

Where should automation help humans do their jobs?

Where does human judgement need to stay at the centre?

A customer care organisation that is adding AI chat systems, for instance, must choose whether the automation should only handle simple questions or whether it should also pass on more complicated issues to human agents who can show empathy and comprehend the situation.

In an AIWoW organisation, work design is not a one-time activity. It becomes a **continuous process of reflection and adjustment**.

Teams regularly look at how systems work, how individuals feel about their jobs, and if the system's initial purpose is still being met.

When humans stop thinking about things, organisations steadily lose sight of their goals. Conscious design stops this from happening by making sure that intelligence, automation, and human responsibility all grow at the same time.

31.7 Conscious Acceleration

Acceleration has always been a goal of organisations: faster decisions, shorter production cycles, and quicker market entry.

AI removes much of the friction from speed. Analysis, coordination, and execution can now happen almost instantly.

However, this creates a new risk: **unconscious acceleration**.

Systems may move faster than humans can understand, supervise, or govern.

AIWoW introduces **conscious acceleration**.

Conscious acceleration is speeding up a system only when humans can understand it, regulate it, and be ready for it morally.

Banks, for instance, utilise AI to quickly find transactions that look suspicious, but humans still need to look at high-risk cases. AI helps hospitals quickly look at medical photos, but doctors still have the final say.

The idea is simple.

Instability happens when you speed up without being ready.

Ready acceleration makes progress that lasts.

31.8 Preserving Humanity While Scaling Intelligence

AI systems scale very quickly.

Human capacity does not.

As smart systems spread throughout organisations, three concerns start to show up:

Impact abstraction - decisions are made without thinking about how they will affect real humans.

Less time to think about things - faster processes don't give you much time to stop and think.

Diffusion of responsibility: When judgements incorporate automated systems, it's hard to know who is responsible.

AIWoW doesn't see humans as feelings; it sees them as an organisational skill.

Human systems must keep:

- Decision
- Understanding
- Being responsible
- What work means

For instance, AI diagnoses in healthcare systems still need clinicians to explain the results and talk to patients. The technology makes analysis better, but humans are still the most important part.

So, organisations need to make sure that humans can learn and evolve together with smart technology.

Systems may become powerful but more fragile if intelligence grows without making humans's judgement and responsibility stronger.

31.9 The Transformation Phases of AIWoW

The transition toward AIWoW usually unfolds gradually. Organisations rarely move directly into a mature model. Instead, they pass through several recognisable phases as intelligence becomes embedded in operations.

Phase 1: Intelligent Expansion

The journey typically begins with rapid AI adoption.

Automation spreads across processes.

Decision support tools become widely used.

Productivity appears to increase quickly.

Many organisations experience early efficiency gains during this phase. However, hidden pressures often begin forming beneath the surface as systems accelerate faster than humans adapt.

Phase 2: Human Strain

As intelligent systems deepen their influence, human systems begin to feel the pressure.

- **Burnout Rises**
- **Trust Begins To Decline**
- **Ethical Discomfort Appears**
- **Decision Ownership Becomes Unclear**

At this stage, the limiting factor becomes **human absorption capacity**. The organisation realises that intelligence is scaling faster than human systems can comfortably manage.

Phase 3: Conscious Redesign

Organisations that recognise this imbalance begin redesigning their systems deliberately.

Leadership shifts from pure supervision toward **mentorship and guidance**.

Metrics expand beyond speed and cost to include responsibility and long-term impact.

Operational design begins by emphasising **regeneration instead of extraction**.

Human judgement and intelligent systems are intentionally structured to work together.

Phase 4: The AIWoW Enterprise

Over time, organisations stabilise into a more mature operating model.

They demonstrate:

- AI **guided by human intent**
- **Distributed decision authority based on capability**

- **Regeneration across humans, materials, and capital**
- **Conscious acceleration as a normal practice**

At this stage, organisations are not only efficient.

They become **resilient, trusted, and capable of sustaining intelligent systems responsibly over the long term.**

31.10 What Disappears During Transformation

As organisations move toward AIWoW, several long-standing assumptions begin to fade.

- Management as supervision
- Speed as the ultimate competitive advantage
- Performance as the only success metric
- Growth through exhaustion

These ideas were effective in earlier industrial and digital systems where control, output, and rapid execution defined success.

However, in AI-driven environments, these assumptions gradually lose effectiveness. Intelligent systems already increase speed and automate many supervisory tasks. What becomes valuable instead is judgement, coordination, and responsible decision-making.

As a result, these old assumptions do not disappear because organisations reject them.

They fade because **they no longer work in systems where intelligence operates continuously and at scale.**

31.11 What Emerges in the AIWoW Enterprise

As organisations transform toward AIWoW, new patterns begin to replace older management assumptions.

- **Leadership Becomes Mentorship**

  Leaders focus on guiding judgement and developing humans rather than supervising tasks.

- **Judgement Becomes The Most Valued Capability**

  As AI handles routine analysis and execution, human value shifts toward interpretation, ethical reasoning, and contextual decision-making.

- **Metrics Guide Learning Rather Than Punish Performance**

  Measurement systems help teams improve and adapt instead of functioning only as control mechanisms.

- **Organisations Behave Like Adaptive Ecosystems**

  Departments, technologies, and human teams interact dynamically, learning and adjusting based on feedback.

- **Trust Becomes A Competitive Advantage**

  Organisations that use intelligence responsibly earn trust from employees, customers, and society.

In an AIWoW enterprise, long-term organisational fitness depends on maintaining a balance between **intelligence and humanity**. When systems combine technological capability with responsible human judgement, they remain stable and resilient. Without this balance, even highly advanced systems become fragile over time.

31.12 The Final Choice in the AIWoW Journey

As organisations enter the AI era, they eventually have a fundamental choice.

Should humans adapt themselves to the logic of machines?

Or should machines be designed to strengthen human systems?

This question appears across industries. Organisations introducing AI-driven decision systems must decide whether automation should replace human judgement or support it. Institutions deploying intelligent systems must determine whether efficiency alone will guide decisions or whether human responsibility will remain central.

AIWoW makes this choice explicit.

Intelligence can scale almost without limit through data, computation, and automation. Human systems, judgement, empathy, and responsibility, do not scale automatically.

For this reason, organisations must ensure that intelligence operates **under human guidance**, not beyond it.

In the AIWoW journey, technology expands capability, but **human values remain the governing force that determines how far intelligence should go.**

AIWoW represents a journey:

From extraction to regeneration.

From mechanical systems to living enterprises.

From unconscious acceleration to conscious design.

Because in the age of AI, the future of work will not be defined by the smartest machines.

It will be defined by ***how consciously humans choose to evolve the systems that use them.***

Summary Mind-map

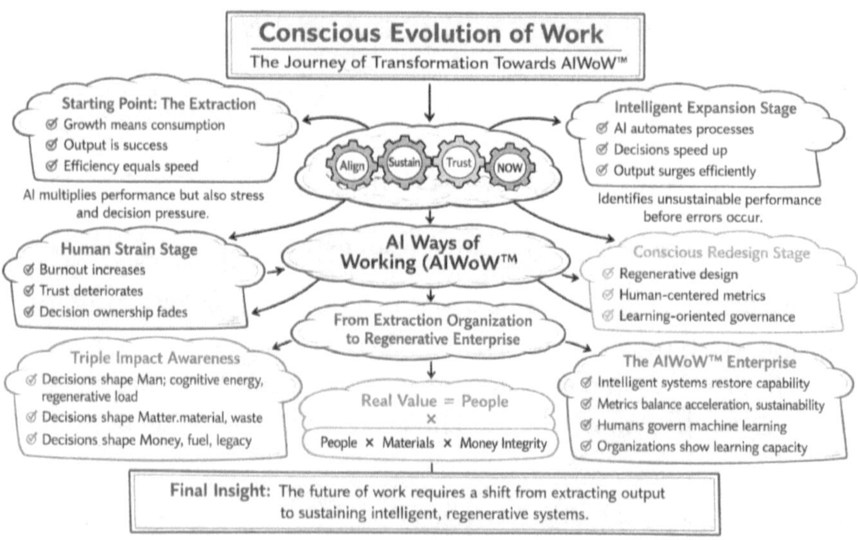

Chapter 32

Practical Adoption of AIWoW Across Real-World Systems

How AI Ways of Working Become Operational in Different Contexts

Throughout this book, AIWoW - AI Ways of Working™ has been explored across many environments where intelligent systems interact with human responsibility. These environments include large enterprises, startups, governments, healthcare systems, financial institutions, education systems, legal structures, media organisations, households, and youth development ecosystems.

Each environment revealed something important.

AI does not behave the same everywhere.

A system that works well in a technology startup may create ethical problems in the healthcare industry.

A method suitable for a manufacturing organisation may not work in the education or law field. AIWoW, therefore, does not propose a single rigid framework.

Instead, it offers a practical adoption approach that adapts to the realities of the domain.

This chapter focuses on how AIWoW can actually be adopted in practice across different areas. The goal is not just theoretical discussion but a practical understanding of how organisations, institutions, and communities can begin applying AI Ways of Working in their routine.

This chapter, therefore, provides a practical adoption lens across the major contexts explored earlier.

32.1 Practical Adoption in Large Enterprises

Stabilising Intelligence at Scale

Large enterprises often have thousands of employees, many departments, and complex decision structures. When AI tools are introduced into such environments, the biggest risk is not technological failure but organisational crumbling.

Different teams may use AI in different ways. Some teams are quite eager to automate, while others are completely against it.

In most large enterprises, the practical use of AIWoW starts with three steps:

- Making it clear what the organisation wants to do with AI
- Setting who is responsible for decisions about AI-influenced changes
- Making sure that automation doesn't take away human oversight in decisions that have a big effect

A multinational retail organisation that uses AI to predict demand might use AIWoW by making sure that forecasting models help planners instead of taking their place. Humans who plan to use AI predictions to make sense of them, check out strange signals, and make decisions on inventories.

The message for businesses is clear: AI needs to grow along with the organisation's responsibilities.

32.2 Practical Adoption in Startups

Speed with Conscious Boundaries

Startups may use AI technologies without having to deal with a lot of red tape, thus, startups adopt it quite quickly. But this speed also makes it more likely that technology and the long-term direction of the product won't be in sync.

When startups employ AIWoW in real life, they focus on keeping things clear while moving swiftly.

Startup teams usually use AIWoW by:

- Making sure that founders are clearly responsible for AI-driven features
- Making sure that AI-driven product decisions can still be explained
- Setting limits on when automation shouldn't take the place of human judgement

For example, a firm that is building an AI-driven hiring platform might let AI narrow down the list of prospects but make sure that humans still make the final hiring decisions.

AI helps startups when they move quickly, yet are still conscious of how automated decisions affect humans.

32.3 Practical Adoption in Government and Public Institutions

Trust Before Efficiency

As the choices public institutions make directly affect citizens, public institutions are under a lot of scrutiny. So, when the government uses AI, it needs to focus on being open and honest.

The government frequently starts using AIWoW in tiny, closely watched ways, such as:

- Sorting documents
- Analysing data that is public
- Better efficiency in administration

More sensitive areas, such as who can get welfare, help from the police, or how public resources are used, need robust human control and oversight.

For example, a government welfare department that uses AI to find fraud would let the system flag situations that look suspicious, but it would need human officers to check the evidence before taking any action.

AIWoW adoption works in public systems when humans can comprehend and question judgements made by machines.

32.4 Practical Adoption in Healthcare Systems

Augmenting Care Without Replacing Clinical Judgement

Healthcare organisations need to be very careful when they start using AI. Mistakes can have serious effects on humans' lives and dignity.

AIWoW adoption in healthcare frequently starts with AI taking on responsibilities that help, such as:

- Recognising patterns in diagnostic tests
- Help with medical paperwork
- Analysing the results of treatment

But skilled doctors must still make the final medical choices.

AI can help hospitals find unusual patterns in scans, but radiologists are still responsible for interpreting the results and telling patients what they mean.

AIWoW in healthcare works when technology helps doctors without making treatment less effective by AI's undue influence.

32.5 Practical Adoption in Financial Institutions

Balancing Intelligence and Risk

Financial systems take care of money, credit, and the economy as a whole. AI can help uncover fraud, figure out credit scores, and make guesses about what will happen in the market. But models that aren't properly handled could put the whole system at risk.

The main point of AIWoW in finance is to make sure that decisions are made honestly and openly.

When banks and other financial organisations use AIWoW, they normally do the following:

- Make sure that credit choices can still be explained
- Have a person make financial decisions that have a large impact
- Watch how the model behaves to see if there is any bias or exclusion that you didn't predict.

An AI-powered loan approval system might look at financial patterns, but it might also enable human loan officers to look at instances when they are near to making a decision.

In financial situations, predictive intelligence must always be responsible.

32.6 Practical Adoption in Education Systems

Using AI to Strengthen Learning Rather Than Replace Effort

Schools should teach students how to think on their own without the use of AI. AI technologies can help students learn in a way that works for them and provide them with feedback straight away. However, if they are not used correctly, they might make students depend on them.

AIWoW is useful in education since it helps keep the learning going.

When schools and colleges employ AIWoW, they often follow rules like these:

- Letting AI help you understand things, but not do your homework
- Getting students to say what they think instead of just sending in finished work
- Creating examinations that measure how well kids think instead of how well they recall things

For instance, a maths teacher would let students ask AI to explain things, but they would have to solve problems on their own.

AIWoW in education makes sure that students use AI to learn, not to get out of learning.

32.7 Practical Adoption in Legal Systems

Supporting Research Without Replacing Judgement

More and more lawyers are using AI tools to help them with court case research, writing documents, and looking at past cases. These tools can make things much more efficient for them.

However, legal decisions have moral and social implications.

The main goal of using AIWoW in law firms and courts is to keep professional responsibility.

Lawyers may use AI to analyse large legal databases or generate draft arguments, but they remain responsible for verifying accuracy and ensuring that arguments reflect the specific context of a case, not hallucinated results provided by AI.

Judges may use AI tools to summarise case material, but must independently interpret legal principles and issue judgements, as those summaries can be with some predetermined thought process or influence.

AIWoW adoption in legal environments succeeds when **AI assists preparation but never replaces judicial reasoning.**

32.8 Practical Adoption in Media and Creative Industries

Preserving Authenticity in the Age of Synthetic Content

More and more, writers, filmmakers, singers, and media houses are utilising AI to develop things, edit them, and look at audience data.

These tools help production run more smoothly, but they also make consumers concerned about fake news, manipulation, and authenticity.

When it comes to employing AIWoW in the media, the goal is to be open and let humans be creative.

Organisations that use AIWoW a lot:

- Tell individuals that you employ fake media items
- Make sure that humans have the last say over what is published
- Make sure that AI-created stories don't fool humans

For example, a news organisation might use AI to summarise intricate stories, but they would still need human reporters to make sure the facts are correct before they publish them.

AI is good for creative professions when it helps individuals be more creative without taking away their voice.

32.9 Practical Adoption in Homes and Everyday Life

Supporting Families Without Intruding on Human Relationships

AI is becoming more widespread in homes through things like voice assistants, smart devices, and digital recommendation systems.

Humans who use AIWoW in their homes are mostly worried about keeping their privacy, their mental health, and their familial bonds.

Families that regularly apply AIWoW ideas:

- Use AI tools to help you remember things or make plans.
- Don't let AI make too many choices for you about parenting or relationships.
- Collect data in private places, but only up to a point.

A family might utilise AI to help them remember their grocery lists or keep track of how much energy their home uses, but they also need to make sure that humans are at the centre of family communication and decision-making.

AIWoW makes sure that technology assists families instead of taking over their lives.

32.10 Practical Adoption for Youth and Young Learners

Teaching Responsible Intelligence Early

AI tools are always available to young humans, making them the first generation to have them.

The major reason to use AIWoW with kids and teens is to teach them how to think in a responsible way.

Parents and teachers who utilise AIWoW encourage kids to:

- Before approaching AI for help, try to do things on your own.
- Don't trust what AI says.
- Ask them to describe their thoughts in their own words.

This strategy helps kids feel more confident in their intelligence instead of just using automated solutions without saying anything.

AIWoW makes sure that the next generation learns how to use their brains instead of giving up their own ideas.

32.11 The Emerging Pattern of AIWoW Adoption

Across different domains, enterprises, governments, healthcare, education, finance, and everyday life, a similar pattern appears when AIWoW is adopted responsibly.

Organisations and communities usually move through four practical steps.

Step	Purpose
Clarify Intent	Why AI is used
Define Responsibility	Who owns decisions
Set Boundaries	Where automation stops
Observe Impact	How humans are affected

This process stops automation from getting out of control.

First, it's clear what AI is supposed to do.

Second, it's still clear who is responsible for decisions.

Third, boundaries make sure that automation doesn't take the place of important human judgement.

Lastly, the effect on humans and systems is always being watched.

By following this process, groups and businesses may slowly add AI while still being in charge, responsible, and having humans watch over the results.

32.12 The Next Evolution of AIWoW Begins

This book has introduced the foundations of AIWoW - AI Ways of Working™ and demonstrated how organisations can begin integrating intelligent systems responsibly. The frameworks and ideas presented throughout these chapters show that AIWoW is not merely about adopting new technology, but about shaping how humans and intelligent systems collaborate in structured, accountable, and productive ways.

However, the evolution of AIWoW extends far beyond individual organisations. As intelligent systems become embedded in everyday tools, services, and decision environments, the nature of work and institutional functioning will inevitably change. The central challenge will no longer be access to intelligence, but the responsible orchestration of human judgement and machine capability.

The next stage of AIWoW, therefore, expands into broader societal domains, including:

- **Enterprises & Industrial Systems**
- **Government & Public Institutions**
- **Healthcare & Human Care Systems**
- **Education & Learning Ecosystems**
- **Financial & Economic Structures**

- **Legal & Governance Institutions**
- **Media, Creativity, & Information Systems**
- **Homes, Families, & Everyday Decision-Making**
- **Youth Development & Future Workforce Preparation**
- **Spiritual Leaders & Spiritual Seekers**
- **Political Leadership, Policymakers, And Bureaucratic Institutions**

As AI becomes part of everyday life, AIWoW will guide how intelligence integrates into these environments while preserving human responsibility, judgement, and dignity.

This book has focused on the conceptual foundations of AI Ways of Working. The next phase will move toward practical **AIWoW Operating Models**, exploring how these principles can be implemented across institutions and systems.

As this book explained **why AIWoW is necessary**, the next will explore **how society can operate with it in practice**.

Because the true impact of artificial intelligence will not be determined by the sophistication of machines, but by the wisdom with which humanity chooses to work alongside them.

And that is where the next evolution of **AIWoW** begins.

"Where machines evolve to think, humans must evolve to feel together.

Intelligence may power the future, but only wisdom can guide it.

AIWoW exists to ensure that as machines become smarter, humanity becomes wiser."

References

This book is expansion of Author own research work **Citation :** Anand Rathore, *"Empathic Intelligence (EI) and the AI Lifecycle Loop: The Future of Organisational Ways of Working"*, Volume 14 Issue 12, December 2025, International Journal of Science and Research (IJSR), Pages: 897–900,

https://www.ijsr.net/getabstract.php?paperid=SR251211182049,

DOI: https://dx.doi.org/10.21275/SR251211182049

PREFACE & INTRODUCTION

1. Bhagavat Geeta – Geeta Press, Gorakhpur

2. **On Karma Yoga and conscious action:** Vivekananda, S. (1999). *Karma yoga.* Advaita Ashrama. (Original work published 1896)

3. **On human-in-the-loop AI governance (referenced conceptually):** Amershi, S., Weld, D., Vorvoreanu, M., Fourney, A., Nushi, B., Collisson, P., Suh, J., Iqbal, S., Bennett, P. N., Inkpen, K., Teevan, J., Kikin-Gil, R., & Horvitz, E. (2019). Guidelines for human-AI interaction. *Proceedings of the ACM Conference on Human Factors in Computing Systems (CHI 2019).* https://doi.org/10.1145/3290605.3300233

CHAPTER 1 The Automation Paradox

1. **On automation history and the paradox of productivity:** Autor, D. H. (2015). Why are there still so many jobs? The history and future of workplace automation. *Journal of Economic Perspectives, 29*(3), 3–30. https://doi.org/10.1257/jep.29.3.3 Brynjolfsson, E., & McAfee, A. (2014). *The second machine age: Work, progress, and prosperity in a time of brilliant technologies.* W. W. Norton & Company.

2. **On speed without comprehension/decision velocity:** Kahneman, D. (2011). *Thinking, fast and slow.* Farrar, Straus and Giroux.

3. **On the automation of logistics (DHL / UPS examples):** McKinsey Global Institute. (2017). *A future that works: Automation, employment, and productivity.* McKinsey & Company. https://www.mckinsey.com/mgi

4. **On algorithmic trading and noise:** Lewis, M. (2014). *Flash boys: A Wall Street revolt.* W. W. Norton & Company.

CHAPTER 2 From Automation to Conscious Acceleration

1. **On organisational speed and sense-making:** Weick, K. E. (1995). *Sensemaking in organisations.* SAGE Publications.

2. **On the shift from industrial to information to AI era:** Toffler, A. (1980). *The third wave.* William Morrow and Company. Castells, M. (1996). *The information age: Economy, society and culture. Vol. 1: The rise of the network society.* Blackwell.

3. **On conscious acceleration as an organisational discipline:** Doz, Y., & Kosonen, M. (2010). Embedding strategic agility: A leadership agenda for accelerating business model renewal. *Long Range Planning, 43*(2–3), 370–382. https://doi.org/10.1016/j.lrp.2009.07.006

CHAPTER 3 From Tools to Teammates

1. **On AI as a participating system:** Russell, S., & Norvig, P. (2021). *Artificial intelligence: A modern approach* (4th ed.). Pearson.

2. **On the shift from command to collaboration:** Wilson, H. J., & Daugherty, P. R. (2018). Collaborative intelligence: Humans and AI are joining forces. *Harvard Business Review, 96*(4), 114–123.

3. **On human-machine dependency risks:** Parasuraman, R., & Riley, V. (1997). Humans and automation: Use, misuse, disuse, abuse. *Human Factors, 39*(2), 230–253. https://doi.org/10.1518/001872097778543886

Skitka, L. J., Mosier, K. L., & Burdick, M. (1999). Does automation bias decision-making? *International Journal of Human-Computer Studies, 51*(5), 991–1006. https://doi.org/10.1006/ijhc.1999.0252

4. **On redefining teamwork with AI:** Deloitte Insights. (2020). *The social enterprise at work: Paradox as a path forward.* Deloitte.

CHAPTER 4 Limits of Existing Work Philosophies

1. **On Lean Production:** Womack, J. P., Jones, D. T., & Roos, D. (1990). *The machine that changed the world: The story of lean production.* Free Press.

2. **On Agile and Scrum:** Beck, K., Beedle, M., van Bennekum, A., Cockburn, A., Cunningham, W., Fowler, M., Grenning, J., Highsmith, J., Hunt, A., Jeffries, R., Kern, J., Marick, B., Martin, R. C., Mellor, S., Schwaber, K., Sutherland, J., & Thomas, D. (2001). *Manifesto for agile software development.* Agile Alliance. https://agilemanifesto.org/

3. **On DevOps:** Kim, G., Humble, J., Debois, P., & Willis, J. (2016). *The DevOps handbook: How to create world-class agility, reliability, and security in technology organisations.* IT Revolution Press.

4. **On Scientific Management (Taylorism):** Taylor, F. W. (1911). *The principles of scientific management.* Harper & Brothers.

5. **On Design Thinking:** Brown, T. (2008). Design thinking. *Harvard Business Review, 86*(6), 84–92.

6. **On AI changing assumptions of existing frameworks:** Raisch, S., & Krakowski, S. (2021). Artificial intelligence and management: The automation–augmentation paradox. *Academy of Management Review, 46*(1), 192–210. https://doi.org/10.5465/amr.2018.0072

CHAPTER 5 The Human Cost of Uncontrolled Intelligence

1. **On cognitive overload:** Sweller, J. (1988). Cognitive load during problem solving: Effects on learning. *Cognitive Science, 12*(2), 257–285. https://doi.org/10.1207/s15516709cog1202_4

2. **On burnout as a system outcome:** Maslach, C., & Leiter, M. P. (2016). Understanding the burnout experience: Recent research and its implications for psychiatry. *World Psychiatry, 15*(2), 103–111. https://doi.org/10.1002/wps.20311

3. **On empathy erosion:** Nummenmaa, L., Glerean, E., Hari, R., & Hietanen, J. K. (2014). Bodily maps of emotions. *Proceedings of the National Academy of Sciences, 111*(2), 646–651. https://doi.org/10.1073/pnas.1321664111

4. **On sustained decision pressure:** Baumeister, R. F., Bratslavsky, E., Muraven, M., & Tice, D. M. (1998). Ego depletion: Is the active self a limited resource? *Journal of Personality and Social Psychology, 74*(5), 1252–1265. https://doi.org/10.1037/0022-3514.74.5.1252

CHAPTER 6 Empathic Intelligence (EI) in AIWoW

1. *Śānti Mantra (Peace invocation)* - Brihadaranyaka Upanishad 1.4.14

2. Goleman, D. P. (1995). *Emotional intelligence: Why it can matter more than IQ for character, health and lifelong achievement.* Bantam Books. **ISBN:** 978-0-553-37506-0 **OCLC:** 32430189 **Publisher location:** New York

3. **APA 7th Edition Citation:** Rogers, C. R. (1980). *A way of being.* Houghton Mifflin. **Publisher location:** Boston

4. Mayer, Salovey & Caruso — Emotional Intelligence: New Ability or Eclectic Traits? **APA 7th Edition Citation:** Mayer, J. D., Salovey, P., & Caruso, D. R. (2008). Emotional intelligence: New ability or eclectic traits? *American Psychologist, 63*(6), 503–517. https://doi.org/10.1037/0003-066X.63.6.503

CHAPTER 7 Conscious Leadership in the Age of AI

1. **On conscious leadership:** George, B. (2003). *Authentic leadership: Rediscovering the secrets to creating lasting value.* Jossey-Bass.

2. **On leadership under uncertainty and AI:** Schoemaker, P. J. H., Krupp, S., & Howland, S. (2013). Strategic leadership: The essential skills. *Harvard Business Review, 91*(1–2), 131–134.

3. **On awareness as a leadership function:** Scharmer, C. O. (2009). *Theory U: Leading from the future as it emerges.* Berrett-Koehler Publishers.

4. **On decision-making velocity in AI environments:** Eisenhardt, K. M. (1989). Making fast strategic decisions in high-velocity environments. *Academy of Management Journal, 32*(3), 543–576. https://doi.org/10.5465/256434

CHAPTER 8 AI as Partner, Not Replacement

1. **On augmentation over replacement:** Daugherty, P. R., & Wilson, H. J. (2018). *Human + machine: Reimagining work in the age of AI.* Harvard Business Review Press.

2. **On automation bias (replacement risk):** Mosier, K. L., & Skitka, L. J. (1996). Human decision makers and automated decision aids: Made for each other? In R. Parasuraman & M. Mouloua (Eds.), *Automation and human performance: Theory and applications* (pp. 201–220). Lawrence Erlbaum Associates.

3. **On aviation as a human-machine partnership model:** Billings, C. E. (1997). *Aviation automation: The search for a human-centred approach.* Lawrence Erlbaum Associates.

4. **On medical AI and partnership (diagnostic support):** Topol, E. J. (2019). High-performance medicine: The convergence of human and artificial intelligence. *Nature Medicine, 25*(1), 44–56. https://doi.org/10.1038/s41591-018-0300-7

CHAPTER 9 Timeless Philosophy in Modern Systems

1. **On karma and leadership (Bhagavad Gita):** Prabhupāda, A. C. Bhaktivedanta Swami. (1972). *Bhagavad-gītā as it is.* Bhaktivedanta Book Trust. Easwaran, E. (Trans.). (2007). *The Bhagavad Gita* (2nd ed.). Nilgiri Press.

2. **On ancient wisdom and modern organisations:** Senge, P. M. (1990). *The fifth discipline: The art and practice of the learning organisation.* Doubleday/Currency.

3. **On ethical governance in AI (AI ethics boards):** Fjeld, J., Achten, N., Hilligoss, H., Nagy, A., & Srikumar, M. (2020). *Principled artificial intelligence: Mapping consensus in ethical and rights-based approaches to principles for AI.* Berkman Klein Centre Research Publication. https://doi.org/10.2139/ssrn.3518482

4. **On autonomous vehicle ethics and conscious action:** Bonnefon, J. F., Shariff, A., & Rahwan, I. (2016). The social dilemma of autonomous vehicles. *Science, 352*(6293), 1573–1576. https://doi.org/10.1126/science.aaf2654

CHAPTERS 10–12 The AIWoW - AI Ways of Working™ Manifesto & Principles

1. **On organisational values and manifesto thinking:** Collins, J. C., & Porras, J. I. (1994). *Built to last: Successful habits of visionary companies.* HarperBusiness.

2. **On ethical intent in system design:** Floridi, L., Cowls, J., Beltrametti, M., Chatila, R., Chazerand, P., Dignum, V., Luetge, C., Madelin, R., Pagallo, U., Rossi, F., Schafer, B., Valcke, P., & Vayena, E. (2018). An ethical framework for a good AI society: Opportunities, risks, principles, and recommendations. *Minds and Machines, 28*(4), 689–707. https://doi.org/10.1007/s11023-018-9482-5

3. **Ethical intent**: Kant, I. (1785). *Groundwork of the Metaphysics of Morals* (M. Gregor, Trans.). Cambridge University Press. (Original work published 1785)

4. **On learning loops and organisational learning:** Argyris, C., & Schön, D. A. (1978). *Organisational learning: A theory of action perspective.* Addison-Wesley.

5. **On accountability as structural law:** Bovens, M. (2007). Analysing and assessing accountability: A conceptual framework. *European Law Journal, 13*(4), 447–468. https://doi.org/10.1111/j.1468-0386.2007.00378.x

CHAPTERS 13–15 AI Lifecycle Loop, Adoptability & Control

1. **On continuous learning systems:** LeCun, Y., Bengio, Y., & Hinton, G. (2015). Deep learning. *Nature, 521*(7553), 436–444. https://doi.org/10.1038/nature14539

2. **On AI governance and control:** Amodei, D., Olah, C., Steinhardt, J., Christiano, P., Schulman, J., & Mané, D. (2016). *Concrete problems in AI safety.* arXiv preprint arXiv:1606.06565. https://arxiv.org/abs/1606.06565 Russell, S. (2019). *Human compatible: Artificial intelligence and the problem of control.* Viking.

3. **On technology adoption:** Rogers, E. M. (2003). *Diffusion of innovations* (5th ed.). Free Press. Davis, F. D. (1989). Perceived usefulness, perceived ease of use, and user acceptance of information technology. *MIS Quarterly, 13*(3), 319–340. https://doi.org/10.2307/249008

4. *Mr. Deepak s/o Shivkumar Bahry v. Heart & Soul Entertainment Ltd.*, 2026:BHC-AS:828, Bombay High Court, Justice M.M. Sathaye, January 7, 2026

5. *Gummadi Usha Rani & Anr. v. Sure Mallikarjuna Rao & Anr.*, Supreme Court of India, Justices PS Narasimha & Alok Aradhe, February 27, 2026

6. *Heart & Soul Entertainment Ltd. v. Deepak s/o Shivkumar Bahry*, Supreme Court of India, Justices Rajesh Bindal & Vijay Bishnoi, March 20, 2026

7. **On intent mapping and value alignment:** Gabriel, I. (2020). Artificial intelligence, values, and alignment. *Minds and Machines, 30*(3), 411–437. https://doi.org/10.1007/s11023-020-09539-2

8. **On ethical interlocks:** Mittelstadt, B. D., Allo, P., Taddeo, M., Wachter, S., & Floridi, L. (2016). The ethics of algorithms: Mapping the debate. *Big Data & Society, 3*(2), 1–21. https://doi.org/10.1177/2053951716679679

CHAPTER 16 Human-AI Responsibility Matrix (HAR Matrix)

1. **On accountability in sociotechnical systems:** Nissenbaum, H. (1994). Computing and accountability. *Communications of the ACM, 37*(1), 72–80. https://doi.org/10.1145/175222.175228

2. **On distributed responsibility in AI:** Matthias, A. (2004). The responsibility gap: Ascribing responsibility for the actions of learning automata. *Ethics and Information Technology, 6*(3), 175–183. https://doi.org/10.1007/s10676-004-3422-1

3. **On audit trails and algorithmic transparency:** Wachter, S., Mittelstadt, B., & Russell, C. (2017). Counterfactual explanations without opening the black box: Automated decisions and the GDPR. *Harvard Journal of Law & Technology, 31*(2), 841–887.

CHAPTER 17 Empathic Control Framework (ECF)

1. **On emotional boundaries and organisational wellbeing:** Hochschild, A. R. (1983). *The managed heart: Commercialisation of human feeling.* University of California Press.

2. **On ethical guardrails in AI systems:** Cummings, M. L. (2004). Automation bias in intelligent time-critical decision support systems. *AIAA 1st Intelligent Systems Technical Conference.* https://doi.org/10.2514/6.2004-6313

3. **On conscious overrides in human-machine systems:** Endsley, M. R. (1995). Toward a theory of situation awareness in dynamic systems. *Human Factors, 37*(1), 32–64. https://doi.org/10.1518/001872095779049543

CHAPTER 18 AIWoW - AI Ways of Working™ **Role Evolution Model**

1. **On role evolution in AI-augmented workplaces:** Acemoglu, D., & Restrepo, P. (2019). Automation and new tasks: How

technology displaces and reinstates labour. *Journal of Economic Perspectives, 33*(2), 3–30. https://doi.org/10.1257/jep.33.2.3

2. **On the AI ethics council/governance roles:** Jobin, A., Ienca, M., & Vayena, E. (2019). The global landscape of AI ethics guidelines. *Nature Machine Intelligence, 1*(9), 389–399. https://doi.org/10.1038/s42256-019-0088-2
3. **On human skill evolution alongside AI:** World Economic Forum. (2020). *The future of jobs report 2020.* WEF. https://www.weforum.org/reports/the-future-of-jobs-report-2020

CHAPTERS 19–22 — Metrics, AI-ROH, CPWU, Empathy Debt

1. **On rethinking success metrics:** Mayer, R. C., Davis, J. H., & Schoorman, F. D. (1995). An integrative model of organisational trust. *Academy of Management Review, 20*(3), 709–734. https://doi.org/10.5465/amr.1995.9508080335 Kaplan, R. S., & Norton, D. P. (1992). The balanced scorecard: Measures that drive performance. *Harvard Business Review, 70*(1), 71–79.
2. **On AI's impact on workers (return on humanity concept):** Brynjolfsson, E., & Mitchell, T. (2017). What can machine learning do? Workforce implications. *Science, 358*(6370), 1530–1534. https://doi.org/10.1126/science.aap8062
3. **On wellbeing as an economic resource (CPWU):** Frey, B. S., & Stutzer, A. (2002). What can economists learn from happiness research? *Journal of Economic Literature, 40*(2), 402–435. https://doi.org/10.1257/002205102320161320
4. Dolan, P., Peasgood, T., & White, M. (2008). Do we really know what makes us happy? A review of the economic literature on the factors associated with subjective wellbeing. *Journal of Economic Psychology, 29*(1), 94–122. https://doi.org/10.1016/j.joep.2007.09.001
5. **On emotional labour and empathy erosion:** Hochschild, A. R. (1983). *The managed heart: Commercialisation of human feeling.* University of California Press.

6. **On burnout as systemic (Maslach):** Maslach, C., Schaufeli, W. B., & Leiter, M. P. (2001). Job burnout. *Annual Review of Psychology, 52*(1), 397–422. https://doi.org/10.1146/annurev.psych.52.1.397

7. **On ethical drift:** Bazerman, M. H., & Tenbrunsel, A. E. (2011). *Blind spots: Why we fail to do what's right and what to do about it.* Princeton University Press.

8. **On DGCA pilot fatigue regulations (used as CPWU illustration):** Directorate General of Civil Aviation (DGCA), Government of India. (2024, January). *Revised Flight Duty Time Limitations (FDTL) for flight crew* [Civil Aviation Requirement, CAR Section 7 Series J Part III Revision 2]. Ministry of Civil Aviation. https://www.dgca.gov.in

CHAPTERS 23–24 — Maturity & Adoption Models

1. **On technology maturity models:** Paulk, M. C., Curtis, B., Chrissis, M. B., & Weber, C. V. (1993). Capability maturity model for software (Version 1.1). *Software Engineering Institute, Carnegie Mellon University*. CMU/SEI-93-TR-024.

2. **On organisational transition and failure modes:** Kotter, J. P. (1995). Leading change: Why transformation efforts fail. *Harvard Business Review, 73*(2), 59–67. Christensen, C. M. (1997). *The innovator's dilemma: When new technologies cause great firms to fail.* Harvard Business School Press.

3. **On scaling AI responsibly:** Cihon, P., Maas, M. M., & Kemp, L. (2020). *Fragmentation and the future: Investigating architectures for international AI governance.* Global Policy. https://doi.org/10.1111/1758-5899.12890

CHAPTERS 25–29 — Hybrid AIWoW (DevOps, Agile, SAFe)

1. **On DevOps principles:** Kim, G., Humble, J., Debois, P., & Willis, J. (2016). *The DevOps handbook.* IT Revolution Press. Forsgren, N., Humble, J., & Kim, G. (2018). *Accelerate: The science of lean software and DevOps.* IT Revolution Press.

2. **On Scrum:** Schwaber, K., & Sutherland, J. (2020). *The Scrum guide: The definitive guide to Scrum: The rules of the game.* Scrum. org. https://scrumguides.org/
3. **On Kanban:** Anderson, D. J. (2010). *Kanban: Successful evolutionary change for your technology business.* Blue Hole Press.
4. **On SAFe (Scaled Agile Framework):** Leffingwell, D. (2011). *Agile software requirements: Lean requirements practices for teams, programmes, and the enterprise.* Addison-Wesley Professional.
5. **On cognitive flow and deep work:** Csikszentmihalyi, M. (1990). *Flow: The psychology of optimal experience.* Harper & Row. Newport, C. (2016). *Deep work: Rules for focused success in a distracted world.* Grand Central Publishing.
6. **On DevSecOps:** Boehm, B., & Sullivan, K. J. (2000). Software economics: A roadmap. In *Proceedings of the Conference on the Future of Software Engineering* (pp. 319–343). ACM Press.

CHAPTERS 30–32 — Global Movement, Conscious Evolution, Practical Adoption

1. **On movements vs. methodologies:** Gladwell, M. (2000). *The tipping point: How little things can make a big difference.* Little, Brown and Company.
2. **On institutionalising ethics:** Floridi, L., & Cowls, J. (2019). A unified framework of five principles for AI in society. *Harvard Data Science Review, 1*(1). https://doi. org/10.1162/99608f92.8cd550d1
3. **On open-source community as a movement model:** Raymond, E. S. (1999). *The cathedral and the bazaar: Musings on Linux and open source by an accidental revolutionary.* O'Reilly Media.
4. **On AI's societal impact:** Harari, Y. N. (2018). *21 lessons for the 21st century.* Spiegel & Grau.
5. **On regenerative organisations:** Laloux, F. (2014). *Reinventing organisations: A guide to creating organisations inspired by the next stage of human consciousness.* Nelson Parker.

6. **On practical AI adoption in healthcare:** Obermeyer, Z., & Emanuel, E. J. (2016). Predicting the future — Big data, machine learning, and clinical medicine. *New England Journal of Medicine, 375*(13), 1216–1219. https://doi.org/10.1056/NEJMp1606181

7. **On AI adoption in government:** OECD. (2019). *Recommendation of the Council on Artificial Intelligence* (OECD/LEGAL/0449). OECD Publishing. https://legalinstruments.oecd.org/en/instruments/OECD-LEGAL-0449

8. **On AI in education:** Holmes, W., Bialik, M., & Fadel, C. (2019). *Artificial intelligence in education: Promises and implications for teaching and learning*. Centre for Curriculum Redesign.

www.ingramcontent.com/pod-product-compliance
Lightning Source LLC
LaVergne TN
LVHW091522200926
848483LV00002B/282
* 9 7 9 8 9 0 4 3 1 7 1 8 8 *